Epochs of Modern History

THE

AGE OF ANNE.

BY

EDWARD E. MORRIS, M.A.

OF LINCOLN COLLEGE, OXFORD

HEAD MASTER OF THE MELBOURNE GRAMMAR SCHOOL, AUSTRALIA

WITH MAPS AND PLANS

NEW YORK:
CHARLES SCRIBNER'S SONS,
743 and 745 BROADWAY.

GRANT, FAIRES & RODGERS.
Electrotypers & Printers.
52 & 54 North Sixth Street, Philadelphia.

PREFACE.

It would not be fair to this little book to send it forth to take its chance in the world without a preface, however much I should prefer that course. My aim in writing the book has been so definite, my object so distinct, that I particularly wish it not to be tried by an unsuitable standard, nor condemned upon wrong grounds.

In the field of history, as with other kinds of knowledge, there are two orders of workers. On the one side are the original writers, who make researches, and delve for new ore; on the other, those who perform the humbler but equally needful office of teaching, of spreading knowledge, and working into shape the material which the former produce. This book is not a contribution to the general fund of historical knowledge. Those who before knew the history of its period will find here no new light. It is offered as an effort to assist in the teaching of history in schools. It is written in the light of a theory, according to the soundness of which and the measure with which it has been followed my book must stand or fall.

Much as I should like to study history as it ought to be studied, to ransack Record offices and public libraries for new information, and with its help to place in new aspect facts known before, I can claim no credit for such work. I have had neither the time nor the opportunity. The demands upon a school-master's hours leave him little leisure, and the undue pressure of examination, with which nowadays each school-time closes, destroys the working power of at least a portion of his holidays. But a schoolmaster may fairly be expected to know the kind of book that will be good for the purpose of teaching. This is the reason for my venture; but I clearly recognise its limits.

The theory on which the book is based is the cardinal theory of the whole series called Epochs of History. I was led some years ago to believe that, in spite of the flood of school histories pouring from the press, there was room for a series, in which short periods could be studied with that fulness without which history is comparatively unprofitable. I had the good fortune to find publishers in the first to whom I applied, and to secure the cordial co-operation of several distinguished writers. As long as I remained in England I edited the series.

It would be ludicrous to claim originality for this method. I have always found that schoolmasters who are really educators accept the doctrine. But I am very anxious to state it clearly, for history lessons have been and are continually ruined by the intrusion of cram—names that are mere shadows, and a profusion of dates.

History is not taught in schools that the excellent virtue of accuracy may be learnt. To teach this is the function of other lessons that occupy a much larger portion of the pupil's time. History should be taught for the sake of its human interest. For this reason I have made it my first object to avoid being dull. I have been very biographical, taking care to introduce formally all new characters of importance as they come upon the stage. Again, I have not feared the accusation of being a "drum and trumpet historian," for war, unfortunately, is an intrinsic part of history, and always stirs the interest of the young, acting as the bait which may draw them on to the study of other matters.

Disclaiming originality, I wish to indicate the sources from which I have drawn. The end of Lord Macaulay's history overlaps the period, but, unfortunately, only the end: all must lament that he was not spared to write the history of a time with which his acquaintance was so intimate. His essay on Lord Mahon's early book is almost as valuable as that book itself for the war in Spain. In the same way Lord Mahon's History of England from the Peace of Utrecht is helpful for the couple of years at the end of my period. The volume which the same historian wrote as Earl Stanhope, to cover the ground between the close of Macaulay's history and the opening of his own, I am inclined not to value so highly as his larger work; but I have no wish to depreciate a book that has been one of my chief authorities. "A History of Great Britain during the Reign of Queen Anne," lately published by Mr. F. W. Wyon, is more thorough in its research and more interesting. His judgment is independent, and his knowledge of French memoirs very complete. It is a matter for regret that he seems to ignore or to despise the work of German historians. I have found Noorden's

"Spanische Erbfolgekrieg" a very mine in which to dig, though I fancy no man could read the book through. The period is unfortunately beyond the point where the great Ranke writes with fulness, but his sketches are of more value than the details of others. Gfrörer's "History of the Eighteenth Century" is suggestive.

I have used Burnet's "History of His Own Time" with necessary caution, and the Lives of Marlborough by Coxe and Alison. Considering the purpose for which the book is intended, I have not hesitated to use my authorities freely, nor cared to avoid their language. I confess indeed that I have been amused to trace thoughts and expressions from authority to authority, and doubt not that I also have borrowed, perhaps too easily, even the words of others.

To the list which I have given, and which is by no means exhaustive, I must add the following as of use in special portions. M. Duruy's "Histoire de France" ("Rhétorique,") Mrs. Bray's "Revolt of the Cevennes," Dr. Bridges' "France under Richelieu and Colbert," the introduction of Carlyle's "Frederick the Great" and Thackeray's "Esmond" and the "Four Georges." It is matter of regret that in a novel like "Esmond," which gives so excellent a picture of Queen Anne's reign, Thackeray should have placed the Old Pretender in London at the time of his sister's death—a deviation from history not necessary to the development of his plot.

EDWARD E. MORRIS.

THE GRAMMAR SCHOOL, MELBOURNE:
September 4, 1876.

Chronological Table of Contents.

CHAPTER I.

THE SPANISH SUCCESSION.

		PAGE
	Spain still territorially the most powerful kingdom in Europe, though she had outgrown her strength	1
	Her want of vitality shown under the feeble rule of the childless Charles II.	2
	Importance of the question as to his successor	4
	Three claimants:	
	(1) Philip, Duke of Anjou	4
	(2) Joseph, the Electoral Prince	4
	(3) The Archduke Charles	4
	Aggressive policy of France under Lewis XIV. dangerous to Europe	4
	The one great opponent of Lewis—William of Orange	5
1697	The contest stayed by Peace of Ryswick	5
1698	First Partition Treaty	6
1700	Death of Joseph, and second Partition Treaty	6
	Irritation of Spain	7
	The Darien Scheme	8
	Unpopularity of William in England	8
	The Kingdom of Spain willed to Philip of Anjou	9
	"Il n'y a plus de Pyrénées"	9
	Lewis's three mistakes:	
	(1) Reservation of Philip's right of succession to the French throne	10
	(2) Occupation of Spanish Netherlands	10
	(3) Recognition of the Old Pretender	10

		PAGE
1701.	The Grand Alliance of the Hague, result of these mistakes	11
1702	Death of William	11
	His character	12

CHAPTER II.

LEWIS XIV.   1714.

(Contemporary with Charles I., Cromwell, Charles II., James II., William and Mary, Anne, George I.)
Five stages in his reign marked by—

1648	(1) Treaty of Westphalia, which ended the Thirty Years' War	14
1668	(2) Treaty of Aix-la-Chapelle, which, forced on Lewis by the Triple Alliance, ended the war of Succession in Brabant	18
1678	(3) Treaty of Nymwegen, which ended the invasion of Holland	20
1697	(4) Treaty of Ryswick, which ended the war against the Grand Alliance	24
1713	(5) Treaty of Utrecht.	139

Three impolitic acts of Lewis:

1681	(1) Seizure of Strassburg	21
1685	(2) Revocation of Edict of Nantes	21
1688	(3) Ravaging of the Palatinate	23

CHAPTER III.

THE NEW DRAMATIS PERSONÆ.

Queen Anne	25
Her Succession	25
Character	25
Husband and Children	26
Lady Marlborough	27
Duke of Marlborough	27

Chronological Table of Contents.

	PAGE
Character	27
Lord Godolphin, Lord High Treasurer	31
Prince Eugene (Eugenio von Savoie)	31
Heinsius, Grand Pensionary of Holland	32

CHAPTER IV.

"THE GRAND ALLIANCE."

The Emperor	33
The nine Electors	34
How they ranged themselves:	
(a) On the French side	35
Bavaria	35
Cologne	35
(b) On the side of the Grand Alliance	35
Brandenburg (kingdom of Prussia)	35
Bohemia	35
Hanover	35
The Palatinate	35
(c) Neutral	35
Mayence	35
Trèves	35
Saxony	35
The central powers of the Grand Alliance	36
England and Holland	36
Other allies:	
Minor princes of Germany and Denmark	36
Also, after the first year, Savoy and Portugal, who deserted France	37

CHAPTER V.

OPENING OF THE WAR.

SECTION I.—*Marlborough in Flanders.*

1702	His object	42
	To clear the Netherlands of the French	42

		PAGE
1702	Result of the first campaign	43
	French cut off from lower valley of the Rhine. Venloo and other towns taken	43
	Capture of Bonn on the Rhine and Huy on the Meuse	43-44

SECTION II.—*Campaigns in Germany and elsewhere.*

(*a*) On the Upper Rhine 44
Landau taken by Prince Lewis of Baden . . 45
(*b*) In North Italy 45
Victory of Cremona won by Prince Eugene, and passes into Tyrol secured 45
(*c*) In Bavaria 45
Imperialists routed by the French 45
(*d*) In West Indies 46
English under Admiral Benbow worsted . . 46

SECTION III.—*Spain.*

(*a*) Failure of attack on Cadiz 46
(*b*) Treasure ships taken by the English at Vigo . 47
1704 (*c*) Earl of Galway commands the allies against Duke of Berwick 48
(*d*) Capture of Gibraltar by Sir George Rooke . 49

CHAPTER VI.

RISING IN THE CEVENNES.

	The strength of the Huguenots in the valleys of the Loire and the lower Rhone	50
	The Camisards ("Wearers of the white frock,")	52
1703	Rise under Jean Cavalier and others	52
1684	The Dragonnades urged on by Madame de Maintenon	54
1704	Failure of the English fleet to help the Camisards	56
	The weakness of the Empire in Hungary and Transylvania	57

CHAPTER VII.

BLENHEIM.

		PAGE
1704	Object of Lewis to attack Vienna	58
	Marlborough's plan—to strike across the Rhine, meet Eugene, and prevent the junction of the French armies in Bavaria	59
	Battle of Blenheim	62
	The results of the victory	67
	The power of Lewis XIV. broken and prestige of French arms destroyed	67

CHAPTER VIII.

LORD PETERBOROUGH.

	His character	68
	The provinces of Catalonia and Valencia chosen by the allies as points of attack	70
	Capture of Monjuich	72
1705	Capture of Barcelona	73
	Exploits of Peterborough	75

CHAPTER IX.

THE YEAR OF VICTORY—1706.

SECTION I.—*Ramillies.*

1706	May 23 The battle	79
	Its results	80
	Fall of Brussels, Antwerp, Menin, Dendermonde	80–81

SECTION II.—*Turin.*

	Siege of Turin	83
1706	Sept. 7 Battle of Turin	84

		PAGE
Results of Turin	.	84
(1) Disheartening effect on French army	.	84
(2) The French driven from Piedmont	.	85
(3) Naples cut off from France	.	85

SECTION III.—*Barcelona and Madrid.*

	The French besiege Barcelona	85
	The siege raised by Peterborough	86
1706	Madrid entered by Earl of Galway	86
	Success of the allies checked by the chivalrous loyalty of the Spaniards to Philip.	87

CHAPTER X.

THE YEAR OF DISASTER—1707.

	Neutrality of Charles XII. of Sweden secured by Marlborough	90
1707 March	The allies defeated by Duke of Berwick at Almanza	92
	Archduke Charles reduced to single province of Catalonia	93
	Naples secured by the Emperor	93
	Failure of attack on Toulon	94
	Defeat of allies on Rhine by Villars	94
	Sir Cloudesley Shovel lost off the Scilly Islands	95

CHAPTER XI.

LATER FIGHTING IN THE LOW COUNTRIES.

SECTION I.—*Oudenarde and Lille.*

Brabant inclining to French	96
Siege of Oudenarde	96
Eugene joins Marlborough	97

CHAPTER XV.

PEACE OF UTRECHT.

		PAGE
	Negotiations	138
1706	(a) After Ramillies	138
1709	(b) At the Hague	138
1710	(c) At Gertruydenburg	139
1711	(d) At Utrecht	139
1713	March. Peace of Utrecht signed	139
1714	The Emperor makes a separate peace at Rastadt	139
	Results of the Peace of Utrecht	**139**
	To France:	
	The Spanish monarchy left in the hands of the Bourbons	140
	To England:	
	The possession of Gibraltar and Minorca, Hudson's Bay Territory, Newfoundland, and Nova Scotia	140
	To Spain:	
	The loss of possessions in Italy and the Netherlands	141
	To Prussia:	
	The acknowledgment of its status as a kingdom	141
	To the Dutch:	
	Gain of a barrier in the Austrian Netherlands against France	142
	Arguments for the Treaty:	
	(a) The war a great burden to England and increase of national debt	142
	(b) Strength of patriotism in Spain enlisted on the side of Philip V.	142
	(c) The union of Spain and Austria more dangerous than that of Spain and France	143
	Against the Treaty:	
	(a) Necessity for seizing the opportunity of preventing danger from France for the future	143
	(b) Worthlessness of renunciations	143
	(c) The scanty fruits of such splendid triumphs	143

A

		PAGE
	The war a just one, but should have been finished after Ramillies	143

CHAPTER XVI.

THE UNION WITH SCOTLAND.

SECTION I.—*The Union itself.*

1704	The Scotch Act of Security passed in opposition to the English Act of Settlement	145
1706	Commission appointed to treat, with Lord Somers as its president	146
1707	The Union accomplished	146
	Opposition in Scotland	147
	Principles of representation	148
	The Scotch law unchanged	149
	Adoption of the Union Jack	149
	Good results of the Union	150
	Compared with union with Ireland	150

SECTION II.—*Attempt for the Pretender.*

1707	Jacobite rising	151
	Sketch of the old Pretender	151
	Failure of the attempt	153

CHAPTER XVII.

PETER THE GREAT AND CHARLES XII.

SECTION I.—*The North-Eastern State System.*

| View of Russia, Denmark, Sweden, and Poland | 155 |

SECTION II.—*Peter the Great.*

His early life	158
His policy	159
In pursuance of it he travels in Western Europe	160
He visits Holland and England	160
St. Petersburg founded	161

		PAGE
	The Patriarchate abolished	162
	European fashions introduced	162
	The institution of the Tchin	163

SECTION III.—*Charles XII.*

1697	Charles succeeds to the throne	164
	His character	165
	He fights Denmark, Poland, and Russia in succession	166
1700	His victory at Narva	167
	He becomes the arbiter of Europe	168

SECTION IV. *Pultowa.*

1708	Charles marches to meet Mazeppa in the Ukraine	169
1709	July 8 Battle of Pultowa	170
	The power of Charles XII. broken	171
	He takes refuge with the Turks	172
1711	Peter the Great crosses the Pruth, and is defeated by the Turks	172

SECTION V.—*End of Charles XII. and of Peter.*

	Charles XII. expelled from Turkey	173
1718	Dec. 11 His death at the siege of Fredericshall	173
	Peter the Great makes a second journey through Europe	174
1725	Feb. His death	174

CHAPTER XVIII.

THE PROTESTANT SUCCESSION.

	Measures to secure the succession of the nearest Protestant heir	175
1597–1690	The Electress Sophia	177
	Her mother Elizabeth, daughter of James I.	177
	Her father Frederick, Elector Palatine	178
	Her brother Prince Rupert	179
	Sketch of her life	179

xx   *Chronological Table of Contents.*

		PAGE
	The Jacobites the extreme wing of the Tory party	180
	The Tory ministers charged with Jacobite leanings	181
1714	Quarrels in the Ministry	182
	The last week of Anne's life	183
	Previous career of Shrewsbury	184
	His appointment as Lord High Treasurer	185
	The Protestant succession secured	185
1660–1728	Sketch of George I.	186
	His merits as a king for England	187

CHAPTER XIX.

END OF LEWIS XIV.

1715 Sept. 1	Death of Lewis XIV.	187
1643–1715	Events in England parallel with his reign	188
	His later life clouded by trouble	188
	Death of the Dauphin	188
	Death of the Duke and Duchess of Burgundy	188
	Lewis XIV.'s reign an evil one for France	189
	Policy of the Regent, the Duke of Orleans	192

CHAPTER XX.

THE FRAGMENTS THAT REMAIN.

	Later career of the Duke of Marlborough	192
1722	His death	193
	Fate of the Catalonians	193
1716	Victor Amadeus becomes king of Sardinia	193
1724	Philip V. of Spain abdicates, but on the death of his son resumes the government	194
	Later events in the Life of the Emperor Charles	195
1740	His death	195

CHAPTER XXI.

ECONOMIC AND SOCIAL.

SECTION I.—*Population, Towns, Architecture.*

	PAGE
Population in time of Anne roughly estimated at between five and and seven millions	195-196
Population and wealth greatest in the south and east	196
Important towns (London, Bristol, Norwich, York, Exeter, Shrewsbury, Worcester, Derby, Nottingham, Canterbury)	197
Steady growth of London	197
Sketch of London life of the period	198
The City and Westminster	199
The London Exchange the centre of the commerce of the world	199
Sir C. Wren the architect of St. Paul's	201
His style	202
Sir John Vanbrugh, the architect	203
Description of Bath	203

SECTION II.—*The Poor. Statistics*

Gradual improvement in the condition of the poor	204
Pauperism in the reign of Anne	206
Prices and wages	207
Distribution of land	207
Corn the staple produce	208
Wool next in importance	208
Cotton manufacture in its infancy	209
Other manufactures	209
High standard of comfort	209
Consumption of beer diminished by introduction of tea and coffee	210
The "Spectator" on luxuries	211
Claret driven out by port	212

SECTION III.—*National Debt.*

General principle of a debt	213
Later history of the debt	215

	PAGE
The policy of repudiation attributed to the Pretender by the Whigs	215

SECTION IV.—*Strength of Parties.*

The Tories, their strength in the country	217
The Whigs, their strength in the towns	217
Oxford, the Tory university—Cambridge the Whig	218
The clergy below the present standard	218
Their position improved by Queen Anne's Bounty	219

CHAPTER XXII.

LITERATURE.

SECTION I.—*French Literature.*

	Influence of patronage and rules of art	219
	Literature greatest in first half of reign of Lewis XIV.	220
	Strength of the drama	221
1622–1673	The comedies of Molière	221
1606–1684	The tragedies of Corneille	221
1639–1697	The tragedies of Racine	221
	Development of French prose	221
1627–1704	Absolutism in religion advocated by Bossuet	222
1623–1662	Revolt of Pascal against this absolutism	222
	Reform advocated by the saintly Fénelon	223
	Influence of French on English literature.—Later reaction on French literature	223-224

SECTION II.—*English Literature.*

	Literature all-powerful and in close alliance with politics	224
1688–1744	Alexander Pope	225
1711	"Essay on Criticism"	227
1712	"Rape of the Lock"	227
1715–1725	"Homer"	227
1732–1734	"Essay on man"	227
	Pope's style and influence	228

Chronological Table of Contents.

		PAGE
	The age of Anne strongest in prose	228
	Party spirit gives an impulse to pamphlet-writing	230
1667–1745	Jonathan Swift	230
1704	"Tale of a Tub"	231
	"Conduct of the Allies"	231
1724	"Drapier's Letters"	232
1726	"Gulliver's Travels"	232
1661–1731	Daniel Defoe	233
	"The True-born Englishman"	233
	"Shortest way with the Dissenters"	234
1719	"Robinson Crusoe"	234
	Joseph Addison	235
1705	"The Campaign"	236
	Character of Addison	237
	"Cato"	238
1671–1729	Sir Richard Steele	238
1711	Joined by Addison in the "Tatler" and the "Spectator"	239
	Influence of the "Spectator"	240
INDEX		243

MAPS.

EUROPE, 1700	*To face title page*
	PAGE
BATTLE OF BLENHEIM, AUGUST 13, 1704	62
BATTLE OF RAMILLIES, MAY 23, 1706	78
ITALY, 1700	*to face* 82
THE NETHERLANDS	" 95
WESTERN EUROPE: SHOWING THE PRINCIPAL CHANGES EFFECTED BY THE TREATIES OF UTRECHT AND RASTADT	140
EUROPE: ILLUSTRATING THE WARS OF CHARLES XII. AND PETER THE GREAT	155

THE AGE OF ANNE.

CHAPTER I.

THE SPANISH SUCCESSION.

IN the last years of the seventeenth century the minds of all European statesmen were turned towards Spain. Spain had once been the most formidable of monarchies, dangerous to the peace of Europe. As far as this formidableness depended on material resources and extent of territories, there was no reason why she should not be so again. In the reign of the Emperor Charles V., who was also known as Charles I. of Spain, the Spanish king ruled not only over Spain, but over the rich provinces of the Netherlands, over large districts of Italy, and over undefined territories in America, rich in silver mines. It is true that from his son Philip II., husband of our Queen Mary, the provinces of the Netherlands revolted, excited by his malignant hostility against the Protestants. Some were successful in their revolt, and formed the country which, released from the Spanish yoke, had since prospered under the name of the United Provinces, or Holland. Portugal, also, which Philip had seized, had again established itself as a separate kingdom.

The Spanish monarchy.

France had wrested three provinces from Spain. But the greater part of the dominions of King Philip were still joined together, Spain and the Netherlands, Italy and the Indies; and the crown of this ill-assorted monarchy was upon the head of Charles II.

As long as he should continue to live, no anxiety would be excited in the mind of any statesman. In mind and body he was, perhaps, the feeblest man in his dominion. In infancy it had been doubtful whether he could be reared. Ever since, he had been an invalid; he suffered from a malformation of his jaw, which prevented the mastication of his food. He was terribly ignorant, and as superstitious as he was ignorant. The kingdom of Spain had been misgoverned before, but in his time it was going to ruin. Every department of the State was in disorder; the law courts, the army, the finances. As long as he could be kept alive, no foreign statesman would feel in the least afraid of Spanish ambition; but his death was imminent, and great uneasiness was felt as to the succession to his crown.

Charles II.

Charles was childless. The crown would therefore devolve upon the descendants either of one of his sisters or of his aunt. Their respective claims will be best explained by a reference to the accompanying table. According to the ordinary rules of inheritance, the dauphin, as son of his eldest sister, had the best right; but Lewis XIV. and Maria Theresa had on their marriage renounced for their posterity all claims to the succession, and ratified this renunciation with the most solemn oaths On the marriage of Leopold, the emperor, to her sister, a similar renunciation had been made, though, according to the notions of the day, the oaths were less sacred, and the agreement was regarded as less binding. The issue of

The claimants.

CLAIMANTS TO THE SPANISH THRONE.

PHILIP III.
King of Spain.

- **Philip IV.** King of Spain.
  - **Maria Theresa** = **Lewis XIV**, d. 1714.
    Solemn renunciation of rights to Crown of Spain made at this marriage.
    - **Lewis the Dauphin.** He waived his claim in favour of 2nd son, d. 1711.
      - **Lewis, Duke of Burgundy,** d. 1712.
        - Lewis, created duke of Anjou, afterwards Lewis XV.
      - **Philip, Duke of Anjou,** to whom Charles willed his crown. Candidate of French and Castilians in the war. Philip V. Left King of Spain at end of war. Ancestor of line that reigned to 1868.
      - **Charles, Duke of Berry,** d. 1714.
  - **Margaret** = **Léopold I.**, Emperor. He waived his claim in favour of 2nd son.
    A renunciation made, apparently not so solemn. *1st marr.*
    - **Joseph. Emperor, 1705.**
  - **Charles II.,** d. 1700, without issue.
- **Mary Anne** = **Ferdinand.** Emperor.
  No renunciation of rights at this marriage.
  - (Léopold I. *2nd marr.*)
    - **Charles.** The Archduke Charles. Claim weakest by descent, but barred by no renunciation. In 1711, on his brother's death, elected Emperor Charles VI.
  - **Maximilian** = **Mary Antoinette.** Elector of Bavaria.
    - **Joseph.** The Electoral Prince. Proposed by 1st Treaty of Partition that he be King of Spain, d. 1699.

this marriage was a daughter, who had married the Elector of Bavaria. Her claim would pass to her son, Joseph, the Electoral Prince of Bavaria. The third claimant was the emperor himself, the cousin of King Charles. His claim was the weakest by descent, but the strongest in that, at his mother's marriage, no renunciation had been effected.

The King of France and the emperor were fully aware that an absolute union of the Spanish Crown either with that of France or with the empire would never be permitted. The dauphin, therefore, and the emperor, agreed each to waive his right in favor of his second son. The three claimants stood forth as Philip, Duke of Anjou; Joseph, the Electoral Prince; and the Archduke Charles.

Second sons.

It was manifest that it would be best for the peace of Europe that the crown should pass to some prince of small power, or one whose power was distant from Spain. Anxiety was especially felt lest it should fall to a French prince; for France was now occupying the position in Europe once held by Spain, and the prospect of a union of the two countries under princes of the same family caused a genuine alarm, especially amongst Protestant statesmen. Lewis XIV. is called in French history "the great king." He was the founder of that policy of the aggrandisement of France at the expense of her neighbors which has marked French history since. Earlier French statesmen and French kings had the notion of an equilibrium in European politics, France being one amongst equal States; but Lewis wished to give her supremacy. Owing to her wise interference on behalf of toleration in Germany, in the Great Thirty Years' War, France had, about the time of the accession of Lewis, attained very

France.

considerable power. By unscrupulous encroachments, by interfering in the affairs of Germany—weakened as she was by her long struggle—and by vigorous fighting under most skilful generals, Lewis had increased that power. There was, indeed, reason to fear for the liberties of Europe if Spain were joined to France; nor was there room for doubt that this power would be hostile to the cause of Protestantism. The wise toleration which Henry of Navarre had granted to the Huguenots by the Edict of Nantes had been cancelled by the revocation of that charter. The influence of the Jesuits was plainly visible on the French Court.

Lewis had one great opponent, William of Orange. His ancestor, William the Silent, had opposed Philip of Spain whose power was dangerous to Europe and to Protestantism; and young William devoted his life to the same cause—the defence of the liberties of Europe, especially in religion. At first he stood forward only as the ruler of Holland; but when the Revolution placed him on the throne of England, that country, which, under Charles II., had been but the vassal, the paid servant of France, resumed her rightful position at the head of the Protestant cause. It is not necessary here to recapitulate the different events that mark stages in the contest between William and Lewis. The last tedious war, in which England had, for the most part, been successful at sea, and France on land, was ended with the Treaty of Ryswick, which, whilst it acquiesced in many of Lewis's conquests, yet settled the Jacobite question. Lewis had undertaken to recognise William as King of England, and nevermore to assist the exiled James in his attempts to regain the crown.

The peace was eagerly welcomed. England and

France alike were tired of war; and the rulers of the two countries, reluctant that the peace of Europe should be disturbed by this new question with respect to the succession to the crown of Spain, desired to arrange it without fighting.

Peace of Ryswick. A.D. 1697.

The negotiations between William and Lewis upon this subject were long and anxious. They began when Bentinck, Duke of Portland, once William's greatest friend, and still one of his most trusted advisers, was sent on an embassy to Versailles. They continued when Tallard, a distinguished French nobleman and general, was sent by Lewis on a special embassy to England. They were brought to a point at Loo, William's favourite Dutch palace, to which, when released from cares of State in England, he always hastened. The result was the First Treaty of Partition. When Lewis found that the English and the Dutch would not consent to the Spanish dominion passing to a French prince, even if shorn of some of its territories, he agreed that it should fall to the Electoral Prince of Bavaria, provided that France received an equivalent for this concession. The price was Naples and Sicily, as a separate kingdom for the Duke of Anjou, and the province of Guipuscoa, in the north of Spain, to be added to France. The Archduke Charles was to have the Milanese.

First partition treaty.

Had the King of Spain died, as was expected, soon after the signing of this treaty, there is little doubt it would have been quietly carried out. But, instead of the death of King Charles, who had long been ill, and whose death was constantly expected, the young prince Joseph fell ill of the small-pox and died at Brussels. All the agreements that had been made were useless; and

Death of Joseph and second partition treaty.

the old difficulty returned. Negotiations began again (1700). The claimants were now reduced to two—the dauphin's son, Philip of Anjou; and the Archduke Charles, the son of the emperor. The price of France therefore rose. England and Holland supported the claim of the Archduke Charles. It was therefore at length determined that the archduke should be King of Spain; that Philip of Anjou should have Naples and Sicily as before; that not only Guipuscoa but also the Milanese should fall to France; and it was intended that France should exchange the latter province for Lorraine, which lay more convenient.

It was natural that these treaties should produce great soreness in Spain. The Spaniards had long been at the head of a great power in Europe; and now their territories were to be divided, and their consent was not even asked. The Castilians were the proudest of all Spaniards, and had long been the ruling class in the country; they felt it the most. The dishonor to Spain was well expressed in a famous political satire, published towards the end of Queen Anne's reign, "Arbuthnot's History of John Bull," from which the popular name for an Englishman is taken. Old Lord Strutt, the King of Spain, is dying; and there assemble with measuring poles and ink-horns to divide his estate, Lewis Baboon (France), his neighbor, John Bull (England), his tailor, and Nick Frog, (Holland), his runaway servant. But the real question as to the iniquity of the partition is not settled here. The peace of Europe was more important than the honour of the Castilians, and the object of the treaty was to keep the nations at peace.

Irritation of Spain.

The soreness in Spain, however, vented itself in anger not against Lewis, but against William. The ill-feeling

Darien. with respect to him, unfortunately, was aggravated by another matter. The Spaniards claimed for themselves the whole coast of Central America. It had occurred some years before to a visionary Scotchman, named William Paterson, who had not always shown the qualities of a visionary, for he was the founder of the Bank of England, to lead a settlement to Darien, on the Isthmus of Panama. He represented in glowing terms to his countrymen the splendor of the country, where Nature produced her fruits little assisted by the labour of man, and the almost certain wealth that would accrue to Scotland. Paterson predicted that the whole trade with India would be diverted from its existing channels and pass across the Isthmus of Panama. The scheme created the greatest enthusiasm throughout Scotland. Everyone was anxious to obtain shares in the company which was formed. Two ships were fitted out, and the Darien company obtained a charter from William's representatives, the government in Scotland. The expedition failed, as it was sure to fail, seeing that the settlers knew nothing of the climate or of the country in which they were to settle. It failed utterly and entirely. Many fell victims to disease and starvation; a few escaped with their lives. This failure brought the ill-will of Scotland against William; the attempt roused the ill-will of England, jealous for her Indian trade, as well as the fierce anger of Spain.

Moreover, the English people did not want to interfere in the affairs of Spain. They were tired of fighting, **Opposition to William in England.** and on that account hostile to the policy of William. A House of Commons had been returned, pledged to a considerable reduction of the army, and determined to secure that in the

English army there should be no foreigners. William's favourite Dutch regiment, the Blue Guards, had to leave England. There was also indignation against William because he had granted to his Dutch friends estates that had been forfeited to the Crown. The opposition to the king had, indeed, been carried so far that he threatened to resign the crown, and had actually written the speech with which he should resign it, a speech which is still extant. Fortunately he never carried out this threat; but the conduct of the Spaniards, singling him out for their indignation about the Partition Treaties, shows that his power was not the same three years after as it had been when the Peace of Ryswick was signed. The Spaniards knew well the humiliation which the Parliament was inflicting on him.

The ruling classes in Spain, whose one great thought was how to keep the vast monarchy together, found it necessary to select one of the two claimants, and selected the more powerful. There were two parties at the Spanish Court, the larger and more earnest party in favour of the French succession, and another in favour of the House of Austria. But the French party prevailed. When the event so long expected at last took place, and King Charles died, it was found that he had recently signed a will, by which he left his kingdom undivided to Philip, Duke of Anjou, the second son of the dauphin. William was in no position to resist. Lewis, bound neither by his oaths of renunciation nor by the sacredness of treaties, without hesitation permitted his grandson to accept the inheritance; and the temper in which he did so was well illustrated by the speech with which he is said to have dismissed him to take up his crown—*Il n'y a plus de Pyrenees*—" The Pyrenees exist no longer." Philip

The will of Charles II.

Philip V. of Spain. went to Spain, where he was crowned and quietly received by the people as Philip V.

It would seem as if Lewis were going to have his own way; and if he had been careful neither to offend the people of England, nor to alarm the Dutch, it is more than possible that there would have been no war. William, and the leading statesmen of Holland, might have felt indignation at the undoing of their work, and might have given their sympathies to the Archduke Charles. But they were powerless, until Lewis committed a series of mistakes, which brought the war upon him. (1.) When Philip went to Spain, his grandfather, by letters patent, reserved his right of succession to the French Crown. By this the fear of a union between the two countries was increased. (2.) King Lewis put French garrisons into towns of the Spanish Netherlands, showing that he regarded those towns as now so closely united with France, that he might treat them as his own. He even proposed that the Netherlands should be ceded to him, as his government was so much nearer and more convenient than that of Spain. By this the fears of the Dutch were excited. But, however strongly William might feel this, the English people were still indifferent. (3.) When James II., the exiled King of England, died at St. Germains, Lewis, visiting him on his death-bed, was moved to promise that he would recognize his son as the King of England. On the death of James, his son James, usually known as the Old Pretender, was, with all due formality, recognised at Versailles; and the English people were at last aroused. The English ambassador was recalled from France; the French ambassador quickly received orders to leave London. The Parliament that had grudged supplies to William

Lewis makes three mistakes.

was dissolved. Amid the greatest excitement, another was elected, giving a large majority to the friends of William, and the country in many ways was now as eager as it had previously been disinclined for war

For such an occasion as this William had waited. However much he might deplore that the peace of Europe should once more be broken—although he knew that his own health was feeble, and that he could not live much longer, the stern purpose of his life did not desert him. That purpose had been opposition to the growing power of Lewis. Since the death of King Charles he had laboured to excite resistance to France among the European powers. The backwardness of the English had tied his hands; but now, through the chivalrous folly or insolence of Lewis, this difficulty had been removed. The league of the European powers, known as the Grand Alliance, was revived, the objects of which were to place the Archduke Charles on the throne of Spain, and to keep down the power of France. It declared first, that France was not to retain the Netherlands, nor to acquire the West Indies, and secondly, that the Crowns of France and Spain were never to be united.

The Grand Alliance of the Hague.

But the Grand Alliance was no sooner formed than its creator died. William had never been a strong man, he had suffered from many complaints, and was hardly ever free from asthma. His indomitable spirit had carried him through scenes of toil and fatigue which would have brought even strong men low His restless energy and his unceasing work had at last worn him out. All his doctors told him to prepare for death, and indeed he was ready for it. "You know," he said to a friend, "that I never feared death; there have been times when I should have

Death of William. A.D. 1702.

wished it; but, now that this great new prospect is opening before me, I do wish to stay here a little longer." He was riding on his favourite horse Sorrel in Hamptoncourt Park, when the horse stumbled upon a mole-hill. The king was thrown, and broke his collar-bone. An illness ensued, which ended in a fever, and the fever proved fatal.

About the character of William the Third many a battle has been fought. His name has been made a cry

Character.
wherewith to rouse animosities which are better left at peace. As no man is perfect, so in William's government, doubtless, mistakes may be found: perhaps they deserve even a harsher name. But the service that he rendered to England is undoubted and priceless, and it was not well repaid. During his later years his life was embittered by opposition from the English, who no longer felt the pressing need of his services against Stuart tyranny. He was constantly reproached with favouring his foreign friends. Would Englishmen have thought better of him if he had left his old and faithful friends unrewarded?

It is not, however, only or chiefly as an English king that William is to be judged—rather as a European

A European statesman.
statesman. As our fathers fought against Napoleon to preserve the liberties of Europe, and therewith our own, so William, from his earliest years to his death-bed, held constantly before him the one thought, how best to keep the power of France within bounds Germany had been left so divided at the peace of Westphalia that there was no one great State in Europe which could resist Lewis. The only chance was an alliance: but for an alliance it was necessary that there should be some one to propose and to maintain it; one who could humour this ally, and

persuade that; one who, penetrated with the greatness of the cause, could forgive petty insults, and by his own warmth make up for the coldness of others. Such an one was William.

Though William died, his work lived on. The machine, it has been said, was put together on true principles, and it continued in motion, though the master-workman was gone.

CHAPTER II.

LEWIS XIV.

It is impossible to understand any period of history without bearing in mind the character of the earlier times. Although this little work is intended as a history of only one and that a short period, the first fourteen years of the last century—it is advisable to give some account of the years that preceded it. *No period isolated.* The war, which gave the chief significance to the period, was the fifth and last act of a long political and military drama, in which, with almost poetical justice, the villain of the play receives his deserts. Of this drama, France and all that borders on France is the theatre. The chief actor is the King of France.

Lewis XIV. succeeded to the throne in 1643, being then only a little boy. He died in 1714. During almost all the seventy-two years of his reign France was at war. There were five general treaties of pacification, which mark five stages *Reign of Lewis XIV.* in the reign, and form the termination of the five acts in the drama. They are called the treaties of Westphalia, Aix-la-Chapelle, Nymwegen, Ryswick, and Utrecht. Of the last of these, a much fuller account will be found in its place further on in this volume. The earlier history will be best followed by keeping these treaties as dividing points, and filling up the intervals.

The peace of Westphalia was the peace which ended the Thirty Years' War. By judicious interference in the later part of that war France had been able to gain her object. Germany was divided into many independent states, jealous of each other. By the treaties a balance of power was established in Germany between the two forms of religion, the Roman Catholic and the Protestant. The Protestant party consisted, moreover, of two sections, who bitterly opposed each other—the Lutherans and the Calvinists. The result was, that Germany was weak, and that France had no danger or shadow of danger to fear from that side. It was not until 1870 that Germany recovered from the exhaustion and disunion which were the cruel and lasting effects of the Thirty Years' War.

Peace of Westphalia.
A.D. 1648.

As Lewis was so young on succeeding to his father's throne, he was, of course, at first merely a nominal ruler. The work of his predecessors, and of the ministers who governed France during his minority, prepared the way for his future policy of ambition. On the death of Mazarin, the greatest of these regents, Lewis, then aged twenty-three, came to his council of ministers and informed them, much to their astonishment, that henceforth he would manage his own affairs. From 1661, until his death, Lewis shaped his own policy, and is alone responsible for it. He had able ministers and was well served by them; but he was their master. This policy can only be described as a course of unvarying ambition, and of per-

Minority.

petual attempts to enlarge and exalt France at the expense of her neighbours.

In the history of some countries the personal character of the sovereign is not an important element in calculations. The policy of England for several years wavered less and was more vigorously carried out when the feeble Anne was on the throne, than under the energetic and able William. But with French history the case is different, especially with Lewis XIV. *L'etat, c'est moi!* " The State, I am the State!" was his favourite motto, which he carried out to the letter. so that his reign may be regarded as a perfect embodiment of absolutism. His best quality, and one most befitting his position, though not too common amongst kings, was industry. He was indefatigable in the details of work. Indeed, he needed all his industry since he took upon himself the work which had before been done by several Secretaries of State. He had capacity also,—"enough," said Mazarin, a competent judge, "for four kings and one honest man." Some writers have credited him with the virtues of generosity and religion. His generosity, however, was only a form of pride; his religion was bigotry. When James was exiled from England, Lewis received him with magnificence, and provided him with a palace as a residence. But such generosity cost him nothing, and it was pleasant to have kings at his board. His religion was a religion of externals. Had he been a sincere Catholic he could not have treated the Pope with the insolence which he showed towards him. Had he been possessed at all by the real spirit of religion, it must have interfered with his cruelty, with his indifference to the sufferings of subjects or foes, with his reckless and insatiable ambition. " By that sin fell the angels." There is an ambition

Character of Lewis XIV.

which might seem almost worth the price of an angel's fall, but the French king's ambition was only to add to his territory, rood after rood, wrested with or without pretext from his neighbour. In the furtherance of his ambition he was entirely without scruple.

In the forty years that intervened between Lewis' real accession to power and the close of the century, there were three great wars besides minor raids.

1661-1700.

The first was undertaken against Spain for the maintenance of a claim upon the Duchy of Brabant. There was a law in Brabant that all the issue of a first marriage, female as well as male, should succeed to a fief or an estate before even the sons of a second marriage. In virtue of this law, upon the death of the King of Spain and the accession of his son Charles, the weak and sickly prince, whose death caused the contest that filled the commencement of the next century, and who was then an infant, Lewis laid claim to the Duchy of Brabant and to other provinces of the Netherlands in right of his wife, who was Charles's half-sister. The claim was bad for two reasons. Firstly, the law applied only to private property, and had never been held to apply to the sovereign. Secondly, as has been said, before Lewis's marriage to the Spanish princess, solemn renunciation had been made of all rights which might pass to him through it. But on this, as on the later occasion, the arbitrary Lewis did not allow such trifles as oaths or treaties to hinder him from acting as he pleased. He had a strong army, and might with him was enough. But opposition appeared where he least expected it.

First War. Succession to Brabant. 1667.

During the seventeenth century England was under the dominion of the Stuarts, whose foreign policy cannot be described as glorious or successful. During the greater part of their reign, the struggle with their Parliaments gave them neither leisure nor opportunity for foreign affairs.

English foreign policy in seventeenth century.

Whilst the Stuarts were anxious to rule without Parliaments, to be kings indeed, like the French kings, and whilst they were meeting with strong opposition from Englishmen who preferred the old lines of the Constitution, it was not likely that they would engage in foreign war. For wars cost money, and as the raising of money was their difficulty, they were naturally determined to ask for as little as possible. The sympathy of the people of England was very largely with the Protestants of the Continent. Remembering the greatness of Elizabeth's England, the people would very gladly have seen their country take her place at the head of the Protestant cause. When the Thirty Years' War broke out, they would gladly have seen James send support to Elizabeth, his beautiful daughter, for one winter Queen of Bohemia. Four times during the century England came thus to the front, under Elizabeth, Oliver Cromwell, Sir William Temple, and William of Orange.

On the third of these our attention must be fixed now. Sir William Temple might have made his name one of the greatest names amongst the statesmen of England. But he did not enjoy the turmoil of parliamentary struggles, and was fonder of learned leisure than of office. After showing very distinguished talents for diplomacy, he shrank from the effort without which great names cannot be made. It was however he who, at this time, when English ambassador at the Hague, conceived the idea of the Triple Alliance, and carried it into execution. 1668 is the only year in the reign of Charles II. on which an

The Triple Alliance.

Englishman can look back without a feeling of shame. England, Holland, and Sweden, the three chief Protestant powers of the north of Europe, were leagued together to resist the continued growth of France, which they regarded as dangerous to their interests and to liberty. The formation of the League was sufficient to prevent the separation of Brabant from Spain, though in other respects the terms which it obtained were not hard for France. Yet the French king chafed under the Peace of Aix-la-Chapelle.

Peace of Aix-la Chapelle.

He thought the best way to treat England was to buy her king, and by the secret Treaty of Dover Lewis bought Charles. The price paid was a sum of money annually as a pension, and a promise to help him with French troops, if the English Parliament proved troublesome. But against Holland the revenge of Lewis took the shape of one of the worst, because one of the most causeless, wars in history. His army invaded Holland, which was not ready for him, being distracted by party spirit. One party, under the Grand Pensionary, De Witt, was for yielding to so powerful a foe; but the terms that Lewis asked were so outrageous, that the mob in Amsterdam rose in fury, and brutally murdered De Witt. The other party regarded as their leader a young man, to whose family Holland owed priceless services, but not services which could surpass those which, from this time forward, he himself proceeded to render to Holland and to Europe. William of Orange devoted himself to the task of opposing Lewis, the enemy of his country, the enemy of his faith, the enemy of freedom. His heroic ardour, always keenest when danger

Treaty of Dover.

Second War. Invasion of Holland

William of Orange.

seemed darkest, inspired his countrymen to resistance. But so overwhelming seemed the force of the enemy that the Dutch were very near despair. The proposal was seriously entertained by them to leave their country, and, sailing away in their numerous ships to the Dutch possessions in the East, there to establish a new country for themselves. "There the Dutch Commonwealth might commence a new and more glorious existence, and might rear, under the Southern Cross, amidst the sugar canes and nutmeg trees, the Exchange of a wealthier Amsterdam, and the Schools of a more learned Leyden." [1]

This proposal was not adopted, though a resolution almost as heroic was carried out. A great part of Holland lies beneath the level of the sea, from which the land has been rescued by the labour of man. Huge dykes or sea-walls have been erected strong enough to stand against the force of the sea, and high enough to keep out the highest tide. These it was now determined to open, and to sacrifice the labour of centuries rather than submit to the invader. The waters were let in upon the land, and Holland became like a great sea from which only the towns stood out. The French troops were not prepared for this contingency, nor provided with a flotilla of boats. Before the new defender, the waves, they retreated. It is painful to an Englishman to reflect that during this display of heroism his country, with its king in French pay, was on the side of France, though the Parliament shortly afterwards compelled the king to separate from the alliance, and, before the war ended, had certainly shown a change of policy in sanctioning the marriage of William of Orange to Princess Mary, the king's niece.

Cutting of the dykes.

[1] Macaulay.

The war thus shamelessly begun became a European war, into the details of which this is not the place to enter. It was ended with the Treaty of Nymwegen, which aggrandised France chiefly at the expense of Spain. This peace may be regarded as the zenith of Lewis's career. It was after it that courtiers, who knew not wherein true greatness lies, hailed him with the name of Great. This title was formally bestowed on him by the magistrates of Paris. His later treaties mark losses of France rather than gain even in territory: certainly the wars that they closed showed loss of glory.

Treaty of Nymwegen. A.D. 1678. Lewis the Great.

The ancients believed that too great prosperity brought with it the wrath of the gods, and the reason of this belief, probably, is that those who gain great success cease to exercise the vigilance that ensures it, and become careless. It seemed to be a special characteristic of Lewis XIV. that success engendered an insolence which seems to us almost like madness; the madness of one whom, according to the proverb, the gods will to destroy. With mere ordinary care, as has been already shown, he might, later in his reign, have avoided the war of the Spanish Succession; but the insolence that is born of triumph made him insult the English people and their king. So now, in the interval of peace which followed the Treaty of Nymwegen, and which may be compared rather to a sick man's broken slumbers than to the quiet sleep of the healthy, he was guilty of three acts, all unjustifiable and all unnecessary, which brought ruin upon his head.

Nemesis.

Three symptoms of madness.

The first was the seizure of Strassburg.

In the cessions that were made to France by the Peace of Nymwegen was included all the territory belonging to certain towns. Lewis intended this to be construed favourably to himself, and instituted Chambers of Re-union, composed exclusively of Frenchmen, to decide what territories had at any time belonged to these towns. Under cover of their decisions he made many additions to his dominions. One, more daring than the rest, was nothing less than the important city of Strassburg, a free city of the empire. Whilst Lewis declared through his ambassador at the Imperial Court that nothing was meant, a French army, of 40,000 men, approached Strassburg, as if for a review, and before any assistance could be sent from Germany (if any could have been sent by a country so divided) the city yielded to the French. There were only 500 soldiers within: the citizens were at the time stricken with typhus fever, and but few could bear arms. Lewis's Minister of War was present with the army, under whose instructions the fortifications were strengthened by no less an engineer than Vauban himself.

1. Seizure of Strassburg.

If the first act of Lewis's madness was an outrage on the stranger, the second was a violation of justice against his own subjects. It was the revocation of the Edict of Nantes.

2. Revocation of Edict of Nantes. 1685.

A century earlier France was torn by civil wars, based upon religious differences. The Huguenots, or French Protestants, were not very numerous, but they were very earnest and zealous. At length it chanced that the rightful successor to the throne was upon their side, so that their party, materially strengthened by the addition of those who were in favour of the rightful king, whatever his creed might be, and helped also by his valour and generalship, gained the upper hand. But Henry of Navarre found that it would be more for the interests of

The Edict.

the whole people that he should accept the religion of the majority. He became a Catholic, but he did not forget his old friends. By the Edict of Nantes he guaranteed freedom of worship for the Huguenots, and the religious wars ceased. (1598.)

Lewis XIV. had by this time fallen very much under the influence of Madame de Maintenon, who was a bigoted Roman Catholic, and a furious antagonist of the Huguenots. She persuaded Lewis to revoke the edict of his grandfather, and apparently after some hesitation he yielded to her entreaties. A persecution commenced, which drove the Huguenots out of the land, for they were not strong enough to resist. France, in this way, lost many peaceful and industrious citizens, who carried their skill and industry into other countries, especially to England and to Holland. The silk-weavers of Spitalfields, where there is still a street called Fleur-de-lys, are descendants of the Huguenot emigrants. Canterbury, Norwich, and other places received colonies of them Men, also, of a higher rank than the weavers, with names famous in literature, were amongst the emigrants. And not only men of peace, but skilful and practised generals, and many soldiers, left the country that repaid their services so ungenerously, and, joining her foes, were found in later battles commanding or serving against France.

Persecution and emigration of Huguenots. 1685.

Nor yet have we finished count of the injury that the revocation of the tolerant edict brought on France. We must also include the rising in the Cevennes, an insurrection of the persecuted Protestants who lived in the Cevennes Mountains, in the south of France. This took place at a time when France was hard pressed by external enemies, and increased her difficulties in repelling them.

The Cevennes.

But as if these two acts were insufficient, Lewis added to them a third, which was as ill-timed as it was cruel.

Charles II. of England, who had been a confederate of Lewis, was dead. His brother and successor, James, was still more inclined to Lewis, for he was a Catholic, heart and soul. During the whole of his short reign he was making attempts to subvert the English Church, and at length the English people were unable longer to endure them. In the early part of 1688 they were beginning to look hopefully across the water to William of Orange, son-in-law and nephew of the king. When, forty years earlier, the Stuarts had been forcing their will upon the English people, there had been no prominent member of the royal family upon the popular side; but now the people were more fortunate, and a hope was spreading amongst them that William would deliver them from their troubles. If Lewis had been wise, he would have listened to the voices that warned him how strong the opposition to him would be if England were joined to it. He would have devoted himself to the work of watching William, and protecting James, his ally, from attack. Apparently Lewis was blind; he allowed his attention to be occupied in another direction with a crime that he was meditating.

English Revolution. A.D. 1688.

The capture of Strassburg had opened for him a way into Germany. William of Orange set sail for England on November 1; but, in the previous month, Lewis had caused a large army to march into the Palatinate, in order to enforce a claim made by a princess, his sister-in-law, upon those territories, although the case had already been decided against her in the imperial courts. As this army could not continue to hold the country which it had seized, it received deliberate orders to ravage the

3. Ravaging of the Palatinate. 1688.

whole of it, to burn the towns, and to destroy the trees, crops, and vines. The order was as ruthlessly obeyed as it had been barbarously conceived. A thrill of horror passed through Europe.

A league of opposition had been forming against Lewis, known under the name of the "League of Augs-
The Grand Alliance of Augsburg. burg," which, now that William had been successful and the English Revolution had been consummated without hindrance from France, received the accession of England and Holland, and was called The Grand Alliance.

The war that followed, the fourth act in the drama of Lewis' ambition, may be divided into two parts: the one
Third War. —the attempts of Lewis to restore the exiled James, the campaign in Ireland, of which the battle of the Boyne was the centre, and the sea-fights in the Channel; the other—the Continental War. In the former the English may be said to have been wholly successful; for though the French won the battle of Beachy Head, that victory had no permanent results, and was soon and fully retrieved. In the Continental War the results were nearly balanced, for though the French won most of the pitched battles, the peculiar genius of William asserted itself, the qualities which made him more formidable after a defeat than others after victory. Three years before the century closed,
Peace of Ryswick. A.D. 1697. this war against the Grand Alliance was brought to an end by the peace of Ryswick. The nations were tired of war, and welcomed peace; but the ambition of Lewis made it rather a cessation of hostilities than a real peace. Once more it was necessary to form the Grand Alliance: once more to resist his encroachments.

CHAPTER III.

THE NEW DRAMATIS PERSONÆ.

IN accordance with the provision of the Bill of Rights, confirmed by the Act of Settlement, William was succeeded on the throne by his sister-in-law, Anne, daughter of James II. and Anne Hyde, daughter of the Earl of Clarendon. *Succession of Queen Anne.*

In character, and in fitness for the position of sovereign, Anne was very different from William. She had not his discernment, nor his statesmanship, nor his resolution. On the contrary, she was *Character.* without strength of character. She could not be expected to establish a new policy, nor, through good report and evil report, to adhere to one already established. She had always been, and, after her accession she still remained, under the influence of some stronger mind. Such influence was essential to her. There is no feature in her character which is so important to recollect as this, for it explains a good deal of her reign, especially two of its salient events—her adoption and her abandonment of the Grand Alliance.

Anne, however, though no great ruler of men, possessed personal qualities which would have made her highly esteemed in private life, and which endeared her to her subjects. Her private character was irreproachable. She was kind, affectionate, and good; a warm friend, and with a humane heart. But above all she was sincerely religious, like both her grandfathers, and, unlike her father, she was warmly attached to the doctrines and rites of the Church of England. She often shared the unreasonable fears of the High Church party, and was easily shaken by the cry—"The Church is in danger!" She was very popular with the English people, and mainly for this reason, that she was peculiarly an *English* queen, having, as she said in her first speech from the throne, an "entirely English" heart. Coming between a Dutch king, whom many Englishmen had accepted as a necessity, but never loved, and a German prince, who could not even speak their language, the English have always looked back with affection to her reign, and have enshrined her in their hearts as "Good Queen Anne."

Anne had married Prince George of Demark, a man of dull understanding and of coarse habits. "I have

Husband. tried him drunk, and I have tried him sober," said Charles II., of him, "and there is nothing in him." Had he been a man of more capacity, it is not unlikely that he would have been placed upon the throne as William had been; but with him it was impossible. To this husband Queen Anne was

Children. tenderly attached. By him she had a large family, but all of their children had died in infancy, with the exception of Prince William, who, in the last reign, had been created Duke of Gloucester. In him the hopes of the English people were centred. King William appointed Marlborough as his governor, Bishop Burnet as his preceptor. "My Lord," he who seldom paid compliments had said to Marlborough, on entrusting him with his office, "make him but what you are, and my nephew will be all I wish to see." But in the last year of the seventeenth century, the same year which proved fatal to the wretched King Charles of Spain, the young prince died. Upon his death the Act of Settlement was made law, by which it was decided to whom the crown should pass upon the death of Anne, for when Anne came to the throne, aged thirty-seven, she was childless. She now appointed Prince George to the office of Lord High Admiral, an office for which he was manifestly unfit.

It has been said that the queen was entirely under the influence of favourites. At her accession, and for many years before, during the whole of William's reign, and even earlier, she had been under the influence of Sarah Jennings, wife of the Duke of Marlborough, a woman of commanding mind, of great ambition, and with a very imperious temper. Her intimacy with the queen was very close. They were in the habit of corresponding with each other under assumed names. The Queen was Mrs. Morley; the Duchess, Mrs. Freeman; their husbands, Prince George and the Duke, were Mr. Morley and Mr. Freeman respectively. The name Freeman was, perhaps, adopted by the favourite as a symbol of the liberties which its bearer thought herself entitled to take with her friend. It would not be too much to say that she governed the queen. Some, her husband amongst the number, have had the faculty of charming whilst they ruled, so that the ruling was concealed: she had not.

Lady Marlborough.

The real hero of this reign, the successor of King William in his policy of consistent opposition to France, was John Churchill, Duke of Marlborough. In this man were united the noblest and the meanest qualities, and it is therefore difficult to form a just estimate of him. For our purpose it will be sufficient to pass very quickly over his earlier life, and to give a short sketch of his character. Fortunately for us, at this point in his career, "that great man is already shaking off the slough of his baser life." Marlborough, as a young man, was attached to the

Marlborough.

His life.

household of James, Duke of York, through this disgraceful fact that his sister was the prince's mistress. At the age of twenty-three he served in a campaign against the Dutch under the great Turenne, whose favourable notice he attracted. He rose quickly through the different military grades, and shortly after James's accession to the throne he commanded the English troops sent against the Pretender, Monmouth, whom he defeated at the battle of Sedgemoor. James wished him to become a Roman Catholic; but from this step he shrank, and when afterwards the Revolution took place, this proposal was the reason that he gave for his desertion. James, placing implicit trust in him, sent Churchill forward with troops against William's invading army. Instead of fighting William, he joined him. During William's reign he is, at the beginning, in positions of trust, but he himself does not seem certain as to his future, or genuine in his sympathy with the Revolution; for, though he held high office under William, he yet intrigued with the exiled James, probably wishing to be safe whichever side triumphed. William discovered his secret correspondence with the Jacobites, and dismissed him from all his employments. Marlborough boasted of having betrayed to James, and so to the French, the secret of an enterprise that the English were about to make against Brest; which betrayal led to the failure of the attempt, and the loss of the commander with 800 men. Yet before William's death Marlborough was reconciled to him, and as we have seen was entrusted by him with the important office of governor to the young Duke of Gloucester. It is also said that William, when contemplating the War of the Spanish Succession, designed that Marlborough should command the armies of the Grand Alliance.

The New Dramatis Personæ.

It will be evident, from the above sketch, that if we begin with Marlborough's bad qualities, that which taints all his character and all his actions is self-seeking, which did not hesitate to use even treachery as its instrument. Nor was his treachery only a willingness to shift allegiance. The generation amongst which he had been brought up, which had seen the days of the Commonwealth, and of the restored Stuarts, and, finally, had consigned the Stuarts again to exile, must have held but lightly by the duty of allegiance. But Marlborough's was no common treachery, no ordinary laxity of principles in high places. If others left James easily, gratitude should have kept him, at least, by his side. The imparting of information of a military expedition to the rulers of a country with which his own was at war can be excused by no blaze of glory; nor can we palliate the sending of money to assist a rival to his sovereign's throne. The self-interest, which seems to have been the leading motive of conduct both in Marlborough and in his wife, sometimes assumed the baser shape of an inordinate love of money. A nobleman, who was once mobbed by mistake for Marlborough in the time of his unpopularity, indulged in this sarcasm at his expense—"I will easily convince you that I am not my Lord Marlborough. In the first place, I have only two guineas about me, and, in the second place, they are very much at your service." Marlborough even grudged a pension to a servant who had saved his life.

Character.

Yet let no one imagine that Marlborough was altogether a bad man. His great vices tainted his public and his private life; but he had qualities which went far to redeem these, and which enabled him to render almost priceless services to his country and to Europe. He was possessed of consummate

His virtues.

military genius, and courage dauntless yet not rash. He was never defeated in any battle. He was always ready to expose himself to danger provided that it was necessary. He had, also, a virtue more useful than courage to soldier or to statesman—calm patience; he showed no excitement in the heat of battle; he was calm and serene in danger as in a drawing-room. Closely allied with this calmness was a suavity of mind and of manners, which fascinated the most critical judge. Marlborough was a singularly handsome man, gifted with a beautiful face and a most perfect figure. It has been said that his calmness proceeded, to a great extent, from a want of heart; but his affection for his wife was so remarkable that he has often been taunted with being too much under her influence. If she wrote angrily to him, no success in war could make him happy until she had relented. Moreover, as a general, Marlborough was remarkable for his humanity; before the battle he would point out to the surgeons their stations, and would take measures to ensure the proper treatment of the wounded. No general was so courteous and considerate to his prisoners.

Many a character has been written of Marlborough, varying from the strongest praise to the severest blame. It would seem the true course not to temper the praise with the blame, and produce a verdict that should be neither hot nor cold, but to adopt and combine the strong features from each account, and to leave it to the moral philosopher to decide how it came to pass, as it assuredly did, that one man could combine the blackest treachery and the greediest avarice with the courage, the calmness, and the sweetness of Marlborough.

Amongst English statesmen Marlborough had most sympathy with Sydney, Lord Godolphin; and he in-

sisted that Godolphin should be appointed to
the office of Lord High Treasurer. This Lord Go-
office is now in abeyance, or, rather, as the dolphin.
expression runs, it is in commission, that is to say, instead of one minister there are five, who are called the Lords of the Treasury, of whom the Prime Minister is one, and the Chancellor of the Exchequer another. From this time forward Marlborough and Godolphin were firm allies. Lord Godolphin, however, was not a statesman of a high order, but one that would be best described as a shrewd man of business. He was able to give Marlborough very useful support, for an army depends on its supplies, and money is the sinews of war. But in private life Godolphin was not superior to the country squires of his time. He had no taste for literature or art, and his favourite pursuits were racing and cock-fighting.

In the work which now lay before Marlborough he was very materially assisted by two men, Prince Eugene and Heinsius. Prince Eugene was a
younger son of the House of Savoy. He Prince
was born in France, and educated for the Eugene.
priesthood; but he showed even in his studies a taste for the life of a soldier. Instead of theological works he was fond of reading Plutarch's Lives. He was a youth of slender figure, and King Lewis on that account refused him the commission for which he asked, and spoke contemptuously of the little abbé. This insult Eugene never forgot. He immediately left France, and entered the service of the emperor. He was thus an Italian, born in France, and living in Germany. In his signature he united the languages of the three countries, "Eugenio von Savoye."

The empire had for many years been engaged in constant wars with the Turks. In these wars Eugene so distinguished himself that he came to be regarded as first general of the empire. Between him and Marlborough a very warm friendship sprang up, which never cooled. There was no jealousy between them, but, whether they were working together in the same campaign, or at a distance at the head of separate armies, they were always one-minded in their aims and policy. Yet Eugene was very different from Marlborough. He had not the same calmness. His courage was mixed with daring. He was like a Fury in the day of battle, and as prodigal of the lives of his soldiers as he was careless of his own.

The third in this triumvirate, which broke the power of Lewis and delivered Europe, was not a general, but a statesman. As such, his work is in the background, and has not been much noticed in histories. Yet, though not so visible, the work which he did in holding the members of the Grand Alliance together, in keeping Holland faithful to the cause, and in helping Marlborough with advice, was as true and valuable as the more brilliant exploits of others. Anthony Heinsius was a Dutch statesman. Shortly after William of Orange had carried the English Revolution to a successful issue, he became Grand Pensionary, a title which we may translate into our own political language by calling him Prime Minister of Holland. On entering public life he had preferred for his country a close alliance with France, and had been hostile to the princes of the House of Orange. But a visit to Versailles opened his eyes to the fact that the Dutch could have no lasting friendship with the French, who despised their government, and persecuted their religion. He changed sides, joined himself closely to William, and became one of his warmest friends and most trusted advisers. And William felt that there was no man whom he would leave behind him so competent and so willing to carry out his policy as Heinsius.

CHAPTER IV.

THE GRAND ALLIANCE.

THE Grand Alliance being duly formed, it will be well to consider its component parts.

At its head we must place the emperor, rather on account of the ancient dignity of the empire than because of its actual power. The office was still nominally elective. At each vacancy the Electors met at Frankfort-on-Maine, and all the forms of an election were gone through. Sometimes there was a show of opposition, but the empire had now become practically hereditary in the House of Hapsburg. For nearly three centuries no emperor had been elected who did not belong to that family. Though the empire gave dignity to the family, it did not give them power. Whatever they had of power came to them from their proper hereditary dominions, which were very heterogeneous. They were kings, and nominally elective, in Bohemia and in Hungary; archdukes in Austria and in the Tyrol. The family was by no means incapable, but was selfish, and unable to rise to the conception of a union of Germany. Earlier, the princes of this House had been bigoted Roman Catholics, who, indeed, had brought about the Thirty Years' War by this very bigotry. But now the danger of encroachment on the part of France, was great, and they were ready to join and to take advantage of the Alliance, although its members were chiefly Protestant. Lewis XIV. was declared " Hereditary Foe of the Holy Empire." Leopold I. was the emperor at the outbreak of the war, having been emperor for nearly fifty years. Shortly after the commencement, in the year after Blenheim, he died, and was succeeded by his eldest son, Joseph, who had won some fame as a soldier, and who was much beloved in his own dominions, being generous and humane. Leopold's second son, Charles, was the candidate whom the allies wished to place upon the throne of Spain. He was by no means equal to his brother in merit.

As the form of election to the empire was still kept up, we should notice who were the Electors. By the twelfth century the number had been fixed at seven, three of whom were ecclesiastics—the Archbishops of Mayence, Treves, and Cologne; and four lay princes—the Electors of Saxony, Brandenburg, Bohemia, and the Palatinate. In the seventeenth century an eighth Elector was added. Frederick, the Elector Palatine, son-in-law of James I. of England, having given his consent to be elected,— as a Protestant—to the kingdom of Bohemia, was defeated by the Austrian prince, who was also Emperor, and was deprived not only of Bohemia, but also of the Palatinate, and, therewith, of his vote, which was given to the Catholic Duke of Bavaria. The Thirty Years' War followed; and at the peace of Westphalia, which ended that war, it was contended that the vote could not thus be taken from the Elector Palatine. At length, to satisfy both parties, a vote was given to each. In 1692 the Emperor Leopold on his own responsibility gave a ninth vote to the Duke of Hanover, whose descendant now sits upon the throne of England, though this vote was not recognized by the Diet of the Empire for fourteen years, that is, after the outbreak of this war. The recognition was claimed by Hanover as its price for continuance in the war.

Of the nine Electors two, Cologne and Bavaria, were upon the side of France. The other two ecclesiastics, Mayence and Treves, were neutral. *How they ranged themselves.* Bohemia formed part of the Emperor's dominions. The Elector of Saxony had recently been elected King of Poland, and was very busy at the eastern end of Germany; he could not spare energies for fighting against France. Brandenburg, the Palatinate, and Hanover were members of the Grand Alliance. When we remember what the Palatinate had lately suffered, we cannot wonder that it should join against France.

Frederick, the Elector of Brandenburg, named as his price for joining the alliance that his electorate should be made into a kingdom. He was the last of the twelve Hohenzollern Electors of Brandenburg, and had been wishing for some *King of Prussia.* time to be king, especially since his neighbour, the Elector of Saxony, had become King of Poland, and another neighbour, the Duke of Hanover, had been made Elector, with the prospect of his family inheriting the English Crown. He took his regal title from another part of his dominions, and, when the Emperor Leopold yielded, his Ministry, it is said, having been richly bribed, Frederick was crowned King of Prussia (1701). It may be well to remember that he was the grandfather of Frederick the Great, and that this was the beginning of the kingdom (though its earlier history before it was a kingdom is well worth study) which in our own day has extended and prospered, until its monarch has become the new Emperor of Germany.

Some other minor princes of Germany joined in the league, such as Lewis, Prince of Baden, and, for at least part of the war, Denmark also contributed troops. But, after all allowance has been made, England and Holland must be considered the central powers of the alliance.

Other allies.

The names Holland and Dutch are instances of two different laws that affect names—extension and contraction. The word "Dutch" in England is only applied to the people and language of Holland, but it is the same as the name by which the Germans, of whom the natives of Holland are a branch, call themselves and their speech. The name "Holland," properly applied to two out of the seven United Provinces, North and South Holland, has been extended to the whole seven. Holland, when the war broke out, had been a nation for rather more than 120 years. These seven provinces, lying round and to the north of the mouth of the Rhine, had, together with the remaining provinces of the Netherlands, rebelled against the tyranny and persecution of Spain; and under the lead of William the Silent, Prince of Orange, great-grandfather of William III. of England, the northern seven had after vigorous and heroic resistance gained their independence. They banded themselves together in the League of Utrecht (1579) into the Federal Commonwealth of the Seven United Provinces. From the time of their freedom they made great progress. Daring mariners, eager and skilful traders, active colonists, in the course of a century they raised their small State to a high rank in Europe. It was for its size far the wealthiest, far the most populous, and far the most important.

After one year of the war, in 1703, the Grand Alliance was joined by two other powers, which at first had ranked themselves on the side of the French prince,— Savoy and Portugal.

Victor Amadeus II. Duke of Savoy, is one of the most romantic characters of the period. Though his territory was small, the part that he played in history was by no means insignificant. He had more than ordinary capacity, both as general and administrator. The virtues of chivalry, bravery, and generosity distinguished him, and made him warmly loved by his subjects. When a French emissary was taunting him with the destruction of his small army, he answered with spirit:—"I will stamp with my foot upon the ground, and soldiers will spring forth." His little land was overshadowed by its more powerful neighbour, and had for at least half a century before his accession been at the beck of the French king. Lewis sent orders to the duke not to harbour Protestants who had fled from France when the Edict of Nantes was revoked, and to persecute those who were in his dominion. Had not his predecessor done it in Cromwell's time, and stirred Milton's heart with the tales of atrocity that were told? Victor Amadeus was but half-hearted in the execution of Lewis's cruel will, and a French marshal was sent to demand his capital. This drove him into open resistance, and he joined the League of Augsburg (1686), which had been recently set on foot. The armies sent against him were active and powerful, and he lost two battles. But great efforts were made to detach him from the common cause, and at length he made a separate peace with France, which was as honourable to him as if he had been victorious. His territory was to be restored; the Duke of

Savoy.

His part in the war before Ryswick.

Burgundy, the eldest son of the dauphin, was to marry his eldest daughter; he was to be treated like a king. On these terms he changed sides. It was said that he was generalissimo for the Emperor and for King Lewis within one month. But his separate peace was the first of a series, and the Treaty of Ryswick (1697) soon ended the war.

When the second Grand Alliance was formed and the war of the Spanish Succession began, he was at first on the side of the French, but after a very short time he made a change, as sudden as that which he had made in the last war, but in the exactly opposite direction. In order to secure his allegiance, not only had the Duke of Burgundy married his eldest daughter, in accordance with the treaty, but his brother Philip, Duke of Anjou, and now, according to the will of the late king, King of Spain, married his second daughter. The insolence, however, of a French marshal, who apparently despised a Prince of Savoy, and the strictness of Spanish etiquette, which would not allow him to sit by the side of his son-in-law, so vexed him, that he meditated deserting his cause. All hesitation was removed by an arrogant letter which he received from Lewis XIV. The following was their correspondence:—

In the Spanish Succession War.

(The King to the Duke.)

"Monsieur,—Since religion, honour, and your own signature, are of no account between us, I send my cousin, the Duc de Vendôme, to explain my will to you. He will give you twenty-four hours to decide."

(Answer.—The Duke to the King.)

"Sire,—Threats do not frighten me. I shall take the measures that may suit me best, relative to the unworthy proceedings that have been adopted towards my troops. I have nothing further to explain, and I decline listening to any proposition whatever."

Lewis XIV. sent orders that the Savoyard troops should be disarmed. Victor Amadeus thereupon changed sides, and was for the remainder of the war bitterly opposed to France. At first he met with many disasters; but his high courage sustained him through them all, and when Eugene brought an imperial army into Italy, the tide of war turned, and the success of the allies in that portion of the borders of France was by no means the least serious of the blows under which King Lewis staggered.

This sketch, which is continued in the main body of the history, may be found of interest, placed side by side with the account of the kingdom of Prussia. As that is the beginning of the modern German Empire, so the descendant of Victor Amadeus is now King of United Italy. The Duchy of Savoy may be said to be the germ of modern Italy, though, strange to say, it now lies without the borders of that kingdom.

Portugal joined the Grand Alliance in the same year as Savoy. During the Middle Ages Portugal had been a small independent kingdom, which during the latter part of that time had devoted itself to the honourable work of discovery and colonisation. On a vacancy of the throne occurring by exhaustion of the previous dynasty, Philip II. of Spain became a candidate; but, being doubtful of success, he determined not to wait for an election, but to seize the crown by force of arms. For sixty years Portugal remained subject to Spain; and for rather more than sixty years since it had been free. In this war the situation of Portugal gave it an importance which its size could not claim. The king

Portugal.

hesitated at first on which side to declare, thinking that France would win, but recognising, also, that the fleets of England and Holland were strong, and that his coasts lay exposed to them. To secure Portugal, the Archduke Charles promised by a secret treaty to cede certain Spanish cities, and the territory called Rio de la Plata in South America. When this was afterwards divulged it created a strong feeling against Charles in Spain. A treaty, called the Methuen Treaty, after Paul Methuen, the English ambassador at Lisbon, gained over Portugal to the side of the allies. One of the conditions of this treaty was that the wines of Portugal should be admitted into England at a much lower duty than the French wines. Such was the price of the accession of Portugal—a price which the English continued to pay for no less than 131 years. The alliance between England and Portugal was permanent.

<small>Methuen Treaty.</small>

Against this league what chance had the French? The confederacy was very numerous, but no reliance can be placed on the members of a confederacy that they will remain of one mind. France was a monarchy, and a despotic monarchy. It suffered from no divided counsels, but one will ruled over all. Moreover, it had a large and well-disciplined standing army; and was probably able to bring at once into the field a larger force than the whole confederacy. And, lastly, the French soldiers had hitherto been victorious on every field; they believed themselves and others held them to be almost invincible. An unprejudiced spectator at the outset would have said that France with Spain on her side would win in this contest. Such an one could not take into account the as yet unproved genius of Marlborough, or the lavish expenditure of money on the part of England and of Holland.

In the same year that Savoy left her side France gained another ally, the Elector of Bavaria. He had been Governor-General of the Netherlands during the reign of his wife's uncle, Charles II. of Spain. It was a post with an enormous salary, and Brussels, the seat of the government, was a pleasant place of residence, pleasanter than his own capital, Munich. To secure his alliance, a promise was made by Lewis that the Elector should be continued in this post, and so within a year of the outbreak he declared himself on the side of France. His brother, the Elector of Cologne, was a creature of King Lewis, and of course upon his side, but his assistance was of no great value.

At the beginning of the war Philip, the French candidate, was aged seventeen, Charles, the Austrian archduke, fifteen. They were curiously alike in character. Both were dreamy and sleepy in disposition, but capable of obstinate opposition when once aroused, and afterwards became mere puppets in the hands of their wives. Lord Peterborough, an English general, somewhat free of tongue, asked if it was worth while that great nations should fight for such "a pair of louts."

CHAPTER V.

OPENING OF THE WAR.

Section I.—*Marlborough in Flanders.*

IMMEDIATELY upon the declaration of war Marlborough was appointed Commander-in-chief of the British forces. Fortunately the Dutch also were easily persuaded by Heinsius to place their troops under the same command. Indeed, Marl-

Marlborough Commander-in-chief.

borough became almost at once exceedingly popular with the Dutch people, as well as honoured and trusted by the Dutch statesmen. His exquisite manners account for the popularity; William's opinion of him for the trust. The standing danger of a confederacy is division of counsels; and it was, therefore, well for the common cause that the troops of both the Dutch and the English—the most important of the allies in that quarter—should be under one general. The fact that there were more commanders than one ruined the campaigns elsewhere—on the Rhine and in Spain. But it was unfortunate that the confidence of the Dutch did not go so far as the abolition of their custom of sending with the general field-deputies, civilian members of the Government, without whose consent no important action should be undertaken. This was no special device to annoy Marlborough, but in his early campaigns it had the effect of hindering him and tying his hands.

It must be remembered that, immediately on his grandson's accepting the Spanish crown, Lewis had seized all the strong towns in the Spanish Netherlands, and occupied them with French troops. Many of these were fortresses of the first rank, and their fortifications had been repaired by Vauban. Until Marlborough and the allies could wrest these from him, there could be no security for Holland from a French invasion. Before Marlborough arrived to take the command of the united army, the town of Kaiserswerth upon the Rhine, which was under the Elector of Cologne, one of France's few allies, had been taken. Marlborough's object was, starting from this town, to clear as much as he could of the Netherlands. He laid siege to, and captured several towns. At Venloo,

Marlborough's object. First campaign. 1702.

Venloo.

the first of them, much gallantry was displayed in an attack upon a fort. One young English nobleman, who had risen from a sick bed, offered every farthing he had to the man who would lift him over the palisades. There was no resisting such a spirit. The town itself soon capitulated, its surrender being hastened by an accident. The besiegers received orders to fire a salute in honour of a victory which the allies had won upon the Rhine. The defenders thought it was the commencement of a general attack, and they yielded at once. Liege was the seat of an independent prince-bishop, but it did not on that account escape its share of war. The French had placed a garrison in it, and the allies took it by storm.

The result of this first campaign of Marlborough was that he cleared from French occupation a wedge, with Liege as its apex, the Rhine as its base, and the Meuse as one of its sides, and that he had cut the French off from the lower valley of the Rhine, and thereby protected the Dutch frontier at one of its most vulnerable parts.

Result of campaign.

At the conclusion of this campaign Marlborough was very near being taken prisoner. The boat in which he was proceeding down the Meuse was seized by some Frenchmen, and he himself was only saved by the quick wit of his servant, who put into his hand an old passport belonging to his brother. The news of his supposed capture spread the greatest consternation through Holland, where his services were beginning to be appreciated. And great was the joy when it was discovered that the capture had not been effected.

Marlborough in danger.

In honour of his services Marlborough was made a duke, and a solemn Te Deum was played in St. Paul's Cathedral, the queen attending in all state. It was the first real check for many years that the French had received.

The campaign of the second year was by no means so successful. The French were concentrating their strength on their efforts in other parts; but Marlborough was unable to use his opportunity because he was hampered by the field deputies, and by Dutch colleagues, nominally his subordinates. One of these generals distinguished himself by running away from the enemy, and himself bringing news that his own troops were cut to pieces, when the truth was that, relieved of his presence, they had fought bravely, even if they had not actually won a victory. Marlborough's own wish was to make a bold attack on Antwerp, but by these thwartings he was prevented from carrying out his design. The results of his campaign, therefore, were meagre; but he managed to widen the base of his triangular wedge by the capture of Bonn on the Rhine, and to drive it a little further home by the capture of the fortress of Huy, which is higher up the Meuse Valley than Liege, being about half-way to Namur.

At the close of that year the Archduke Charles, on his way to Spain, paid a visit to the Low Countries, and afterwards to England. He presented Marlborough with his portrait and with a sword set in diamonds. Thus early in the war must Charles have recognised that almost his only hope of success lay in Marlborough's generalship.

Section II.—*Campaigns in Germany and elsewhere.*

Besides Marlborough's first campaign in the Low Countries, there was also fighting elsewhere in the first

year of the war. On the Upper Rhine Prince
Lewis of Baden succeeded in taking the Landau.
town of Landau, which was held by the French. It was
in honour of this that the salute was being fired which
led to the capture of Venloo. Prince Lewis was a
soldier of the old school, personally brave, but very
difficult to set in motion, very crotchety about the rules
of tactics, and not apt to imbibe new ideas about them.
He was shortly after this beaten by a French marshal.

There was fighting also in Italy, where the allied
troops were commanded by Prince Eugene. Mantua
and Milan had both declared for Philip of
Anjou, and it was necessary for Eugene to North Italy.
offer battle, in order to secure the imperial interests in
North Italy. He won a brilliant victory at Cremona, in
which the French general was taken prisoner. By this
he protected the Empire for a time from any invasion
by way of the Italian passes into Tyrol.

In the second year of the war Lewis and his war
ministers seemed to have resolved to make a vigorous
attack upon the Empire. The Empire was
the weakest of the allies, because the terri- Attack on
tories of the Empire lay most exposed to   the Empire.
attack. An army was sent to co-operate with the Elector
of Bavaria, who had now declared in favour of France.
It had no difficulty in escaping from Lewis of Baden,
and then, by marching through the Black Forest, it
effected a junction with the Elector of Bavaria. A
campaign in Tyrol ensued, in which the capital Innsbruck, and the strong fortress of Kufstein, commanding
the Brenner Pass, were captured by the Bavarians But
the peasantry rose against the invaders, and   Defeats of
they were forced to retire. A battle was   allies at
fought at Hochstadt, close by the field where   Hochstadt and Landau.

Marlborough defeated the French next year, but the imperialists were routed. Another French army retook Landau, so that the general result of the campaign in Germany was very favourable to the French.

Meanwhile in another quarter the English had been engaged in a fight which did not add lustre to their honour. Admiral Benbow was a brave old sailor, popular with his men but hated by his officers, whom he kept to their work. He was acting against a French squadron in the West Indies, and making a most gallant fight, which he would have won if he had not been deserted by some of his captains. He was himself struck by several shots and mortally wounded, but he survived long enough to bring the traitors to court martial. Two of them were shot for cowardice and one dismissed from the service. But it was believed that the reason for their conduct was as much hatred of their admiral as fear of the enemy's cannon balls.

Section III.—Spain.

It was to be expected that, in a war which was about Spain, an expedition would be made against Spain itself.

Cadiz.

King William had planned an expedition against Cadiz, once the scene of a great English triumph, when Essex "singed the King of Spain's beard," and it was determined now to carry out this plan. Cadiz, was called the golden gate of the Indies, because all the wealth of the mines in Spanish America entered Europe there. The Spaniards were very weak: they were without money and without troops. If the English had made a vigorous and well-directed effort, they would probably have taken Cadiz. The command of the force was given to the Duke of Ormond, who had in William's battles shown great bravery, but who had not the faculty of commanding. The navy was entrusted to a gallant sailor, Sir George Rooke. A contingent of Dutch troops was employed under a Dutch general. But Ormond was wholly unable to preserve discipline, and national jealousy led to disturbances between the English and the Dutch. The orders were not very clear, and Rooke made merry over them. They were to conciliate the Spaniards to the cause of Charles by making an attack on their towns. The Spaniards armed themselves under a brave old nobleman, the Marquis of Villadarias, who, having but few troops wherewith to defend Cadiz, resorted to the expedient of lighting watch-fires sufficient for a large force, and so deceived the allies Two small towns were taken, but the men could not be restrained from plundering them, shamelessly firing even the churches in their Protestant fury. Thus, instead of conciliating, they roused the fierce hostility of the Spaniards. After a month a council of war decided that the enterprise should be abandoned.

Fortunately for the credit of England, on the voyage home a chance was offered for the fleet to distinguish itself. News was brought that the yearly fleet of Spanish galleons laden with treasure had put into Vigo Bay. The law of Spanish trade was that these galleons could unload only at Cadiz. As the English fleet was in front of Cadiz, they had taken refuge at Vigo. If they could have received permission to unload, all the treasure might have been saved for Spain. The jealous officials at Cadiz, however, refused this permission, and although the higher authorities at Madrid granted it, it arrived only after a delay that proved fatal. The Spaniards at Vigo placed a

Vigo and the treasure ships. 1702.

boom or barrier of masts and spars across the mouth of the harbour, where they also manned two small forts.

The hope of plunder and the desire to recover the reputation which they had lost before Cadiz stimulated the allies to great efforts at Vigo. Whilst the English soldiers under Ormond scaled and took the forts, a gallant sea-fight ensued, in which victory fell to the English. The ships charged, and broke the boom. It is uncertain what became of the greater part of the treasure: enough fell into the hands of the assailants to reward them for their enterprise. There are some who think that the remainder still lies at the bottom of Vigo harbour; but others argue that the interval which elapsed between the appearance of the allies and their attack was sufficient to enable much of it to be landed and removed into the interior.

The English Government did not send any expedition into Spain in the next year; but tried first by means of diplomacy to attach the King of Portugal to the cause of the Grand Alliance and of the Archduke Charles. When they had at length succeeded in this, it was determined to attack Spain at the same time from the east and from the west. The army from the west consisted of Portuguese levies and English troops: it did not do much, until the command was given to the Earl of Galway, a French Protestant, who, escaping from the intolerance of France, had been honoured with a commission in the English army by King William, and later with an Irish peerage. He had already earned a reputation for bravery at the Battle of the Boyne, and possessed a certain amount of military skill, but he lacked the power of adapting his skill to new circumstances. Strange to say, whilst the allied army was commanded by a French-

Earl of Galway in Portugal. 1703.

man, the army that was opposed to it was commanded by an Englishman. For against Portugal Lewis had sent a large army into Spain to help to fight the battles of his grandson. This force he placed under the Duke of Berwick, the illegitimate son of James II. and Arabella Churchill, Marlborough's sister—a cold, stern man and an excellent general.

Meanwhile Sir George Rooke had been making an attempt upon the opposite coast of Spain. He had prepared to make an attack on Barcelona, an important commercial city, and one that was believed to have much sympathy with the archduke. But the troops which he had on board were insufficient, and the malcontents in the city, who had expected a large force and the presence of the archduke himself, were disappointed. Rooke, therefore, was obliged to retire. As the force was returning, a very important place fell almost by accident, into the hands of the English. Gibraltar was not then the strong place that the art of fortification has made it since; but it was always very strong by nature; so strong, that the Spaniards left but a small garrison there, and that garrison was careless in its watching. Rooke determined to make an attempt on Gibraltar, and landed some troops on the narrow strip of land by which the Rock of Gibraltar is connected with the mainland The day after the bombardment commenced was a Saint's Day, and the sentinels went to hear mass in a neighbouring chapel. Whilst they were thus employed, some English sailors clambered by a path, which was almost inaccessible, on to the top of the rock, and there hoisted the British flag. In spite of vigorous efforts on the part of enemies to haul it down, that flag has waved over the Rock of Gibraltar from that day (3rd August, 1704) to this.

Capture of Gibraltar, Aug. 3, A.D. 1704.

CHAPTER VI.

RISING IN THE CEVENNES.

Two regions of France seem to have been especially open to the influence of Protestant or Huguenot opinions.

Geography of the Huguenots

One is the lower valley of the Loire, where the doctrines of the Huguenots were accepted by the artisans of the great industrial towns, of which Nantes may be taken as representative. This town, as is well known, gave its name to the Edict of Toleration, by which under certain conditions freedom of worship had been permitted to the Huguenots.

Loire valley.

The district must also be made to include the country to the south of the Loire, as far as La Rochelle, the favourite stronghold of the Huguenots.

Rhone valley.

The other part of France is the lower valley of the Rhone, beginning with Lyons (which in the persecution lost 9,000 of its silk weavers), and the hills which close that valley in. Upon the east side is Dauphiny, the home of the Vaudois; on the western is the province of Languedoc, in which during the twelfth and earlier part of the thirteenth century the sect of the Albigenses was strong. In several points the Albigenses resemble the later Protestants—in their opposition to the Pope, in their indignation against the corruptions of the Church, and in their vehement zeal for a purer form of faith based upon the Scriptures. The Albigenses were put down after a cruel persecution, which is sometimes dignified with the title of the Albigensian Crusade. But it would seem as if memories of this earlier struggle, the seed of religion, which is found in the blood of martyrs, remained in the country where they had laid down their lives. When persecution broke out in the middle of the reign of Lewis XIV., the Huguenots of Northern and Middle France saved themselves by flight to happier countries, or by an acceptance of the dominant faith. The regions where resistance was found were the natural homes of liberty, the mountains of the south, first, among the Vaudois, and, secondly, in the Cevennes.

Cevennes is the name of the range of mountains that runs nearly parallel to the Rhone, at some little distance from its right bank. At the southern end the range separates from the direction of the river, trending towards the Pyrenees, leaving a marshy plain between the mountains and the Mediterranean, in the midst of which is situated the town of Nisme. The hills are of volcanic origin, though the volcanoes are extinct. They are rough and precipitous, with many caves and fissures, yet in many places thickly covered with forest trees. It is just the country in which a few peasants, well acquainted with footpaths and by-ways, might keep at bay a regular army, even though its soldiers were many times more numerous than they.

Cevennes.

Mixed with the pure religion of this simple mountain folk there was certainly much fanaticism. As the persecution increased in intensity, many amongst them professed to be inspired; and shortly after the opening of the new century the inspirations took the form of exhortations to resist. It was remarked that the spirit of prophecy fell chiefly upon the young, and that in the insurrection which followed the leaders were young. In July, 1702, the very year in which the War of the Succession commenced, and shortly after that war had been proclaimed, fifty of the persecuted, excited to resistance by the prophets, met in a forest, under three tall beech trees. There they determined to attack their persecutors.

The Camisards. The insurgents became known as the Camisards, or "wearers of the white frock:" but it is not certain whether this was the ordinary smock-frock of the country peasants, or a special dress, chosen that the wearers might be visible to each other on a dark night. The fighting that arose out of this insurrection, to which the name "War of the Blouses" has been given, cannot properly be called a war: it was rather a series of raids. The Camisards would issue forth from their mountain fastnesses, and make an attack upon a priest who had persecuted them, upon a monastery, or upon a troop of Royalist soldiers. The attack over, or the enemy proving too strong, they would retreat at once to the hill-tops again. They knew all the paths, and they could climb like their own sheep or goats. All the peasants sympathised with them, and would help them to hide from the royalists. Their troops remind one of the regiments of the English Puritans. Before a battle there would be a meeting for prayer, and preaching, and praise, at which men would exhort officers. The Camisards marched to battle, lustily singing a hymn to the God of battles, and when the fighting was over, however great the carnage, on the very field uprose the song of praise and thanksgiving to Him who had given them the victory.

Of all their leaders, the most remarkable was Jean Cavalier. In the very year in which the Edict of Nantes was revoked was born this leader of the rebellion which that revocation caused.

Jean Cavalier.

He was of humble parentage, his father being a shepherd; and his mother had trained him in the Protestant doctrines. At the age of fifteen he had to fly from the country, and took service with a baker at Geneva, then, as always, a hospitable place of refuge for the exile. Whilst in safety, however, he felt for his kinsfolk and neighbours who were suffering, and at length the "baker's boy" determined to return and to rouse resistance. He was only seventeen, when, on account of his manifest fitness for the post, he was recognised as the General of the Camisards. Bravery was a virtue that he shared with all his men: he had other qualities of his own. The education which he had received could have been but little, and not calculated to fit him for his work. Yet he was a born general, and his manœuvring on one occasion extorted from the ablest living marshal of France the praise that "it was worthy of Cæsar."

Three stories from his life in these two years will serve to illustrate his daring, his chivalry, and his uprightness:—

1. On one occasion, as his men wanted powder, he rode, disguised as a merchant, into the town of Nismes to buy some. On entering he found all in confusion, for a rumour had just reached the town that the Camisards were preparing to attack it. The gates were immediately shut. *His character. 1. Daring.* But Cavalier, having procured the powder that he wanted, and carrying it about his own person, went to the officer commanding a troop of cavalry that was going forth against the rebels, and asked permission to ride with it. The officer complimented the supposed merchant on his courage, but warned him at parting, lest he should meet with the dangerous Cavalier.

2. Riding in disguise, as was his wont, he once acted as guide to a young royalist officer, conducting him to a place of safety and then revealing himself to him as they parted. *2. Chivalry.*

3. Some banditti took advantage of the disturbed state of the country, and, pretending to be Camisards, plundered and murdered a lady. Immediately on hearing of it Cavalier set to work to find the men, and, having found them, hanged them without ceremony.

3. Uprightness.

Not hastily, nor without provocation, had the Camisards taken up arms. During all the seventeen years of Cavalier's life the persecution had been terible. Nor had it been limited to these years. The revocation of the Edict was not a sudden reversal of policy, but rather with its results the culmination of one long-continued. It was known that cruelty and severity towards Protestants were a passport to the favour of the French king; but a legal sanction was given by the formal revocation, made within a few days of the king's secret marriage with Madame de Maintenon, who, instigated by the Jesuits, urged him on to it. What the king had allowed before he ordered now; all bands of humanity were withdrawn. A regiment of dragoons was considered the best body of missionaries. If they could not convert, they could at least kill, and attention was paid to no complaint against these instruments of Holy Church. It was in the province of Languedoc, in the earlier wars against the Albigenses, that when one asked how to distinguish the heretics from the true believers, the savage answer was made—"Kill all! God will know his own." Peaceful valleys were turned into scenes of slaughter; and the most cruel tortures, the wheel and the rack, as well as the stake, completed the work that the sabres of the dragoons had begun.

Dragonades.

It is hardly to be wondered at, though it is much to be deplored, that the Camisards, when at length they turned upon their persecutors, retaliated with a fearful retribution. Cavalier himself was not cruel; but many of the bands of Camisards under other leaders took terrible and cruel revenge, nor was he able to stop it.

Retaliation.

All the early attempts to put down the rebellion were by means of severity. There was a feeling of irritation, both amongst the local authorities and at the king's court, that so insignificant a body of peasants—for the insurgents seem never to have numbered 10,000—should dare to resist the royal authority. More troops to catch the rebels, more tortures for them when caught, were the only cures that occurred to their minds. As yet the external war did not press very heavily upon France, and it was thought that the rebellion could soon be crushed. Thus for about two years the insurrection continued with varying success; the insurgents making raids, the royalists sometimes intercepting them, but oftener failing.

Severity used to put down the rebellion.

Meanwhile the Camisards, knowing about the war with the allies, made appeal to foreign Governments for assistance, and especially to England and Holland. With touching simplicity they declared that they were not rebelling against their prince, but exercising a right of nature. "We arm ourselves but to resist force. We follow but the dictates of conscience. We are not to be frightened by numbers. We will meet them. Yet will we harm no persons if they do not harm us. But just reprisals will we ever make upon our persecutors, and in this we are sanctioned by the law and by the Word of God, and the practice of all nations." At first the foreign Governments turned a deaf ear to their appeals; but it was evident that, if a force of the allies could effect

Appeal to foreign Governments.

a junction with these insurgents, a great blow would be struck at the French power. At length, in 1704, a force of ships was sent, under the command of Sir Cloudesley Shovel, a gallant and famous English admiral, who had risen to that dignity from the position of a cabin-boy. When the fleet arrived in the Gulf of Lyons the appointed signals were made, which were to be answered from the shore. But correct information had not been brought to Cavalier, and, though he saw the signals, he did not understand them. The admiral had received strict orders to land no troops unless the signals were answered. He, therefore, sailed away.

English fleet sent.

The rebellion had now lasted for so long a time (upwards of two years) that Lewis determined to send against the Camisards the first marshal of France. He, probably, selected Villars on account of his military skill; but the selection was good for other reasons. Villars was no bigot, and seems from his first appointment to have resolved upon a policy of clemency. He entertained a great admiration for young Cavalier. He opened negotiations with him at once, and the result was that a treaty was made, by which freedom of conscience, and liberty of worship, except in fortified towns, were granted, together with a free pardon for all the insurgents who accepted the treaty, and immunity from taxes for a certain period, until the district should have recovered from the effects of the war. Some of the Camisards were very indignant with Cavalier for signing this treaty because the possession of certain strongholds was not granted as a guarantee for its fulfilment. They still held out; but by his acceptance of the treaty the rebellion was now very much diminished, and was

Marshal Villars' clemency.

End of the war.

without great difficulty put down. The spirit of the treaty was not strictly observed, and a great many of the inhabitants of the Cevennes emigrated. The success of Lewis was in the spirit of the maxim—"*Solitudinem faciunt, pacem appellant.*"

Cavalier himself took service with the English Government, by whom he was sent into Spain. At the head of a regiment of his fellow-exiles he was engaged in the famous battle of Almanza. The story is told how in that battle the Camisards caught sight of a regiment of their former persecutors, and rushed upon them with the bayonet with a fury such as shocked even men accustomed to fierce battles. Of 700 Camisards only 300 survived, and Cavalier himself, severely wounded, was left among the dead. He afterwards became a general in the English army, was Governor of Jersey, then of the Isle of Wight, and died an old man at Chelsea.

Cavalier's later life.

As France had a weak point in the disaffection of the Huguenots, so the Empire was weak on its eastern side. From one opponent—the Turks—it had, perhaps, not much to fear; for the Turks had suffered severely at the hands of Eugene in the last war, and were, moreover, obliged now to turn their eyes in another direction, towards the growing power of Russia. But in wars against the Empire the Turks had always found allies in Hungary and Transylvania. The disaffection in these two provinces was due, partly to the pressure of taxation, partly to differences in religion, but chiefly to that desire for separation from Austria which has so often shown itself in Hungary. The taxes were very heavy throughout all the Austrian dominions. The Protestants in Hungary had been persecuted by the Emperor, and

Similar trouble in Austria.

Hungary.

this had led to the last Hungarian insurrection, when the Turks, instigated by the Hungarians, had invaded Austria and besieged Vienna. The desire for separation was constant During the War of the Succession, the condition of Hungary might be compared to a fire that is composed of smouldering embers, ready at any moment to break into a flame. Here and there flames showed themselves when a turbulent noble headed an insurrection. But, as the Empire was on the winning side elsewhere, these rebellions never became formidable

---

CHAPTER VII.

BLENHEIM.

IN the spring of 1704 Lewis determined to make a great effort. He raised as many troops as he could, and sent different armies against different members of the Grand Alliance. But his chief attempt was to be against the Emperor. He determined to make a vigorous lunge at Vienna, the heart of the Empire, and to compel the Emperor to make peace under the walls of his own capital. To this object two things helped. Bavaria was Lewis's single ally; and Bavaria could be used by the French as an advanced outpost, in an attack on the Austrian dominions. Moreover, whilst the Austrians were thus exposed in front, they were also weakened in the rear by the revolt of the Hungarians. The Hungarians had been long in revolt, which had been sedulously fomented with French gold. They were at present quiet; but it was hoped that the appearance of a French army before

Object of France in making the campaign.

Vienna would be the signal for a general uprising of the Hungarians; and Hungary lies dangerously near Vienna. Already a French army under Marshal Marsin was in Bavaria with the Elector; to this others were to join themselves, and then the advance was to be made.

Though this well-concerted plan was not divulged, Marlborough with the instinct of genius understood the meaning of the preparations, and determined to defeat them. He communicated his design to only one man, Prince Eugene, whom he promised to meet in Bavaria, that with their united armies they might face the invading French, and thus save the Empire and with it the Grand Alliance. Marlborough used his influence in England both to have 10,000 men added to the English army, and to have his instructions drawn up with some latitude. He turned the opposition of the States of Holland by marching with the allied army towards the Moselle, and only then revealing to the States his intention to march to Bavaria to help the Emperor—with the Dutch troops, if they gave the permission, but if not, without them. The States saw that it was too late to oppose, and not only gave the desired permission, but generously sent reinforcements and supplies. Across the Moselle, and across the Rhine, then up the valley of the Maine Marlborough marched; the enemy, and even his own soldiers, only conjecturing the object of the enterprise. In the Duchy of Wurtemburg he met Prince Eugene, and they spent three days together. It was the first time they had seen each other; and now was laid the foundation of the lifelong and unclouded friendship which forms so noble a feature in the character of each.

Marlborough's plan.

He joins Eugene

Here they were joined by Prince Lewis of Baden, a

German general of the old methodical school, who claimed precedence over the others. Marlborough proposed that he should devote himself to the task of watching the French frontier, and preventing the expected union of another French army with those already in Bavaria. But Prince Lewis declined, and Eugene had reluctantly to depart upon this duty, for which, however, it was manifest he was much better suited. Marlborough then acquiesced in an arrangement by which Prince Lewis and he should divide the command, taking it on alternate days.

Lewis of Baden.

The first achievement of the allied army was the storming of the Schellenberg, a hill just above the town of Donauwörth upon the Danube. The Bavarians occupied it in force, and the allied troops, when they came up, were tired with a long march. But it was Marlborough's day, and he knew not what the prince would do upon the morrow. Moreover, though the hill was strongly fortified, the intrenchments were not quite completed. So Marlborough gave to his wearied troops the order to attack. Twice they charged up the hill, and twice they were repulsed. The third time they were reinforced by some German soldiers, and led by Prince Lewis himself, of whose personal courage there was no doubt, whatever might be the feeling as to his generalship. This time the Bavarians were routed. In their flight a new disaster fell upon them. They were hurrying across the Danube, over a long wooden bridge, and when some 2,000 had crossed, the weight of the fugitives broke the bridge, and many were hurled into the swift stream.

Storming of Schellenberg.

The day after this engagement Marlborough heard that, in spite of the watchfulness of Prince Eugene, a considerable French army, under Marshal Tallard,

Blenheim.

one of the most distinguished French generals, and the same who had been ambassador to King William at the time of the Partition Treaty, had passed through the defiles of the Black Forest, and had effected a junction with the armies of Marshal Marsin and of the Elector of Bavaria. Eugene now joined the others, and it was decided that Ingolstadt should be attacked, a strong and a virgin fortress, and important because it commanded the Danube. His colleagues were glad to find that the attempt upon Ingolstadt was regarded by Prince Lewis as worthy of his dignity; and they were thus relieved from the presence of an undesirable colleague. *(Tallard joins Marsin.)*

Receiving information that the united French forces were at Hochstadt, the scene of their triumph of the previous year, Marlborough and Eugene advanced to meet them. On August 12, the two generals, mounting the church tower in one of the villages on the road, saw the encampments of the French army. It was at once determined to give battle; and the men joyfully prepared for it. Some of the officers ventured to point out the dangers of their position to Marlborough; but he answered that a battle was necessary, and that he trusted in the bravery of his troops. The early part of that night Marlborough spent in prayer; he then received the Communion at the hands of his private chaplain, and, after a short rest, was again in council with Eugene. With the first streaks of dawn on the morning of August 13, at three o'clock, the army was in motion. A haze covered the ground; but at six they were visible to the French, and a cannonade commenced; to which the English artillery replied, whilst the troops on either side were deploying into line. *(Preparations for battle.)*

The village of Blindheim, or Blenheim, which has given its name to this famous battle, is situated on the north bank of the Danube. The river is about one hundred yards broad, and its stream is very swift; just before reaching the village the river makes a loop to the south. A short distance below the village the Danube is joined by a little brook, the Nebel. Almost parallel with the Danube, about three miles distant, is a low range of thickly-

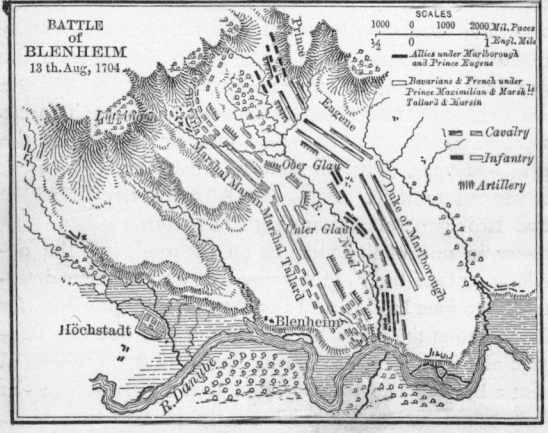

Description of the ground.

wooded hills: they are a continuation at a lower level of the Schellenberg, which at Donauwörth (nine miles down the stream) almost overhangs the Danube. From these hills flows the Nebel, which is but a little stream: in some places a boy could jump across it, divided as it is into several branches. The country is well drained now; but then the land between the branches was little better than a swamp. Two little hamlets are on this brook: the lower, Unterglau, is about a mile from Blenheim; Oberglau is higher up. They are perhaps three-quarters of a mile apart. On an arm of the stream on the slope of the hill is a larger village, Lutzingen, which is not however as big as Blenheim.

When both armies were ready for the battle, the Nebel divided them. Marlborough's forces, which were chiefly English, were on the left of the allies, reaching down to the Danube. To Prince Eugene, with a more composite army, the right was assigned higher up the little brook. Tallard with the troops that he had brought opposed Marlborough. Maximilian, the Elector of Bavaria, and Marshal Marsin were stationed opposite Eugene, the rear of the French left wing being in the village of Lutzingen. But Tallard, though he had a great reputation, was not an able general, and committed a fatal mistake in the disposition of his troops, arising probably from his confident belief that he was destined to have an easy victory. He stationed seventeen battalions of his best troops in the village of Blenheim, where their movements were hampered by want of space. They were too many for the defence of the village, and those not wanted for that purpose were useless for any other. Moreover, the centre of the French army, the line of communication with the other wing, was proportionately weakened. This weakening helped the victory of the allies: the crowding of the troops made that victory more complete.

Position of the armies.

On account of the uneven nature of the ground Prince Eugene took some time to get his troops into position. Marlborough occupied the interval by ordering prayers to be read at the head of each regiment. Then with some of his principal officers he sat down to breakfast. At midday an aide-de-camp galloped up with the message that Eu-

The battle begins.

gene was ready. "Now, gentlemen, to your posts," said Marlborough cheerfully. There was no delay. On the left of the line English troops advanced to attack the village of Blenheim under the command of Lord Cutts, reputed to be the bravest officer in the English army, and so fearless under fire that he had received the nickname of "Salamander." But Blenheim was strongly defended. There was a strong barrier of palisades, and behind them a needlessly large number of the best regiments of French infantry. The English troops were forced back twice, and then received orders to keep up firing, but not again to advance until a diversion had been made.

Allied left.

Meanwhile, on the right, Eugene was attacking Marshal Marsin and the Elector. First he led his cavalry to the charge: the front line of the enemy was broken, and a battery of six guns taken. But the second line stood firm, his cavalry recoiled; and the battery was retaken. Eugene, no longer able to trust his cavalry, galloped off for his infantry, who were chiefly Prussian. It was the steadiness of these Prussian infantry that saved the battle on the right wing.

Allied right.

In the centre Marlborough was superintending the passage of the Nebel by his cavalry; but the passage was a matter of difficulty, because the ground was exceedingly swampy. Fascines were thrown in, and pontoons used where possible. Tallard undoubtedly made a great mistake in not attacking the cavalry during the crossing. He seems to have thought that when over they would fall an easy prey. It was not until the first line was formed that the French charged, but then without any marked result.

Centre.

To the right of the centre a considerable force of the allies had made an attack on the village of Oberglau.

They had taken it, and were then attacked in turn, and driven from it by the Irish Brigade, a valiant regiment of Irish exiles in the service of France. The Irishmen rushed forward, and had broken the line of the allies, and almost severed the communications with Eugene. Marlborough was told, and at once galloped up, and by his exertions restored the battle, driving back with his cavalry the Irish, who were disordered with their success, and posting infantry so as to enfilade them on their retreat.

Oberglau.

The afternoon was now far spent; as yet all that could be said was that there had been an alternation of success, and that both sides were holding their ground. But the generalship and the exertion of Marlborough were about to be rewarded. At five o'clock the whole body of his cavalry had been brought across, and he ordered the advance. At the sound of the trumpet about 8,000 splendidly mounted horsemen moved up the gentle slope, at first slowly and then more and more quickly. Once the advance was checked, and they recoiled for about sixty paces. Then the signal to advance was sounded again, and at a magnificent pace the whole line charged. The French cavalry fired their carbines, wheeled and fled. "The bulk of our cavalry," said Tallard afterwards, in his official report, "did ill, I say it, very ill." Marlborough had won. The French line was cut in two. Some infantry which had been brought up to support the horse were compelled to surrender. The cavalry were in full flight, part towards Hochstadt, part towards Blenheim. Marlborough pursued the latter, sending a Dutch general after the former. Marshal Tallard was caught before he could make his escape into Blenheim. Marlborough put him in his own carriage, and then

Cavalry charge.

Marlborough's report of victory. hastily wrote in pencil a note to the duchess, which his aide-de-camp was to take at once with the news of the victory to England. It is still preserved, and runs thus:—

"August 13, 1704.

"I have not time to zay more, but to beg you will give my duty to the Queen, and let her know Her Army has had a glorious victory. Monsr. Tallard and two other Generals are in my coach, and I am following the rest. The bearer, my Aide-de-camp, Coll. Parke, will give Her an account of what has pass'd. I shall doe it in a day or two by another more att large.

"MARLBOROUGH."

The French battalions in Blenheim, meanwhile, were hemmed in between the English troops and the Danube. Some, and amongst them their commander, *The French in Blenheim.* tried to swim the river, but it was too swift and they were drowned. During the summer evening, and after night came on, the English were firing into the thick masses in Blenheim. Every attempt to escape was stopped. At length it became manifest that nothing could be gained by further bloodshed. Great was the despair of the gallant French soldiers: one regiment burnt its colours. Then they surrendered.

Eugene had made repeated attacks upon his opponents. About the time of the great cavalry charge he advanced, and took the village of Lutzingen; but there was no rout of the Bavarians and French opposed to him. The troops retreated in good order. *Eugene's attack on Lutzingen.* Marlborough ascribed the ill success of Eugene to ill luck; "if his fortune had been equal to his merit," he said, "this day would have finished the war." As a compliment he determined to divide the prisoners, who amounted in all to about 11,000, with Prince Eugene.

There is a good deal of difference in accounts of the battle, especially as to the numbers of the combatants. It would seem from the best authorities that the allies had about 52,000, the French about 60,000 men: and that of these the former lost 11,000, the latter 40,000, in killed and prisoners. *Numbers.*

It is almost impossible to exaggerate the importance of this victory, which broke the power of Lewis XIV., and destroyed the prestige of the French arms. Marlborough was received everywhere with delight. In England the joy was great. The royal manor of Woodstock was conferred on him and his heirs, and the Palace of Blenheim was commenced as a monument of a nation's gratitude. The Emperor made him a prince of the Empire, and bestowed on him the principality of Mindelsheim in Bavaria. *The result.*

CHAPTER VIII.

LORD PETERBOROUGH.

IN 1705 the English Government determined to make a vigorous push in Spain. The command of the new expedition was given to Charles Mordaunt, Earl of Peterborough, one of the most remarkable soldiers of his time, and especially suited for the work now set before him. Born two years before the Restoration, he had served when a boy in the Mediterranean fleet. Changing his profession, as *Life of Peterborough.*

was then often done, he had been subsequently engaged in fighting in Africa. From his seat in the House of Lords he had opposed the will of James II. upon the Test Act. He found it advisable to take refuge in Holland, and was the first English nobleman who pressed upon William of Orange that he should stand forth as the deliverer of England. For the two years that preceded the Revolution he was constantly with him; and when the Revolution was accomplished he was rewarded with the title of Earl of Monmouth, and with the offices of Lord of the Bedchamber, and First Commissioner of the Treasury. Lord Monmouth, however, was not the man steadily to retain the king's favour: and during the reign he lost first his civil, and then all his offices, and was imprisoned in the Tower. His disgrace rested upon doubtful evidence, and he was soon released. In 1697 he succeeded to his uncle's title as Earl of Peterborough; but it was not until Queen Anne's reign that he again took part in public life. He had been offered and had refused the chief command of the forces in the West Indies. It is said that it was at Marlborough's suggestion that this new command in Spain was given to him.

This outline of his life gives but a slight indication of his character. Its predominant feature was activity—
Character. invaluable where energy was wanted; otherwise it took the form of restlessness. Had he any definite work to do there was no man so fertile in resources, none who would do it so quickly. But obstacles would fret him: he had not the patience of Marlborough. When unemployed, he would travel over Europe with astonishing rapidity. It was said that he was faster than any courier. He was not like ordinary men, and would have been better suited for the days of knight-errantry. He had all the virtues of chivalry. He

was very generous and devoted to the fair sex. He could inspire troops with enthusiasm; none was his equal as a leader of irregulars. It must also be mentioned that he had no mean opinion of himself, and that his open, free way of talking made him many enemies.

A few lively lines by Dean Swift give us a very vivid idea of Lord Peterborough: *(Swift's account of him.)*

> Mordanto fills the the trump of fame:
> The Christian worlds his deeds proclaim,
> And prints are crowded with his name.
>
> In journeys he outrides the post,
> Sits up till midnight with his host,
> Talks politics, and gives the toast:
>
> Knows every prince in Europe's face,
> Flies like a squib from place to place,
> And travels not, but runs a race. . . .
>
> A messenger comes all a-reek,
> Mordanto at Madrid to seek:
> He left the town above a week.
>
> Next day the post-boy winds his horn,
> And rides through Dover in the morn—
> Mordanto's landed from Leghorn. . . .
>
> So wonderful his expedition,
> When you have not the least suspicion
> He's with you like an apparition—
>
> A skeleton in outward figure,
> His meagre corpse, though full of vigour,
> Would halt behind him were it bigger.

The commission which Peterborough received from the Home Government was purposely drawn with great

Peterborough's commission.

latitude, and was exactly calculated to suit his peculiar genius. He had full command over the army, and a joint control with Sir Cloudesley Shovel over the navy when he was on board. It was pointed out to him that the provinces of Catalonia and Valencia were believed to be favourable to the cause of the Archduke Charles; and various places along the coast of Spain, and even on the Mediterranean shore of France, were suggested to him as inviting attack. The greatest stress was laid on Barcelona, a large commercial town on the sea-coast and the capital of Catalonia.

Progress of the expedition.

The force amounted to about 5,000 men, two-thirds English and one-third Dutch. It was very badly provided with stores, or with money to purchase them. Peterborough's first act on landing at Lisbon, to which he first sailed, was on his own responsibility to remedy the want of stores. Here, also, two regiments of dragoons were spared by the Earl of Galway to add to the force. The Archduke Charles, who had been with Galway's army in Portugal, now joined himself to Peterborough, and when the force stopped a little later at Gibraltar, the Prince of Hesse Darmstadt joined likewise. He had been popular as governor of Catalonia in the last reign, and it was thought that his presence might win over some of the natives.

Valencia. Peterborough's proposal.

The fleet next cast anchor off Valencia, where Peterborough proposed a bold scheme, a foretaste of the romantic adventures which have made his expedition memorable. He proposed to march at once upon Madrid, which was only 150 miles distant: the road lay through the province of Valencia, which was mainly favourable.

There was no army at Madrid; and if the French army that was now facing Galway, on the frontier of Portugal, should turn to Madrid, to expel the bold invaders, it would be exposed to attack upon two sides at once. If the archduke had not been on board the fleet, Peterborough, having full powers, would doubtless have carried out his plan with a result which, from later experience, it is quite possible to guess. But, in a war waged to place the archduke upon the throne of Spain, it was not possible to act contrary to his wishes. He opposed the plan very strongly when it was laid before him; and it was rejected altogether by a council of war. It was therefore determined to proceed to Barcelona.

But Barcelona was one of the best fortified and strongest cities in Spain. It was absurd that so small a force should think of laying formal siege to it: it was not a quarter large enough even for one line. The garrison was about as numerous as the assailants. The would-be king and the Prince of Hesse were very anxious that an attempt should be made: they especially maintained that the inhabitants of the surrounding country would join. The troops and artillery were landed: some 1,500 Miquelets, as the picturesquely-armed peasants of the province were called, came to the camp. During three weeks there were disputes in the force. The archduke and the Prince of Hesse were taunting Peterborough, and insisting upon an attack. The officers of the navy joined them in regarding it as feasible. The officers of the army declared that it was hopeless, the general of the Dutch contingent going so far as to refuse to lead his men to certain destruction. Peterborough was distracted between them, but he at length gave way to the latter. The heavy guns were again embarked. A public entertainment was

Barcelona.

given in Barcelona in honour of the departure of the force. Next morning, however, the English flag was waving from the fort that commanded the city.

The town of Barcelona lies between the sea and this strong fort or citadel, which is called Monjuich. It is situated on the last of a range of hills, and, as it really commanded Barcelona, it had been fortified with especial care. It was believed to be impregnable: on this account the soldiers of the garrison were negligent. Lord Peterborough, expecting this, determined to attempt a sudden assault.

Monjuich.

To reach Monjuich from the English camp without giving an alarm it was necessary to march about nine miles. The night was dark; the force selected consisted of 1,200 foot and 200 horse. Peterborough, as he was moving out of the camp, stopped at the quarters of the Prince of Hesse, inviting him to accompany them to "see whether they deserved the bad character which he had so liberally given them." Much astonished, he came at once. Two hours before dawn the troops arrived beneath Monjuich, but Peterborough did not intend a night attack. He explained to his men the nature of the fortifications. There was an inner circle of works; round these there was a ditch. The English were to receive the enemy's fire, and then jump into this ditch: the enemy would come forward to attack them, and they were then to advance, driving the enemy back, and following them closely into the inner fortifications. The little force was divided into three columns; Peterborough, with the prince, attacking the most dangerous part, a bastion on the Barcelona side. As he had said, so it happened. All except the innermost fort fell into Peterborough's hands.

Capture of Monjuich.

The Prince of Hesse there lost his life. A reinforcement of dragoons was sent from Barcelona to Monjuich. As they entered they were received with cheers. The prince thought the cheering meant that the place had surrendered, and, hastening to secure it, was shot just as he discovered his mistake. An alarm arose that a large force was coming from Barcelona to the relief of Monjuich. Peterborough went to reconnoitre. In his absence a panic seized upon the troops. Some of the soldiers suggested to the officer who was left in command that they should retreat, and he at once adopted the suggestion. Captain Carleton, who has written an account of the campaign, tells us how he himself heard this, and spurred his horse after Peterborough, who without a word galloped back, shouted to the men that they were marching in a wrong direction, restored confidence by the magic of his presence, and promptly recovered the position which had been so rashly endangered.

The guns were landed again, and in less than three days the whole of the fortress of Monjuich was in the hands of the English. Great enthusiasm was now aroused, when Peterborough at once turned to the siege of the town of Barcelona. The sailors wanted to serve in the batteries on shore: the soldiers vied with them in their efforts. Very soon the town capitulated without there being the necessity for an assault. The Catalans from the neighborhood were so angry that the town had held out against the cause which they espoused that the English general had great difficulty in preserving order, and in preventing terrible violence and plunder.

Capture of Barcelona. October 23.

The results of this brilliant achievement were very important. Almost all Catalonia declared for the Archduke Charles. Soldiers of Philip's army deserted in numbers: new re-

Catalonia for the Archduke,

cruits came in. The belief that Catalonia was still disaffected to the general Government of Spain, and inclined to the House of Austria, because Castile was in favour of the French prince, was fully justified. The example was infectious. The town of Valencia, and the greater part of the province of that name, soon submitted. Peterborough was very anxious to follow up these successes, and to continue the vigorous push which, in accordance with his instructions, he had been making. Had he been properly supported, it is difficult to conjecture what would have stopped his success. But unfortunately those with him, whether Dutch generals or English officers, or the Archduke Charles himself, had not his energy. They determined upon letting the navy retire to Lisbon, and sending the army into winter quarters in the different towns which had espoused their side. These contingents were insufficient to hold the towns, and a considerable portion of the army remained useless in Barcelona.

and Valencia.

On the other hand, the Spanish Government was not prepared to remain idle. They sent 7,000 men, under one of their best generals, to recover San Mateo, a town important, not for its size, but for its situation on a pass between Catalonia and Valencia. In this place an English colonel had been stationed with a force of 500 irregulars. Peterborough marched to its relief with only 1,200 men, and raised the siege. He was always well served by spies; and, by arranging that one should be captured with false despatches, he created in the mind of the Spanish general the impression that the relieving army was much larger than his own. He precipitately retreated towards Valencia; but Peterborough was not content with relieving the town. With his small force, and keeping up the

San Mateo.

same impression, although it was the depth of winter, and in a mountainous country, he pursued the retreating army.

He had not followed it for more than six leagues, when he received doleful news from Barcelona, that no less than three armies were being concentrated upon the town, and all the troops were required that King Charles could muster. After some hesitation Lord Peterborough sent his infantry to the sea-port of Vinarez, that they might thence be conveyed to Barcelona. He determined, with his 200 horsemen, to continue the pursuit. By very rapid movements, his men appearing now on the right, now on the left flank of the enemy, and concealing by various devices his inferiority of numbers, he followed the strong Spanish army. The town of Nules, strongly attached to the cause of King Philip, he took in the following manner. He rode up to the gate and asked for a magistrate or priest. A priest came. Peterborough told him that he gave them only six minutes in which to surrender; else he would, when his artillery came up, assault and give no quarter. They surrendered, but he had no artillery.

Pursuit of Spaniards.

He heard that the Spaniards had determined on besieging the town of Valencia, and he felt it was absolutely necessary to relieve it. He sent, therefore, quickly for his own infantry from Vinarez, and for reinforcements from Catalonia. Wanting cavalry, he converted 600 infantry into horse soldiers. A regiment of foot was being reviewed. Peterborough said to the officers, "How would you like your men to be mounted on good horses?" He led them on a little further. There were 600 horses ready saddled and bridled, which the general had bought at Nules.

Exploits of Peterborough.

At Murviedro the road to Valencia was stopped by a force under an Irish officer in the Spanish service. He was a kinsman of Peterborough, who took advantage of the fact to make proposals to him that he should desert, and when he firmly refused, Peterborough, by means of feigned deserters, spread a report of his treason. The result was, that in the general mistrust Peterborough passed him, and on February 4 entered Valencia. But not yet did he rest there. He heard that a body of 4,000 men was marching to reinforce the Spanish army. At dead of night he set out with one-fourth the number, crossed the river Xucar, attacked and dispersed the force, and returned to Valencia with 600 prisoners. There was no further danger for Valencia. For the remainder of the winter Peterborough and his men enjoyed their well earned repose.

CHAPTER IX.

THE YEAR OF VICTORY, 1706.

Section I.—Ramillies.

THE year 1706 was the most important in the whole war to the cause of the allies, for in that year they won brilliant successes in three different quarters. In Spain there was at the same time the triumphant raising of the siege of Barcelona by Lord Peterborough, and the march of Lord Galway to Madrid. In the Netherlands the easily-won victory of Ramillies led to the recovery of the whole country from the French. In Italy Eugene's brilliant victory brought about the raising of the siege of Turin,

Success in three quarters.

and was followed by the overthrow of the French cause throughout the whole of not only Savoy but Italy.

Marlborough, knowing the critical state of affairs in Italy, had wished to be allowed to repeat the campaign of Blenheim, and, marching his army quickly into Italy, to join with Eugene in raising the siege of Turin; but his army was composed of contingents from different allies, whose leave he had to ask to take them, and this was refused by many of the different Governments. The Dutch were especially afraid that their border would again be left unprotected. Acquiescing in the reversal of his policy, Marlborough set off to meet the enemy "with a heavy heart." Yet he was marching to one of his most brilliant victories.

Marlborough sets out.

He had under him in the Netherlands a force of about 60,000 men, most of whom were English and Dutch. Opposed to him was Marshal Villeroy, with a French army of about the same size as his own. With him was the Elector of Bavaria, ready to fulfil his own saying, when offered terms by the allies, that "since the wine was abroach he was ready to drink it to the lees." The French general seems to have known that the allies were late in making preparations, and to have thought that by a speedy advance he might find Marlborough with his English troops alone, and unprepared. He learnt his mistake when they met on the battle-field of Ramillies.

The armies.

The village which has given its name to this battle stands in the middle of a high plain in Brabant. Three rivers rise close by it. The Little Gheet and the Great Gheet, mere brooks, flow northwards, uniting at some leagues' distance, and then flowing into a tributary of the Scheldt. They are separated

The ground.

by a narrow belt of land, at first not more than a mile in breadth, but expanding as they flow apart. The Mehaigne to the south of the field flows eastward, then some miles further on turns south and joins the Meuse. The French right wing rested on the Mehaigne at the village of Tavieres; their line extended in a large arc, the centre being strongly stationed in the village of Ramillies and at Offuz, which lies a little to its left; the left of the whole line was at the village of Anderkirk on

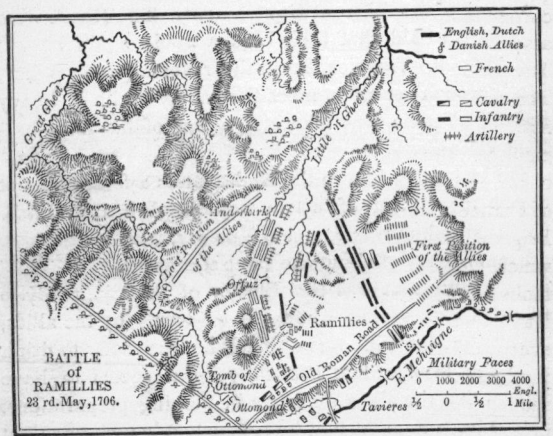

the Little Gheet. Marlborough took advantage of this arrangement. It is manifest that if two armies face each other, one in a concave and the other in a convex order, the latter has this advantage, that troops can be more quickly moved from one flank to the other.

Behind the French line, between the right and centre where the cavalry were stationed, stands an old barrow called the Tomb of Ottomond. Marlborough saw that this commanded the field, and made it his object to break through the line and secure it. To conceal his design he made a vehement attack on the French left, to strengthen which Villeroy sent his reserve and all the soldiers that he could spare. Marlborough then, in such a way that they were not missed, detached a large body of troops, who marched, hidden by a slightly-rising ground, to reinforce his own left.

Marlborough's plan.

But before the attempt to break through the line was carried out, the attack on Anderkirk was followed by assaults on the villages of Ramillies and Tavieres. The latter was quickly carried. The real crisis of the battle was the cavalry fight that followed. The Dutch general charged, and the first line of the French was driven back. But the second line consisted of the finest troops of France—the Maison du Roi—the French Household Brigade, the regiment which had won Steinkirk, and which consisted now, as then, of the young nobles, famous for their valour, and careless of their lives. The Dutch were driven back. Marlborough ordered up every available sabre, and himself galloped to the front. Just as he was coming forward, he was recognised by some of the French dragoons who nearly made him prisoner. Sword in hand he fought himself free, and tried to make his horse leap a ditch, but he fell to the ground. An aide-de-camp brought him another horse, and as a colonel held the stirrup, a cannon ball took off his head. Saved as it were by miracle, Marlborough headed the charge. The famous French regiment was overpowered by numbers, the village of Ramillies was taken, and immediately afterwards the Tomb of Ottomond. The French line was thus cut in two.

Battle of Ramillies, May 23, A.D. 1706.

The French still held Anderkirk, the village on their

left, and the advance of the allies was impeded by the confusion which reigned all over the field.

End of the battle.

Marlborough halted his troops to re-form their lines, and the French bravely attempted to face them. When Marlborough once more ordered the advance to be sounded, a panic seized the French, and they fled. The battle had lasted three hours. Till late into the night the flying French were pursued by the English cavalry. All their artillery, except six guns, fell into the hands of the allies. The French lost in killed, wounded, and prisoners, 15,000 men; the allies less than a quarter of that number.

The battle of Ramillies was by no means so valiantly contested as that of Blenheim. Its results, however, were quite as important. Blenheim saved

Results of Ramillies.

the Empire; Ramillies conquered the Netherlands. Marshal Villeroy and the Elector of Bavaria halted in Louvain; but they decided that they could not hold it, and the town capitulated next morning. Brussels, the capital of Brabant,

Towns fall into hands of Marlborough.

opened its gates to the conquerors, and proclaimed the Archduke Charles as its sovereign. Marlborough, in his name, guaranteed the liberties of the province, as the archduke himself had done in Catalonia. Moreover,

Brussels.

when the Dutch wished to levy a contribution on the inhabitants of Brabant towards the expenses of the war, and the English Government were inclined to adopt the policy, Marlborough protested so warmly, that the scheme was not carried out. Other towns hastened to follow the example of Brussels. The fortresses occupied by French troops alone

Antwerp.

held out. Marlborough first proceeded to

Antwerp, which was expected to cause him trouble; but a quarrel had begun between the French soldiers and the Walloons, who jointly formed the garrison. The latter declared for the allies, and this strong fortress was captured without a blow. Ghent and Bruges, the two chief cities of Flanders, opened their gates. Then Marlborough advanced upon Ostend, and began the siege with such vigour that it surrendered in nine days. Menin is a strong fortress on the Lys, which now serves as a boundary between France and Belgium, for Vauban, the great French engineer, had fortified it with all his art. Lewis had by this time sent his bravest marshal, Vendôme, to restore the fortunes of France on its northern frontier. He approached Marlborough's army as if with the intention of raising the siege of Menin, but the memory of Ramillies was too much for the courage of his soldiers. "Everyone here," he reports to Lewis, "is ready to doff his hat, if one even mentions the name of Marlborough." It took twenty-three days before Menin fell. Dendermonde, which lay to his rear, was Marlborough's real object. It was so situated on the banks of the Scheldt, that by letting out the waters the governor could prevent an enemy's approach. "They must have an army of ducks," Lewis had said, "to take Dendermonde." It surrendered, however, to Marlborough. In his despatch he gives the reason—"That place could never have been taken but by the hand of God, which gave us seven weeks without rain. The rain began the day after we had taken possession, and continued without intermission." Ath surrendered next, after a siege of twelve days, and Marlborough would also have attempted the strong fortress of Mons if the Dutch had been more prompt with supplies. Thus ended the brilliant campaign of 1706, all the results of which may be traced to the victory of Ramillies.

The Emperor and King Charles wished to make Marlborough governor of the country which he had thus conquered. It was a post of importance, and of considerable emolument; the English Government would have gladly seen him accept it. But the Dutch, and even his friends amongst them, made so strong an opposition that the plan was allowed to drop.

Marlborough proposed as governor of Netherlands.

Section II.—Turin.

At the beginning of the year 1706 the cause of the allies in Italy looked very gloomy. It seemed that nothing could prevent the capture of Turin, that then they must be wholly driven out of Italy, and that the Duke of Savoy would be compelled to quit the Grand Alliance, just as he had formerly quitted it before the Peace of Ryswick. Great efforts were therefore made to send strong support. Marlborough even went to Vienna to obtain supplies and reinforcements for Eugene, and his representations were successful, so that Eugene was able to take the field with a larger and better equipped army than before. Just before his arrival in Italy the imperialists had been defeated by Vendôme at Calcinato. The story ran that, to lull the vigilance of the opposing general, Vendôme had pretended to be ill, and suddenly appearing well, and at the head of his army, had routed the imperialists. Eugene's first work was to reorganise the defeated troops.

The allied cause in Italy.

Meanwhile the French began the siege of Turin. It was commenced with true French politeness. The

ITALY
1700

The Year of Victory.

French general, by order of the king, sent to offer safe passports for the princesses of Savoy, and to say that, if the duke would point out his head-quarters, no bombs should be thrown there. The duke sent answer that his daughters were already safe, and that the French might throw their bombs where they thought proper. Having made all preparations for resisting the siege, the duke left his capital, thinking that the presence of a court might hinder the defence, which he entrusted to Daun, the father of one who was afterwards a famous Austrian general in the Seven Years' War. Messages were sent to inform Eugene how critical was the state of Turin. He marched quickly from Tyrol to its relief. Fortunately for the cause of the allies the battle of Ramillies had just been won, and Lewis recalled Marshal Vendôme from Italy, as the only French general who could face the victorious Marlborough. In the place of Vendôme, whom he so highly valued, he sent his Royal Highness the Duke of Orleans, and, as the fashion was, a general to guide him, Marshal Marsin, who had commanded part of the army opposed to Eugene at Blenheim. The Duke of Orleans was merely ornamental. Marsin's reputation did not stand high. It was said that he had been made a marshal only because Madame de Maintenon held a high opinion of his religious character.

Eugene's quick march took him across three rivers, the Po, the largest, giving him most trouble. By a wide circuit to the south he reached the Pass of Stradella, in a spur of the Apennines, running towards the Po. This pass was very important, because it formed the communication between the French and their allies in the peninsula. This occupation of the pass and the victory which followed it have been compared to "a stab in the jugular artery, or a blow on the spinal marrow." Marching from Stradella on Turin, Eugene effected a junction with the Duke of Savoy.

State of the siege.

After surveying the ground from the heights of Superga, whence the city and the whole surrounding country can be seen, the two generals determined on an attack. News reached them that the siege, which had now lasted for more than three months, had reached such a point that the besiegers had twice forced their way within the fortifications, and twice had been repulsed; and that the defenders had fired away their last barrel of powder. The allies were eager for battle. When Eugene's house steward asked him where he would dine the next evening, "at Turin, at Turin," he enthusiastically answered.

Battle of Turin, Sept. 7, A.D. 1706.

The French were stronger than the allies in numbers, and much stronger in position. They were behind intrenchments, to the attack of which the allies had to march across a plain. But bravery and generalship carried the day; the French were signally routed. The duke, accompanied by Eugene, entered his delivered capital amid the ringing of bells and every sign of enthusiasm. Eugene dined that night in Turin.

Results of Turin. 1. The French troops are demoralised.

This was the third victory which secured to the allies important results, indeed hardly less important than Blenheim and Ramillies. The first of these was the effect on the minds of the French. They were taught that Marlborough was not the only general who could rout them. "I am sorry to tell you," wrote one of their own officers, "that I no longer know our men—they are so changed. I will not give you a detail of the disorder in which they fought at Turin, and of the confusion which prevailed among us, when we turned our backs on an army that, even after the battle, was much inferior to ours. I will draw a curtain over this disagreeable scene; but I cannot help telling you that our troops hardly think themselves safe here, divided as they are by the Alps from the enemy." The same feeling was thus prevailing in the French army of the South as in that of the North, and the army of the South also was compelled to withdraw within the borders of France. The second consequence was that Savoy was now secured to the cause of the Grand Alliance. The French evacuated all Piedmont except the fortresses. These they lost one by one—Milan last. The Convention of Milan (March 13, 1707) secured North Italy for the allies. But the kingdom of Naples also was thus cut off from France by land, whilst the English fleets prevented troops being sent by sea. Naples made a separate peace with the imperialists, and was never again united to the monarchy of Spain.

2. The French driven out of Piedmont.

3. Naples makes peace apart from Spain.

Section III.— *Barcelona and Madrid.*

THE successes of the Earl of Peterborough in Spain, and the acceptance of King Charles in so large a portion of that country, produced greater vigour on the French side than had yet been shown. Philip himself commanded an army whose object was to recover Barcelona. Lewis sent a fleet under his natural son, the Count of Toulouse, together with a skilled French marshal, to help the inexperienced Philip. Charles's ministers implored him to escape; but he bravely determined to remain in Barcelona, which was soon blockaded by land and sea. The

The French besiege Barcelona

breaches in the fortress of Monjuich, which Peterborough had taken so quickly, had not been properly repaired; yet it held out for twenty-three days. Meanwhile Peterborough with his small forces, chiefly consisting of irregular troops, tried to raise the siege, but in vain. The English fleet during Peterborough's romantic enterprise had returned to England. It was now back in the Mediterranean, and a new commission had been sent to Peterborough, which gave him the command of the fleet when he was on board ship. At great risk he put out to sea in a small boat; on the first night no ship of the fleet was to be seen; on the second night he was more successful. He did not wish the French admiral to see the whole fleet, but rather desired to entice him to battle with a part, and then to bring up the rest as a reserve. But the Count of Toulouse was well informed, and sailed back from Barcelona to Toulon. The land forces soon followed the navy, and the siege was raised.

Peterborough makes them raise the siege.

The success upon the east of Spain set in motion the army under the Earl of Galway on the west. Berwick, who was opposing it, had forces too small to resist the advance, and fell back on the north. Philip, who was in the north, had hastened to Madrid; but he was obliged immediately to quit it. He was attended on his retreat by his nobles, more faithful to him on account of his adversity. Shortly after Philip had left Madrid, Galway with his English and Portuguese troops entered the Spanish capital.

Entrance into Madrid.

This may be considered the highest point of the success of the allies. On May 11, the day on which the siege of Barcelona was raised, a total eclipse of the sun took place. It was eagerly remarked that the sun in his glory had been

The point of greatest success in the war.

the favourite device of Lewis XIV. In the middle of this year 1706, though victory in Savoy was yet in the future, the allies had been successful in the Netherlands, and both upon the east and west of Spain. They were fighting to keep down the power of Lewis, especially to prevent him from attacking Holland, and to place the Archduke Charles upon the throne of Spain. All the strongholds of the Netherlands, were now in their hands, and the capital of the Spanish monarchy was taken by Galway, who anxiously expected Charles to join him in Madrid. But our account of the year as a year of victory must end here.

When the cause of Philip seemed to have reached its lowest stage, a peculiar feature in the character of the Spanish people, especially in that of the Castilians, was shown. They had not seemed to care for King Philip in his prosperity: *Spanish loyalty for Philip.* he had excited no enthusiasm amongst them—they had obstructed his government by their apathy, if by nothing else. Now that he was in exile they became enthusiastic in his cause. Never was there such loyalty. One story may serve as an illustration. A Castilian priest brought him 120 pistoles from his small village, which had only 120 houses—" My flock are ashamed," said the good priest with tears in his eyes, "that they are not able to send a larger sum; but they entreat your Majesty to believe that in the same purse are one hundred and twenty hearts faithful even to death."

Against this feeling it was useless for the allies to contend. It seems only wonderful that all did not recognise, as Peterborough expressly did, that Charles would never be king in Castile; for Spain was now divided into parties almost as it had once been into kingdoms, and the inhabitants would have gladly acquiesced in a division which would have given Castile to Philip and Aragon to Charles. It was an Englishman, General Stanhope, who protested that this would reduce Spain to nought in the councils of Europe.

Although Madrid was thus held for him, King Charles could not be persuaded to enter. He pleaded that he must enter in state, and that his carriage was not ready. "Our William the third," reasoned General Stanhope, "entered London in a hackney coach with a cloak bag behind it, and was made king not many weeks after." Between the hostility of the natives and the lukewarmness or cowardice of the prince, it was impossible to hold Madrid. As Charles would not come to Madrid, Galway, no longer able to obtain supplies, left Madrid to join the archduke and the forces under Peterborough. Charles marched from Saragossa, Peterborough from Valencia: they joined each other, and the next day effected a junction with Galway at Guadalaxara. We are told how each army saw with astonishment the smallness of the other.

Madrid left.

Junction of Galway and Peterborough at Guadalaxara.

As they left Madrid, Berwick's troops entered; and as the inhabitants were in favour of his cause, his army was received with enthusiasm. It grew day by day in numbers, whilst the forces of the allies kept wasting. The crisis was past. Never again had the cause of Charles such a chance in Spain as on the day when Galway entered Madrid.

Moreover a new difficulty beset the allies. Not only were their troops few, but their generals were many. Rather than serve under Galway, his senior officer, Peterborough, determined to go. A clause in his instructions had ordered him to proceed, if he had an opportunity, to the assistance

Plurality of generals.

of the Duke of Savoy. He set off therefore for Italy, and was chagrined to find that all the officers were glad at his departure. With many qualities that might inspire those under him, Peterborough had something that made him unpopular—a most sarcastic and biting tongue, from which even the prince was not safe.

When Peterborough was gone, however, the cause of the allies did not prosper any better. Before the advancing troops of Berwick they retreated to Valencia, where they wintered.

CHAPTER X.

THE YEAR OF DISASTER—1707.

THE year 1707 was a strange contrast to that which preceded it. In almost every quarter it was a year of inaction or of disaster to the cause of the Grand Alliance. It was strange that the campaign in Flanders which followed that of Ramillies was so unfruitful in successes. The campaign of Turin alone seemed to carry forward its results into the following year; but the selfishness with which the Emperor acted made the success in Italy almost more hurtful than useful to the general cause. In Spain, divided counsels had, even in the latter part of the previous year, produced their natural fruit in failure and retreat. They were in this year to be crowned with the greatest defeat which the allies suffered during the war. In other parts of Europe, also, fortune seemed to have deserted their cause.

When Marlborough assumed the command of the

army in Flanders, he expected such success as would lead directly to a speedy termination of the war. He had indeed many other things to do than merely to command his own army. The Home Government looked to him constantly for advice. It was his work to keep the different members of the Grand Alliance true to the cause, and zealous. In the spring of this year the King of Sweden was causing anxiety to the Emperor. King Charles XII., whose career is described in another part of this volume, was at Dresden with an army not inconsiderable in numbers, but still more formidable from the bravery and reputation of the soldiers. French envoys paid him frequent visits, for Lewis felt that if he could win Charles to his side, he might yet triumph in the war, as the Emperor would be paralysed. Marlborough therefore made a hasty journey to the Court of Charles, to try whether his influence could counteract that of these French envoys. On the way he stopped for forty-eight hours with the Elector of Hanover, who advised him to try the effect of the promise of pensions to the chief ministers of King Charles, and to pay the first year in advance. At Dresden Marlborough did not neglect this advice, but perhaps he relied more on his own power of flattery, for this was his first speech to the king:

Marlborough and Charles XII.

"I present to your Majesty a letter, not from the chancery, but from the heart of the queen, my mistress, and written with her own hand. Had not her sex prevented it, she would have crossed the sea to see a prince admired by the whole universe. I am in this particular more happy than the queen, and I wish I could serve some campaigns under so great a general as your Majesty, that I might learn what I yet want to know in the art of war."

Charles was naturally pleased, and Marlborough was soon convinced that the Grand Alliance had no reason to fear danger in that quarter, as Charles was meditating a very different design. Charles was unmoved when Marlborough spoke of Lewis, but his eyes flashed fire when he spoke of the Czar.

On Marlborough's return to Flanders he was anxious to begin active operations against the French; but he was thwarted by the Dutch deputies, who seemed to have received orders to that effect from their own Government. The Dutch wanted a cession of territory, in order to secure their border the better from attack; but as this cession would have to be made at the expense of the Emperor, they anticipated opposition from him, and determined to thwart the progress of the common cause until they could make terms for themselves. Such instructions, combined with the usual phlegmatic slowness of the Dutch deputies, fettered Marlborough's action. The other allies also were backward in sending their contingents. Month after month passed, and the whole summer slipped away without anything being done.

Marlborough in Flanders.

In the month of March was fought in Spain the battle of Almanza. It was the greatest defeat which the allies suffered during the war, and was inflicted by the Duke of Berwick. The English found some consolation for their defeat in the thought that their conqueror was an Englishman. Berwick indeed had much of the generalship, the coolness in action, and the bravery of his uncle, Marlborough.

Battle of Almanza, March, A.D. 1707.

Almanza in Valencia is a town situated in an open plain. As Berwick was stronger than the allies in cavalry, the country was better

The positions.

suited to him; but Galway was either ignorant of this fact or disregarded it. Anxious to expel the French from Valencia, he advanced to the attack. Berwick had drawn up his troops, with his infantry and artillery in the centre, and his cavalry on the flanks. The various elements of Galway's forces were more mixed; and he has been especially censured for drawing up infantry in line close in the rear of his cavalry.

The battle began about two in the afternoon. Lord Galway, who was as brave in battle as he was cautious in council, led an attack upon the French right which, successful for a moment, was repulsed by the second line under Berwick in person. In the centre the French were at first successful, then driven back: but a French officer prevented any evil result from the repulse by declaring that it was a feigned retreat made by the general's order. Then Berwick came up with reinforcements and restored the battle. The first important disaster befell the allies on their right. The Portuguese cavalry at the charge of the enemy turned and fled, leaving bare and unprotected some infantry of their own countrymen, who were cut to pieces. Some Spanish cavalry also on the other wing made no resistance. The English infantry in the centre, left thus exposed, were attacked on both flank and in front at the same time, were outnumbered and compelled to surrender. A force of thirteen battalions escaped to a wood, but surrendered next day to the French cavalry who surrounded them.

Total defeat of the allies.

Two days after the fight Lord Galway wrote to Marlborough:—

"I am under deep concern to be obliged to tell your lordship we were entirely defeated. Both our wings were broke, and let in the enemy's horse, which surrounded our foot, so that none could get off. I received a cut in the forehead in the first charge. . . . . . I cannot, my lord, but look upon the affairs of Spain as lost by this bad disaster; our foot, which was our main strength, being gone, and the horse we have left chiefly Portuguese, which is not good at all . . . . All the generals here are of opinion that we cannot continue in this kingdom."

Lord Galway did not exaggerate the importance of the defeat. The whole of the provinces of Valencia and Aragon surrendered to the French. The town of Valencia opened its gates to them without any effort at resistance; the few towns which did resist were soon overpowered, and were treated with severity. The Archduke Charles was reduced to the single province of Catalonia, where the inhabitants were still faithful to him; but here his army was so small that he could hardly have withstood an invasion, had one been made.

Results of the defeat.

Once more it seemed as if the cause of the allies was hopeless in Spain. The only chance for that cause was the appointment of a really able commander with adequate forces. Such a commander was Eugene, and such forces could easily have been sent by sea from North Italy to Barcelona. The English and Dutch ministers used their best endeavours to procure the adoption of this policy. But the Emperor, preferring his own interests, despatched a large force into Naples to secure that kingdom. It was easy work. The imperialist troops under Daun, the gallant defender of Turin, were received with welcome, and the few who held out for Philip were besieged and taken in

Eugene should have been sent to Spain.

Emperor secures Naples.

Gaeta. The Island of Majorca also declared for Charles. These victories, however, might have been secured at any time.

It was with difficulty that the Emperor could even be brought to sanction a plan on which Marlborough strongly insisted, the invasion, namely, of France in the south-east, so as to produce a diversion from the war in Spain. There was still hope that the Protestants might rise. The English fleet would co-operate.

Attempt on Toulon.

The place to be attacked was Toulon, and the army was to be under the command of Eugene and the Duke of Savoy. Had the former known how very unprepared the place was, he would probably have attacked it at once and taken it. The engineer whom Lewis sent down to defend Toulon reported that it was not a fortress, but rather a garden, being overspread with large country houses, orchards, and convents. Whilst he was working hard to get ready and defend the place, Eugene prepared to attack it in due form. But his army was straitened for supplies; and, threatened by the advance of a large French force, Eugene and his cousin who had commenced the attempt half-heartedly, determined to raise the siege.

There was yet one other military disaster this year. The imperialist army on the Upper Rhine, which Lewis

Defeat of allies on Rhine by Villars

of Baden had commanded since the year of Blenheim until his death at the beginning of this year, was now commanded by a still more incompetent general, the Margrave of Bayreuth. His army had to defend the lines of Stollhofen; but Villars, the French marshal, surprised him, stormed the strong lines, and entirely routed the German troops. Villars was thus able to break into the Palatinate, and in imitation of the former French conduct he

THE NETHERLANDS
NORTH SEA
UNITED NETHERLANDS
SPANISH NETHERLANDS
FRANCE
Flanders
Brabant
Amsterdam
The Hague
Ryswick
Utrecht
R. Maas or Meuse
Gertruydenburg
R. Rhine
R. Scheldt
Ostend
Antwerp
Ghent
R. Schelde
Dendermonde
Brussels
Oudenarde
R. Lys
Lille
Tournai
Waterloo
Ramillies
Mehaigne R.
Liege
R. Meuse
Namur
Huy
Mons
Valenciennes
Malplaquet
R. Sambre
R. Moselle
CAMPAIGN OF MALPLAQUET 1709
Tournai
R. Scheldt
Conde
Haine R.
Mons
St. Ghislain
St. Amant
French Boundary
Valenciennes
Scheldt R.
Malplaquet
Hon R.
Maubeuge
Bavay
Sambre R.

laid much of it waste. Marlborough induced the Emperor after this to take the command from the Margrave, and give it to a man of greater capacity, the Elector of Hanover, the future King George of England.

Yet another calamity befell the English, but not from the hand of the enemy. Sir Cloudesley Shovel was bringing back his fleet to England from the Mediterranean, when it met with stormy weather off the Scilly Isles. On a dark night in October, three ships, including the admiral's, "the Association," were dashed against the Gilstone Rock, and only one man escaped of their crews. The admiral's body was washed ashore and found by some fishermen, who plundered it and buried it in the sand. His large emerald ring, however, was recognised, and, on the fishermen confessing, his body was taken up, and received a grand funeral in Westminster Abbey. *(Wreck and loss of Sir Cloudesley Shovel.)*

At the end of this year the country was sick of the war, and would have welcomed a peace. During the rest of the war this feeling grew, nor did any military glory again diminish it.

CHAPTER XI.

LATER FIGHTING IN THE LOW COUNTRIES.

Section I.—*Oudenarde and Lille.*

THE discontent felt in England against the war, and the fact that the bonds which held the alliance together seemed to be growing loose, convinced Marlborough that this year (1708) a blow must be struck. He reports that the burgo- *(Need for a blow.)*

master of Amsterdam, who had hitherto been in favour of the war, had warned him that the Dutch were turning towards the idea of making for themselves a separate peace. Moreover, the inhabitants of Brabant, who had welcomed the success of the allies after Ramillies, and who might have been still warm in their favour if Marlborough had been permitted to accept the government of the country, which Charles had offered, and still continued to offer, were becoming dissatisfied. The temporary government was chiefly in the hands of Dutch commissioners, who were by no means conciliatory, as Marlborough would have been. The Dutch boasted that at the peace they would keep the country; and as they were Protestants and the inhabitants staunch Catholics, the boast was very unpalatable to the latter. This feeling was known to the French, whom the inaction of the previous year also put in good heart. They determined now to make an effort to win the country back. Bruges and Ghent opened their gates to French troops. There was disaffection among the soldiers at Antwerp; but Marlborough, having received information of it, was able to prevent any outbreak.

Brabant inclining to French.

The next place which the French attempted to secure was Oudenarde, a strong fortress on the Scheldt. It was important to them on account of its position, standing between Brabant and their own frontier. The French army was nominally commanded by a royal prince, the Duke of Burgundy; but, as the fashion was with French armies, a general of greater skill was sent with him, whose duty it was to guide him and make up by his skill for the prince's inexperience. This was the Duke of Vendôme. But for this arrangement to work well it is absolutely necessary

Siege of Oudenarde.

that the prince and his general should be on friendly terms, or at any rate have a mutual understanding. The feeling between the Dukes of Burgundy and Vendôme was strong repugnance, if not actual animosity. The Duke of Burgundy was a devout Catholic, with the manners of royalty, but lacking military skill. The Duke of Vendôme was an infidel, dirty in his habits, and lazy, but with genius as a general. A kingdom divided against itself will not stand. An army in the direction of which there is discord so apparent cannot succeed.

Marlborough's army was not so numerous as that of the French duke's; but he was destined to receive one auxiliary worth a host. As the war in Italy was finished Eugene was free, and it was arranged that he should join Marlborough at the head of a body of imperialist troops. *Eugene joins Marlborough.* There were, however, the usual delays in starting: and though Marlborough wrote to hasten him, it was evident that his army could not reach Marlborough in time. Scenting the battle from afar, Eugene left first his infantry behind, then his cavalry, and arrived in Marlborough's camp attended only by his personal suite. "My men will be encouraged," said Marlborough, "by the presence of so distinguished a commander."

The two generals were agreed as to their plans. It was determined to march between France and the French army, so that, in case of defeat, the French could not retreat to their own territory. On the approach of the allies, the siege of Oudenarde was raised, the French marching northwards. The French, their faces turned towards Paris, occupied a strong position, defended by some rising ground. *Battle of Oudenarde, July 11, A.D. 1708.* The allies moved to the attack at

H

three in the afternoon of July 11, 1708, greatly to the surprise of the French generals, for the allied army had just marched fifteen miles.

Before Marlborough had even got all his army into position, he ordered his cavalry to charge, so that if the enemy had any thought of retiring without a battle it was too late. In this first charge the Electoral Prince of Hanover, afterwards George II., distinguished himself. The right of the allied army was assigned to Eugene, out of compliment to whom Marlborough made this wing very strong, and placed the English troops in it. He himself commanded the centre, in which no English were fighting, but various corps of the other nations of the Grand Alliance. At the first assault the allied left was broken not long after it had crossed the Scheldt. The enemy, thinking that they were winning, pressed forward to drive the allies back into the river. An obstinate fight ensued, hand to hand, bayonet to bayonet. Indeed a great deal of the battle was of this nature; it was remarked that artillery was hardly employed at all, the fighting being at too close range.

Battle begins.

As the French right thus pressed forward, Marlborough saw an opportunity of cutting it off, and he sent a very strong force under the old Dutch general, Marshal Overkirk, who had fought in William's battles, and in many another. He was now in his last field, for he died this year. The service was well carried out, and the heights behind the French right were occupied. As night came on, Overkirk's men on the allied left and Eugene's men, who had been working steadily forward on the right, almost met. They had even fired some shots into each other's ranks, before the mistake was discovered by the officers. The order was given to cease firing, and through the gap that was still open many of the French escaped, but many more were taken prisoners. The number of slain in the battle was not very great. The Chevalier St. George fought on the side of the French.

The Duke of Vendôme, it is said, wished to fight again the next day, but the Duke of Burgundy and his friends positively refused. "We must then retreat," said Vendôme, angrily; "and I know," he added, looking at Burgundy, "that you have long wished to do so."

A few days after the fight Eugene's army came up, but as the Duke of Berwick, who had been watching it and marching parallel with it, now joined the main body of the French, no real difference was made in the proportion of the armies.

After a victory the important question is—what use shall be made of it? Eugene wished to attack the strong fortress of Lille on the French frontier. Marlborough proposed to disregard it, and march upon Paris. In this project he would have received the support of the Home Government, but Eugene considered it dangerous to leave such strong enemies in the rear, and the Dutch deputies were aghast at the proposal. *Sequel to battle.*

The siege of Lille was looked upon with great interest. In all other quarters the war flagged, whilst men's attention was turned upon this important contest. The fortification of Lille was considered a masterpiece of Vauban. Boufflers, one of the ablest of French marshals, was defending it. It was known that King Lewis was determined to strain every effort rather than let Lille be lost. On the other hand the allied generals were equally determined to take the town. The convoy which brought up the siege train, the heavy artillery and the supplies, was said to have *Siege of Lille.*

been thirteen miles in length. Eugene commanded the besieging, Marlborough the covering army, opposed to Berwick and Vendôme. The regulations which the allied generals jointly drew up for those who were to serve in the trenches are still considered a valuable lesson for the young soldier. Prodigies of valour were performed by the defenders. When powder failed, a body of French soldiers marched through the enemy's lines, each carrying forty pounds of gunpowder. Through the leader speaking Dutch, many succeeded in passing the sentinels; but a casual remark in French from an officer betrayed the rear. At another time a French captain took news into the city, swimming through the allied lines down the river Dyle on which Lille is, with his letter in his mouth, and escaping the notice of the sentinels by swimming under water. He returned to the French camp in the same way.

The chief trouble of the besiegers was to obtain supplies. On one important convoy bringing provisions from Ostend it seemed as if the whole siege would turn to Eugene's camp. The French therefore sent an army to attack it; Marlborough detached General Webb for its defence. The French came upon Webb in the wood of Wynendale, but were beaten back, and the provisions reached Eugene safely. This affair was considered of importance, because Webb, as a Tory, was opposed to Marlborough in politics, and either on that account, or by mistake, Marlborough assigned the glory of the skirmish to another general. In the time of Marlborough's unpopularity afterwards, the Tory House of Commons passed a vote of thanks to General Webb for the victory at Wynendale.

Skirmish at Wynendale.

As a last resource to prevent supplies reaching Eugene

A.D. 1709. *Later Fighting in the Low Countries.* 101

the French opened the sluices, and laid the country under water. Whereupon the allies built large flat-bottomed boats, and brought the supplies by water.

After sixty days of gallant defence, Marshal Boufflers was obliged to capitulate. It was even said that King Lewis wrote that he should not push matters to extremity, but spare the lives of those who had fought so well. Eugene, in admiration of the brave defence, allowed Boufflers to name his own terms of capitulation. Lille was not surrendered until all its powder had been fired away, and the garrison had been for some time living on horse-flesh.

Surrender of Lille.

Section II.—Negotiations.

The winter after Oudenarde and the taking of Lille was a terrible time for France. When the spring arrived the country was in a condition of absolute exhaustion. The efforts, which had been required after such defeats as Blenheim, Ramillies, and Turin, and by the variety of points on which the country was open to the attacks of the allies, had emptied the treasury, and increased to an enormous extent the public debt, had robbed the fields of their cultivators, and caused them to be left untilled. Bankruptcy and famine stared France in the face. There was no money to pay the soldiers; the taxes were unfruitful; no one seemed to have money to lend. The only quarter whence corn could be imported was the Levant; but English cruisers swarmed in the Mediterranean, and intercepted the corn ships. There was nothing for the people to eat but black bread; even the fine ladies at Versailles lived on oat-cakes. The winter was one of especial severity. It was terribly cold in England, where the Thames was frozen over for weeks, but its

State of France.

effects were more terrible in France, for there they were suffering starvation.

Lewis XIV., who claimed to be the father of his people, was touched with their distress, and humbled himself to apply for peace. He sent an ambassador to Holland with proposals very advantageous to the allies. He proposed that his grandson should surrender all the Spanish dominions, except Naples and Sicily, which were to be made into a separate kingdom for him.

Lewis proposes terms.

Marlborough was appointed English plenipotentiary, together with Lord Townshend, an honest but not very able man, who on the accession of George I. became the Whig Prime-Minister. The English insisted on the cession of the whole Spanish monarchy, on the acknowledgment of the queen and the Protestant succession, on the banishment of the pretender, and the demolition of the works at Dunkirk. To these the various allies added other claims, each for their own advantage, at the expense of France. The most important was the Dutch claim for a barrier or chain of strong fortresses to secure them from attack. As to the particular fortresses claimed Marlborough thought the Dutch were asking too much.

The terms of the allies.

When the terms were made known in Versailles the scene at the cabinet is described as most melancholy. The princes of the blood royal even shed tears on the condition of France; but it was determined to proceed with the negotiations. M. de Torcy himself, the minister for foreign affairs, was sent to the Hague to see whether he could procure easier terms. He has described several interviews which he had with Marlborough, to whom he was empowered to offer a large

Embassy of Torcy.

Conference of the Hague.

bribe. But the French minister himself tells us that Marlborough would not listen to the disgraceful offer. The allies adhered to their proposals, adding to rather than abating from them.

The conditions with which Torcy returned to Versailles were harder than before: that the whole Spanish monarchy should be ceded to the Archduke Charles, and that the Dutch should have all the frontier towns for which they asked.

Intolerable proposal.

It was known that Philip would not quietly surrender his hold of Spain, where he had won the love of the Castilians. "God had placed him on the Spanish throne," he said, "and he would maintain himself there with the last drop of his blood." A clause was therefore added, saying that, unless Spain and Sicily were surrendered within two months, King Lewis was to join the allies in driving his own grandson from his throne. However crushed France was, these terms were intolerable. However much king and people might long for peace, it was not to be bought thus. Madame de Maintenon indeed wanted Lewis to accept this condition, but another cabinet meeting was held, at which bolder counsels were heard. "If I must continue the war," said Lewis with a spirit that brings back his earlier days, "I will contend against my enemies rather than against my own family."

Appeal to the people, May 1709.

He made an appeal to his people to meet the emergency, sending a circular to all the governors of provinces, intending that its contents should be made public. He spoke of his own desire for peace and his efforts to secure it: he was prepared, he said, to make humiliating sacrifices, but the more he showed himself disposed towards them, the more did the allies rise in their demands; they seemed determined to open to themselves avenues by which they might penetrate into the heart of France; even if he had consented to all their conditions it would not have procured peace. "Seeing," he continued, "that our enemies in their pretence to negotiate are palpably insincere, we have only to consider how to defend ourselves, and show them that France united can resist the united powers of Europe in their attempts, by fair means or by foul, to ruin her. All the ordinary sources of revenue are exhausted. I come before you for your counsel and assistance, at a time when our very safety as a nation is at stake: let us show our enemies that we are still not sunk so low but that we can force upon them such a peace as shall consist with our honour and with the good of Europe."

Marlborough and the allies did not expect an answer such as this appeal produced, or such a result to their intolerable and humiliating demands. The French were touched by these words from one whom they had regarded as almost superhuman. Poorly clad and half-starved recruits flocked to the standards, but there was a new spirit in their eyes. A war which had been the French king's war became the French people's, and a larger army was set on foot than ever during the war before.

The answer to it.

Section III.—Malplaquet.

Marlborough, who knew the effort that France was making, and the importance which on that account attached to the approaching campaign, pressed upon the English Government the necessity of strengthening his army. He used his best endeavours also to obtain more troops from the other nations of the confederacy. He knew well the military maxim, that in a desperate struggle, victory

Preparations.

will fall to that side which can bring up reserves when its enemy no longer can. Marlborough succeeded in persuading the home Government to send some extra troops, and not to recall certain regiments from Antwerp: the Dutch also sent 4,000 German troops who were in their pay. But the number of men under arms was already very large, larger than ever before, and reaching more nearly to the size of modern armies. Those with the French standards were about as numerous as those in the allied army. There were about 110,000 men in each. But the French were badly supplied; the distress in France showed itself in the army in the scarcity of bread. If a detachment had to march, it was said, it could only have a full breakfast by diminishing the breakfast of the troops that were to halt.

The command of the French army was now given to Villars, the only French marshal who had not as yet been defeated in the war. The soldiers believed in his luck, which it was hoped would not now desert him. Boufflers, who had won himself glory by his brave defence of Lille, offered, although senior to Villars, to serve under him: and this noble example, part as it were of the wave of enthusiasm which was sweeping over France, did much to kindle the ardour of the soldiers, who, mostly consisting of raw levies, were opposed to the veterans under Marlborough and Eugene. Villars was the able general who had shown clemency to the Camisards. He was much addicted to boasting on assuming command. The first thing that he did was to announce that his army was much larger than it really was; the second was to give a ball.

Villars and Boufflers.

The plan of campaign which the allied generals set before them was a continuance of that which had made the siege of Lille a necessity. It was to force their way into France, leaving no stronghold behind. The only formidable fortresses which stood between were Tournai, Mons, and Valenciennes. They would also have to fight the army of Villars, whose business was likewise twofold—to prevent the capture of these towns, and to prevent the army of the allies from penetrating across the frontier. With this latter object he began to make strong works behind the rivers Scarpe, Scheldt, and Trouille.

Plan of campaign.

Marlborough made an advance, as if to attack the army of Villars, who thereupon hastily withdrew troops from Tournai to strengthen his forces. Then by a night-march the allied troops quickly invested Tournai thus weakened. The place was as bravely defended as it was strongly fortified, and the citadel was especially strong. Vauban's skill had been employed on all these towns along the French frontier, and Tournai was considered his masterpiece. The town was taken in a month; the remains of the garrison then retired into the citadel, which resisted for five more weeks. The terrors of the siege were increased by the fact that in none of the other sieges were mines so much employed by the besieged. Just when a breach was made in the walls, and the allies were advancing towards it, a mine would be sprung and 300 soldiers blown into the air. Or when a party of the besiegers had discovered a mine, and were congratulating themselves on the discovery, they were blown up by the explosion of another mine beneath it. On September 3, however, the garrison surrendered, and Marlborough in consideration of their bravery let the defenders march out with the honours of war.

Tournai.

The next object of attack was Mons; but to invest

this it was necessary to break through some part of the French lines, and to cross the river Haine.

On the night of the surrender, an advance guard was sent to seize St. Ghislain, if possible; but it was too strong for them. A second and stronger force under the Prince of Hesse pushed further on, and crossed the river above the town of Mons; and then finding a gap between the town and the lines of the French behind the Trouille, which joins the Haine just below Mons, the prince advanced, and invested Mons on the southern side. This movement, which succeeded almost without opposition, was of great service. It made an opening through the French lines, and placed the allies between Mons and France. If Villars wished to stop the siege of the town, his only chance was by risking a battle. He advanced therefore towards Mons from the south, and took up a strong position at Malplaquet. The allied generals were, however, as ready as he was for a battle. They had followed close upon the heels of Hesse, and on September 9 held a council of war. The Dutch deputies were of course opposed to fighting. Marlborough was for an immediate attack before the enemy could intrench himself; but Eugene, who also wished to fight, was yet willing to delay, until more battalions which were expected from before Tournai should come up. This, as a middle course was adopted, but there can be no doubt that Marlborough was right. The stubborn resistance that the French made two days later was greatly assisted by the intrenchments which they had thrown up; and the right policy would have been to attack at once or not at all.

The ground round Malplaquet was very thickly wooded. It was originally part of a large forest, which in many places had yielded to cultivation.

Description of ground. To the north, the direction in which Mons lay, there were two woods, Laniere and Taisniere, and between them a glade or open space, which was called the Trouée of Aulnoit. At the southern end of this glade Villars intrenched himself: he had used the two days well. When the English soldiers advanced, they murmured—"So we have still to fight against moles." Villars had also occupied the woods.

The battle that followed was terribly bloody. It was won, not by strategy, but by downright hard fighting. Each wing of the allies was once repulsed.

Battle of Malplaquet, September 11, A.D. 1709. The right had to fight its way through the wood of Taisniere. The left was under the command of the Prince of Orange; and when, after most terrible slaughter, it was at length driven back, Marlborough told the prince that this attack was only intended to be a feint. It is uncertain whether this was intended as a consolation to the prince for his repulse, or was really a part of Marlborough's plan. Prince Eugene was wounded in the battle, being shot behind the ear; but when his officers begged him to retire and have the wound dressed, he said "there would be time enough for that in the evening, if he survived." On the other side Villars was wounded more seriously, but he also showed the same spirit. He ordered a chair to be brought, that he might continue to direct the battle, but he fainted in it, and was removed from the scene. Boufflers, on whom the command devolved, found that after four hours' hard fighting his centre was broken, and the intrenchments carried. The French, however, were able to retreat in good order from the field. The loss of the allies in thus dislodging the French amounted to about 20,000 men, or nearly one-fifth of the force that they brought into the field. The French, who fought behind intrenchments, lost a little more than half that number. These two facts, the excellent retreat and the loss of the allies, made Malplaquet a very different defeat for the French from Blenheim, Ramillies, or Oudenarde. Lewis's circular had borne good fruit, and there was truth in Villars' boast: "If God vouchsafe that we should lose such another battle, your majesty could count your enemies destroyed." Some such feeling may have influenced also the mind of Marlborough, as well as the loss of his old friends and comrades. He is said to have been unusually distressed after this battle. He became seriously ill, and a report, afterwards expressed in a triumphant song, was spread amongst the French that he was dead.

But the victory remained with the allies. The siege of Mons was not raised. That fortress surrendered on October 26; and the allies went into winter quarters. Marlborough recovered from his fever; but had he died then, he had, perhaps, been happier in the opportunity of his death. His last great field was fought, his last great victory won.

CHAPTER XII.

LATER CAMPAIGNS IN SPAIN.

Section I.—The Three Years that followed Almanza.

THE battle of Almanza was a singularly decisive battle, and its effects were long felt. Certainly for three years the allies remained on the defensive, and languid campaigns were the result of that defeat. Lord Galway, the defeated English

Effects of Almanza.

general, was recalled from his post, and appointed to the command of the English auxiliary troops in Portugal. In his place, as the Emperor could not be persuaded to send Prince Eugene, an English and a German general were appointed. Of these two, Stanhope, the Englishman, was the abler. As minister at the Court of Charles he had obtained an intimate acquaintance with the state of affairs in Spain. As a general we find him usually in favour of bold plans, and brave in their execution. Without military genius he seems to have had respectable talents for war: in later times he occupied no mean position as Prime-Minister, in the reign of George I. Staremberg, his German colleague, was a methodical general, very slow and cautious in his plans, who, without a spark of genius for war, had tried, but in vain, to make up for the deficiency by study.

Stanhope.

Unsuccessful on the mainland, the allied generals were more successful in the Islands of the Mediterranean. Sardinia declared for Charles almost immediately upon the appearance of the English fleet before it. A more important conquest was that of Minorca. Every winter the English fleet had been obliged to return to England for the winter. On this account the English Government pressed upon the attention of their commanders, that they should endeavour to secure some port in the Mediterranean, so as to prevent the necessity for this return. As the attempts on Toulon had hitherto failed, it was suggested that Port Mahon, the harbour of Minorca, considered the best harbour in that part of the sea, would do equally well. Marlborough had strongly advised Stanhope to make an attempt to secure this harbour. "I conjure you, if possible, to take Port Mahon."

Minorca.

Stanhope found opposition amongst the naval men to this project, for it was known that Port Mahon was strongly defended. He therefore got together transports, embarked his troops, and then sent word to the navy that he was going. The men of war soon followed. His artillery consisted of ships' guns and mortars; his force amounted to 2,600, including marines. On account of the rocky and steep nature of the coast, it took him twelve days to land his cannon, and get it into position; but so vigorous then was his attack, that within one day he had effected a breach, and made an entry into the outer works, whilst within four days the place had surrendered. Stanhope thought so highly of the harbour which he had thus captured, that he filled it only with English troops, and advised the English Government not to surrender it to the Archduke Charles, but to hold it as security against the large sums of money which he owed them. Charles did not like the plan, but made a virtue of necessity.

Port Mahon taken.

Meanwhile, Berwick had been succeeded as commander-in-chief of the French forces in Spain by the Duke of Orleans, an ambitious and bad man, whom we have already seen at the siege of Turin. He was nephew of King Lewis, after his death and during the minority of his successor, Regent of France, and ancestor of the House of Orleans, which has given a king to France during this century. From him, Stanhope, on returning from Minorca, received a proposal, which the Duke of Orleans suggested might be made the basis of an arrangement that would finish the war. He proposed that the allies should withdraw Charles—the French, Philip—because neither party would consent to the candidate of the other reign-

Duke of Orleans.

ing as King of Spain; that both parties should then accept in that capacity him, the Duke of Orleans. Stanhope answered that he could not betray Charles, but suggested that it might be possible to make an independent kingdom for the duke out of Navarre and Languedoc, part of the south of France, where the Protestants had been in rebellion.

This was probably intended to keep the duke quiet at least for a time. But his correspondence with the enemy was discovered and carried to King Lewis, and it was impossible that he could any longer be the French general in Spain. Indeed, in order to support his negotiations for peace, Lewis had withdrawn or professed to withdraw all his troops from Spain. He had a way of withdrawing with one hand and giving back with the other: it was hinted to the men that they might desert the French for the Spanish standards. But for the present Lewis did not send another French general.

French withdrawn from Spain.

In the spring of the next year the army of Portugal, which consisted chiefly of Portuguese troops, but contained also some English regiments under Lord Galway, fought an action on the frontier between Spain and Portugal, at a place called La Gudina. The battle was indeed but a repetition of Almanza on a small scale. There was the same cowardice on the part of the Portuguese horse, not shared in any way by their infantry; the same personal courage and the same military incapacity in Lord Galway; the same stubborn bravery on the part of the English troops. Fortunately, the battle was on a smaller scale. Its results were also rendered less serious than they might have been by a threatened attempt by Stanhope on Cadiz.

La Gudina.

Section II.—*The Final Campaign.*

In the spring of 1710 General Stanhope succeeded in obtaining from the English Government larger forces than had yet been employed in Spain. Using these as arguments, he with great difficulty persuaded Staremberg, his colleague, to consent to vigorous action, and the Archduke Charles to make a bold stroke for the crown that might be his. He even induced Charles to promise that when the army was ready to advance he would join it. Since Almanza the allies had been confined within the single province of Catalonia, which was always faithful. The attempt was now to be made to extend their bounds.

Stanhope's advance.

The river Noguera, during some part of its course the boundary between Catalonia and Aragon, falls into the Segre at Lerida, and is a branch of the Segre which falls into the Ebro. The Spanish army—under the command of Villadarias, the gallant veteran who had stirred up the resistance to the allies at Cadiz, now drawn from retirement by his country's need—was prepared to dispute the entrance of the allies into Aragon. For the greater part of the months of June and July there was no action of importance. Stanhope was always in favour of bolder counsels, and always met with resistance from Staremberg and Charles. At the end of July the allies advanced, and had just crossed the river Noguera, when the enemy came in sight. The others were still unwilling to fight, and at about six in the evening the Spaniards sent some squadrons of cavalry down the hill as it were to defy the English to an engagement. A loud cry of shame broke from the English ranks. Stanhope at length obtained a reluctant consent. Though there was but half an

Battle of Almenara.

hour's daylight left, he drew up his cavalry in two lines and charged, himself at their head. Stanhope himself engaged the general in command of the Spanish cavalry, and killed him with one blow of his sword. This almost Homeric incident is portrayed on the medal struck in honour of the battle. The charge was wholly successful, the enemy were routed, and their camp taken. Philip himself was in great danger, and only escaped through the bravery of his friends. The half-hour was sufficient, though Stanhope wished for more time. "If we had had but two hours more of daylight," he wrote, "you may be assured that not one foot soldier of their army could have escaped." "If God had granted us," wrote one of his subalterns, "the same favour that He did to Joshua, to stop the sun two or three hours, none of their infantry, and very few of their cavalry would have escaped." The infantry of the allies was not engaged at all.

The result of the battle of Almenara was that even Charles and Staremberg consented to advance; but one month later Stanhope had almost the same difficulty to induce them to fight again. The scene of the next battle was Saragossa, the ancient capital of Aragon, famous in later history for its stubborn resistance to the French. Stanhope managed to take his army across the Ebro without any resistance, though resistance then might have proved a serious obstacle. The armies were separated by a deep ravine. Their numbers were nearly equal, the Spanish army being rather the larger, and amounting to 25,000. The battle of Saragossa was fought in full view of the people of the town from which it takes its name. The English and allied troops had to fight without their breakfast, because the convoys had miscarried. The battle began

Battle of Saragossa.

early with cannonading. As seems usual in these battles in Spain, there was a body of Portuguese horsemen on the left of the allies, who made no resistance to the Spaniards opposing them. The latter pursued them with impetuosity, and thus gave Stanhope an opportunity of pressing forward into the gap. The main body of the allies fought their way across the ravine. Some of the Spanish newly-levied troops ran; but one body of veterans would hardly surrender when surrounded. Cannon and standards fell to the conquerors. Almanza was avenged.

That night Charles occupied Saragossa, and there the army rested for a short time. Charles and his German advisers seemed to wish to remain there; but Stanhope dwelt upon his instructions that something decisive must be done. He *The allies advance,* wished to advance upon Madrid, and summon thither the allied army from the other side of Spain, the army from the command of which Galway had just been removed. Once more Stanhope prevailed. The knowledge that the campaigns were fought to a great extent by means of English money must have weighed with Charles.

It is characteristic of Stanhope's eagerness, that on the advance to Madrid he himself commanded the vanguard of light horse. There was hardly a fortnight's interval between the time when *and occupy Madrid.* Philip left Madrid and Charles's entry. But the difference between the return of the defeated Philip and the arrival of the victorious Charles was instructive. It ought to have taught this lesson—the lesson repeated in our own day—that these Castilians were not a people on whom a king could be thrust by the will of foreigners. One marvels that Charles should have sought to reign over a people who so manifestly hated him. Once before the allies had occupied Madrid, and the archduke could not then be persuaded to go thither. Perhaps it had been better had he then gone, and obtained a convincing proof how unpopular he was in that city, and how hopeless his cause: for the allies were received in Madrid on their second visit in the same way as on their first. The same affection was displayed for a defeated king, which his subjects had been slow to show when he was prosperous; the same depths of seemingly sluggish natures were stirred. Everyone who could leave Madrid had retired with the king to Valladolid. Delicate and high-born women went on foot rather than stay. The streets were empty; the shops were shut. There was no demonstration of joy unless for payment; there were signs of grief on every side. "This city is a desert," Charles angrily exclaimed, and left it.

Thus the cause of the heretics, as the allies were called, was at its worst just when it seemed to be most successful. They could with difficulty obtain supplies in Madrid. The enemy's light horse cut off foraging parties. The allied army in Portugal was then under a Portuguese general, for its new English commander, Galway's successor, had not yet arrived, and it could not be induced to move. Notwithstanding these difficulties Stanhope determined to winter in these parts, with his head-quarters at Toledo. It was said that as Charles left Madrid the inhabitants rang the bells for joy.

Retreat to Toledo;

The position of the allies, however, in Castile became more and more untenable. Charles himself was anxious to return to his queen at Barcelona. He started off with an escort of 2,000 horsemen, a force which, as the allies had before been

then to Catalonia.

weak in cavalry, they were ill able to spare. It was now determined that they should return to Catalonia; but on account of the difficulty in obtaining supplies the troops were divided into three bodies, which were to march at the distance of some thirty miles apart. It was hoped that they would thus be able to draw supplies from a wider range of country. The Catalans and Portuguese marched on the right; Staremberg with the Germans in the centre; Stanhope and his English on the left.

In most wars it is found that successful armies increase, whilst defeated armies have a tendency to dwindle. Yet since the defeat at Saragossa Philip's army had grown, that of the allies had dwindled. Such was the effect of Castilian pride, of Spanish enthusiasm. Moreover Lewis had no longer reason even to appear to withhold help from Philip. He did not send soldiers, but he sent him a general. He sent Vendôme, the general who had lost Oudenarde, because he was no match for Marlborough, but who would win victories in Spain, for neither Stanhope nor Staremberg was a match for him. The faults in Vendôme's character have been noticed before; this was an occasion when, anxious for his reputation, he exerted himself to the utmost. The indolent marshal showed vigour such as none other had shown. He was with his army on the alert before the allies marched towards Valencia. When once they were retreating, he marched after them at an incredible pace. *Vendôme sent to Spain.*

He first came upon Stanhope and the English in the town of Brihuega, where they had stopped for the purpose of baking bread. The English had no notion that Vendôme was so near. Never expecting that the Spanish troops could march so swiftly, Stanhope does not seem to have *Defeat of English at Brihuega.*

even stationed the usual outposts. First some horsemen showed themselves on the heights above Brihuega, which is a small town with an old Moorish wall, and almost surrounded by hills; next, but on the same day, infantry appeared. With difficulty could Stanhope send an aide-de-camp to inform Staremberg of his position, for Vendôme's troops quickly invested the town. The night was spent by Vendôme in preparations for an attack, while Stanhope prepared for defence. The English built barricades in the street, made loopholes for musketry, and passages from house to house. They had no artillery, and every street was commanded by Vendôme's cannon. A summons to surrender was met with a refusal; but a breach was soon made in the old Moorish wall. When the Spanish troops entered the town there followed a street fight, the English making a most stubborn resistance. When their ammunition was all spent they fought with the bayonet, until, seeing that further resistance was useless, Stanhope capitulated. The troops became prisoners of war upon honourable terms.

Meanwhile, where was Staremberg? He had received the message from Stanhope's aide-de-camp, but had apparently delayed, until he could call in the right wing; when, on the morning after the siege, he came near to Brihuega, he heard no firing, and therefore understood that Stanhope had capitulated. The Spanish army was now manifestly the stronger in numbers, but was fatigued after the severe fighting of the previous day. Yet Vendôme was anxious for a battle; Staremberg was not. To prevent the retreat of the German marshal, Vendôme ordered a charge of the Royal Guards. Philip himself headed it, and, fired by his presence, the Spanish cavalry upon the

Battle of Villa Viciosa.

right entirely routed their opponents, and captured their cannon. This wing was carried too far in the pursuit, and meanwhile Staremberg himself, upon the German right, was leading a triumphant charge, followed by another equally successful on the centre. He recovered his own, and captured all the Spanish cannon; then the victorious Spanish right returned from their pursuit, and the battle was renewed, until night put an end to it. The battle, which is usually called after the small town of Villa Viciosa, may be counted as drawn. The Spanish lost all their artillery, but had captured some standards. On the night after the battle, Philip's baggage had not come up, and there was no bed for his majesty. "You shall have the most glorious bed that ever monarch slept on," said Vendôme, as he sent for the captured standards, and had them spread before him. Staremberg certainly, even if the battle be counted his, was in no position to profit by it. Early next morning he spiked all the cannon and retreated quickly, harassed on his march almost as far as Barcelona, which he entered with 7,000 men, the sorry remnant of the army of the allies.

This was the last campaign in Spain. Madrid twice occupied, and twice abandoned for the same reason, the allies saw that it was impossible to hold Spain for Charles, as long as the feeling of the Spaniards remained unchanged. And when the news was brought to Lewis, he also felt that no other attempt would be made, that the point for which he had been fighting was gained. His grandson would remain King of Spain. So there was joy at Versailles, and men sang before the king a song of triumph.

End of the war in Spain.

CHAPTER XIII.

THE FORTUNES OF PARTIES.

It may be doubted whether the fortunes of English parties have ever had so great an effect upon the history of Europe as in the reign of Queen Anne. The development of parties in that reign is also important as the beginning of influences which extend to our own days. It has on these accounts been thought advisable to speak of them at some length, and to collect their history into one chapter. It was indeed at an earlier time than this reign that the two great parties ranged themselves in opposite camps under the names of Whigs and Tories. These parties represent two different principles in the human mind. Some men are more disposed to attach importance to authority, some to liberty. The former will rally round a monarchy, the latter round a republic. In one great earlier contest in English history matters had been pushed to extremes, and one principle had triumphed in the Civil War, the other in the Restoration. But men had learnt a lesson from the history of the seventeenth century, and there were very few on either side who were not content with a more moderate application of their principle. It may be well to sum up the points of contrast between the two parties at this time. Both parties were content with the shape which the English constitution had assumed. Thus both acquiesced in the monarchy and in government by means of a Parliament. The memory of 1660 secured the monarchy from attack; the memory of the long contests between the Stuarts and their Parliaments, confirmed by the victory of 1688, secured the privileges of Parliament. The opposition between the parties was therefore narrower. The Tories believed in the divine origin of the monarch's authority; the Whigs did not. The Tories wished the sovereign to have greater power; the Whigs wished him to have less. According to the French epigram, in a constitutional monarchy the king reigns, but does not govern. The Whigs held this view of a king's duty; but the Tories would have made a monarchy more of a reality.

The Tories felt that the Revolution of 1688 was a necessity, but one which they disliked. They would have preferred not to disturb the Stuarts: and the Jacobites, as those were called who wished to restore the Stuarts, may be regarded as the extreme section of the Tory party. That revolution was the work of the Whigs, who always attached to it the epithet of "Glorious." William was their favourite king, and the representative of their ideas. Yet William had a much larger share of political power than is thought in the present day to lie within the province of the sovereign. He had a very great influence in shaping the foreign policy of England.

Party views of the Revolution.

But it was on matters connected with religion that the distinction between the parties was most widely marked. The Tories were the Church party: those to whom the rites and doctrines of the Established Church were dear. They were very hostile to Dissenters, and perhaps scarcely less hostile to the Roman Catholics. The Whig party was in favour of toleration: to this party the Dissenters belonged (for they owed to it all the rights which they possessed),

Religious parties.

as well as those Churchmen who, preferring the doctrines of their own Church, yet considered other forms of government and modes of worship lawful. Bishop Burnet tells us that in this reign the distinction between High and Low Church was first known, but, when he proceeds to explain it, we see that it is almost the same as the difference between Whigs and Tories.

Queen Anne was a Stuart: by nature and training her inclinations were towards the Tory party. It is the duty of a sovereign in this country to belong to no party. Queen Anne really strove to rise to the height of this duty, of the importance of which she was fully aware. More than once she herself expressed it. But sometimes her inclinations were too strong for her sense of duty, and whenever this was the case her inclinations led her to favour the Tory party.

The queen's views.

On being called to the throne she gradually removed the ministers of her predecessors who belonged to the Whig party, and supplied their places with others of her own selection. She did not change the whole ministry; for neither in William's reign, nor in the early part of Anne's, was it considered necessary that all the ministers should belong to one party. She was under the influence of the Marlboroughs. Whilst important places in the royal household and about the queen's person were given to his wife, very high offices in the State were conferred on the Earl of Marlborough, and it was in accordance with his desire that Godolphin was appointed to the office of Lord High Treasurer, which corresponded to the modern position of Prime-Minister.

Her first ministry, Tory.

Godolphin and Marlborough were Tories, but they threw themselves heartily into the war in accordance with the plans of King William. Because it was William's policy, the war was dear to the Whigs. Because it was opposed to Lewis, who was protecting the Stuarts, the Tories were but lukewarm in the prosecution of it. *Godolphin and Marlborough change.* It therefore came to pass that the ministers received warmer support from their opponents, the Whigs, than from their natural allies, the Tories. Nor was it wonderful that under these circumstances a change came over their own views, and that Godolphin and Marlborough gradually passed over into the Whig camp.

A measure called the Occasional Conformity Bill may be used to gauge their change. According to the Test Act no one could hold office under the Crown, or be a member of a corporation, without taking the Sacrament according *Occasional Conformity Bill.* to the rites of the Church of England. It had come to be the practice that many who were really Dissenters qualified for office by obeying the Act. They were called Occasional Conformists, and were very obnoxious to the Tories and High Churchmen. A zealous Tory in the House of Commons brought in a Bill punishing this Occasional Conformity very severely. By it anyone who had taken the Sacrament according to the Test Act, and afterwards attended a Dissenting place of worship, was to be prevented from holding his appointment, and fined 100*l.*, besides 5*l.* a day for every day that he had discharged the duties of his office after going to the conventicle. This measure quickly passed through the Commons, but in the House of Lords it met with sturdy resistance. The Government strained every effort to overcome the opposition. Even Prince George of Denmark, the queen's consort, himself a Lutheran and Occasional Conformist, was urged to come down to the House of Lords to vote for the Bill. "My heart is vid you," he is reported to have whispered to some who were voting in the opposite lobby. But notwithstanding the zeal of the Government, the Whig Lords so altered the Bill that the Tory Commons refused to accept it. A prorogation stopped further dispute.

In November of the same year (1703) this measure was brought forward again, but this time the support of

Brought forward a second time.

the Bill by the Government was very lukewarm. Godolphin and Marlborough were separating themselves from the High Tories, and beginning to look to the Whigs for at least some support. They tried to dissuade their friends from bringing the bill in, but in the division they voted in its favour. It was defeated in the Lords.

Next year the Bill was introduced again, and some members of the House of Commons, indignant that the

Brought forward a third time.

Bill which they favoured had so often been rejected in the Upper House, proposed to "tack" it to the Bill of Supply; so that if the Lords threw out the Bill they would have the responsibility of cutting off the supplies of the Government. It

The Tackers.

is a rule of Parliament that the House of Lords may not make any alteration in a Money-Bill. They can reject it, but cannot amend it. The practice, therefore, of tacking—that is, joining another Bill to a Money-Bill—would, if unscrupulously employed, enable a majority in the Commons not only to defeat the Lords, but to deprive them altogether of their constitutional right of making amendments. On this account the practice has been made illegal. The proposal to tack, however, was on this occasion rejected in the Commons; and when the Bill came before the Lords, Marlborough and Godolphin gave their votes against it, though neither of them spoke. In the elections of 1705 the ministers used their influence against the tackers. "Give them no quarter," was Marlborough's advice. The result of that general election was that the Whigs obtained a majority: and the Occasional Conformity Bill for the present slept.

The leaders of the Whig party at this time were five Whig peers, who were called "the Junto." Four of them had been ministers of King William. The man of greatest eminence among them was Lord Somers. There was no Englishman in whom King William had placed such confidence, and no one who had so well deserved it. The son of a Worcester attorney, he had risen to the post of Lord High Chancellor; yet he so conducted himself that he seemed born in the purple. He was remarkable for the gentleness of his manners and the benevolence of his disposition. His opinions were strongly Whig; yet he was always remarkable for the moderation of his counsels. His virtue and wisdom had raised up enemies against him. Towards the end of King William's reign it was discovered that he had lent money to a sea captain who became a pirate, and was well known as Captain Kidd. It was not proved that Somers knew of any evil intentions on the part of the sailor. But the storm against him raged so furiously that when King William made him a grant of Crown lands the feeling against him was renewed, and, as the easiest way of quieting the storm Lord Somers was dismissed from office. He lived in dignified retirement, watching the course of public affairs. With or without office he was the leader and guide of the Whig party.

Of the five members of the Junto, Charles, Earl

of Sunderland, son-in-law of Marlborough, was the youngest, and had also the reputation of being the most violent Whig, When the two ministers, Marlborough and Godolphin were depending more and more upon the Whigs for support, the Junto stipulated that Sunderland should be made a Secretary of State as the price of this support, and as a security that measures would not be introduced hostile to the principles of the Whigs The first ally that the Junto secured amongst the ministerialists was the Duchess of Marlborough. She was disappointed at the lukewarmness with which the Tories had carried out the war policy. She persuaded her husband, and then both of them urged the appointment of Sunderland upon the queen, who resisted long and strenuously. Sunderland received another office, that of ambassador at Vienna: but the pressure for the original appointment was continued. Eighteen months later it was made, and marks a distinct point in the change of the ministry from Tory to Whig.

Lord Sunderland.

An influence, however, was at work which was undermining the Government. It was always said of Queen Anne that it was necessary for her to be under the influence of some stronger mind. While she was Princess Anne, as well as in the early part of her reign, her friend, her second self, was the Duchess of Marlborough. But the favourite's temper was imperious, and she presumed upon the queen's friendship for her. Her own political views had by this time changed, but she could not bring the queen to alter her views so readily. The queen seems to have been prepared to discard her ancient friend, when she was provided with another upon whom to lean. The duchess had placed about the queen's person a cousin of her own,

Abigail Hill.

who was poor and in need. She never fancied that this act would prove hurtful to her own power. But Abigail Hill, the queen's waiting-woman, was a lady of quiet and pleasant manners, a great contrast to her cousin, the duchess. The first intimation of the decline of her power that the latter received was the intimation that Miss Hill had privately married Mr. Masham, a gentleman of the queen's household, and that the queen herself had been present at the marriage.

Abigail Hill, or Mrs. Masham, as she must now be called, was not only a cousin of the Duchess of Marlborough, she was also upon the other side cousin of a prominent Tory politician, Robert Harley, whose influence with her was very strong. *Change of the queen's favourite.* Accordingly the new favourite of the queen used all her power in favour of the Tory party, which was already preferred by the queen. This was not then merely a question of court intrigue, of a woman's private likings or dislikings, but a matter fraught with important political consequences. The influence of Mrs. Masham over the mind of Queen Anne led ultimately to the dismissal of the Whig ministers and to the reversal of their war policy. It led to the ministry of Harley and Bolingbroke, and to the peace of Utrecht. Thus it came to pass that "the insolence of one waiting-woman and the cunning of another" changed the fortunes of Europe.

It must not, however, be supposed that these changes followed immediately, although in the same summer in which Mrs. Masham was married the queen took the first step in opposition to her ministers. Without even asking their opinion or telling them, she appointed two bishops, men who were excellently fitted for the duties of their office, but were high Tories.

But in the following year (1708), while the queen was

turning more and more against the guidance of her ministers, she was compelled, in order to please them, to make changes in various offices, which were by no means agreeable to herself. While the ministry was not yet wholly Whig, and while Robert Harley was still a Secretary of State, and Henry St. John Secretary at War, a clerk in Harley's office was found guilty of treasonable correspondence with the French: an unsuccessful attempt was made to implicate Harley in the treason. Marlborough and Godolphin represented to the queen that Harley must be dismissed from office. When she refused, on the ground that Harley was a good Churchman, they declined to attend a meeting of the Council, and prepared even to resign their offices. The queen would have found it difficult to continue without the services of Marlborough; but she held the meeting of the Council, and, as was then the custom, presided herself. It was on a Sunday: as the queen entered the chamber there were black looks. Harley, however, opened his portfolio and began business. "I do not see how we can do anything," said one, "in the absence of my Lord Treasurer and my Lord General." It was evident that the other ministers would stand by Godolphin and Marlborough, not by Harley. Soon afterwards Harley and St. John resigned.

Yet the ministry is made more Whig.

During the autumn of this year the poor queen was much tried by the illness of her husband, whom she tenderly nursed. His illness was asthma. After his death Somers was admitted to the ministry, being appointed to the office of President of the Council. It was evident now that the ministry was entirely Whig. It is a rule of modern English politics that all the members of a government

Cabinet government.

shall belong to one party, that they shall prepare their measures in common, be jointly responsible for all mistakes, and, as the expression runs, stand or fall together. This, which seems an axiom now, was not so regarded at the beginning of Queen Anne's reign. She herself wished to have a ministry recruited from the moderate men of both parties, what in modern political language is called a coalition. Her personal feelings had in this arrangement at first assigned the preponderance of power to the Tory, or, as she called it, the Church party. The course of events had shifted this balance. For the next two years there was a Cabinet entirely Whig, and this was followed by another entirely Tory. King George III. tried to form a government from both parties, but the experiment was not attended with success. There have also been other coalitions; but all have been unable to stand, and from the year 1708 homogeneous party Cabinets have been the rule in England. A Cabinet is a Committee of the Privy Council, in which all the chief ministers have seats. Though an important element in English political life, its existence is not recognised by the law.

Strange to say, it was almost exactly at the time when the Whigs had secured all the seats in the Cabinet that the causes which led to their ruin began to work. The alienation of the queen from the Duchess of Marlborough was almost complete. It was said that at a public ceremonial the duchess spilt a glass of water, as if by accident, over the gown of her rival, and she was not again invited to Court. The Duke of Marlborough, fearful lest he should also lose the queen's favour, conceived the idea of having his appointment as Commander-in-Chief confirmed to him for life. It is quite possible,

Marlborough's request to be made Commander-in-Chief for life.

indeed, that his motive was patriotic, and that he may have desired the permanent appointment to secure the allegiance of his country to the cause of the Grand Alliance. He was warned by his friends that such an appointment was contrary to the constitution: and one of them, the Lord Chancellor, told him that he would not put the great seal to such a patent. Marlborough persevered, and actually applied to the queen, who firmly and without hesitation refused. These events ought to have made Godolphin and his ministry careful. Yet their next step seemed most heedless.

A not very wise clergyman, named Dr. Sacheverell, a college friend of Addison's, who though of Low Church parentage, had won himself a reputation for extreme High doctrines, preached in London before the Lord Mayor and in Derby at the assizes two sermons in which he attacked the Revolution, maintaining that resistance to a king was never justifiable, and declaring that the Church was in danger "even in her majesty's reign." Not content with this general teaching, he alluded to Godolphin under a nickname borrowed from one of Ben Jonson's plays, of "Volpone," or "the Fox." His sermons were published. The matter was brought before the Cabinet, when its wisest members, such as Somers, were in favour of letting the sermons alone, or at best prosecuting the preacher in a court of law; others, however, and Godolphin most strongly, were for impeachment before the House of Lords. The result was that an important State trial was made out of this trumpery matter. Thinking him persecuted, people took the Doctor's side. He was condemned indeed when the impeachment came before the Lords, but his punishment was almost nominal, for he was only prohibited from preaching for three years,

Sacheverell's sermon.

and his book was burnt by the hangman. As the condemned clergyman travelled through England, his journey was like a triumph. Crowds came forth to see him and to ask his blessing; he was received everywhere with enthusiasm.

Before this feeling had subsided there was a general election. With the Tory sympathy for Sacheverell was united a general weariness of the war, and the result of the elections was the return of a powerful Tory majority. The queen gladly took advantage of it to get rid of her Whig ministers. The long services of Godolphin, and a little later the distinguished services of Marlborough, were repaid with almost ignominious dismissal. The Duchess of Marlborough, who had for some time been kept at a distance from Court, was dismissed from her office, and had to leave her apartments in St. James' Palace. She was so angry that she tore down the mantel-pieces and had the brass locks removed from the doors. *[margin: General election. Tory majority. Dismissal of Whigs.]*

The queen did not wish all her former ministers to resign. She pressed Somers to continue in office, for she said "he had never deceived her." Five times she gave back the seals into Cowper's hands. But they stood staunchly by their colleagues, and the new principle prevailed. A new government was formed under Harley and St. John

The work of this new ministry remains to be narrated. One incidental result of the change was that the Occasional Conformity Bill, which had for some time slept, was now passed almost without opposition. *[margin: Occasional Conformity Bill passed.]*

CHAPTER XIV.

FAG-END OF THE WAR.

OF the two men who were now the leading advisers of the queen and acknowledged chiefs of the Tory party Harley was in the higher position, though Bolingbroke was really the abler man. Robert Harley belonged to a Whig family; his father had even been put in prison on suspicion of being implicated in Monmouth's conspiracy. Entering Parliament for a Cornish borough immediately after the Revolution, Harley was very strongly opposed to the Tory party, which he afterwards joined. In William's reign he was elected Speaker of the House of Commons. When Godolphin was dismissed, his place as Lord High Treasurer was, at first, not filled up; the office was put in commission, and Harley was appointed Chancellor of the Exchequer, but was practically Prime-Minister. Harley was neither eloquent nor a man of genius, but he possessed powers which have sometimes availed more than eloquence or genius—the arts of a courtier. He was more at home in the queen's antechambers than in either House of Parliament. He was ambitious, unscrupulous, strong in worldly wisdom.

Harley.

An event which nearly cost him his life had the effect of increasing his popularity. A French refugee, who called himself the Marquis of Guiscard, had made frequent proposals for descents upon the coast of France. Afterwards he had carried on intrigues with France. He was arrested, and

Attack on his life.

under examination before the Council, when he suddenly seized a penknife from the table and stabbed Harley with it. A scuffle ensued, in which the Frenchman was mortally wounded, and it was then found that Harley's wound was but slight. Great sympathy was expressed for Harley, and shortly afterwards the queen made him an earl, with the double title, Oxford and Mortimer. She then raised him to the office of Lord High Treasurer.

Made Earl of Oxford.

Henry St. John was a man of very different character. In that age, famous for its wits and its literary men, he could hold his own with any of them. He was very intimate with the chief authors of the day, especially with Pope and Swift, and the poet-diplomatist, Matthew Prior. He was an accomplished classical scholar, very eloquent, and renowned as an elegant writer. As a politician he was distrusted, and could never have kept his party together. He was brilliant rather than safe. As a writer, he was very hostile to Christianity. It was nearly a year later than Harley's promotion that St. John was elevated to the peerage, and he was then only made a viscount. His title was Viscount Bolingbroke. It is said that this inequality of rewards led to ill-will between these members of the same Government.

St. John.

Made Lord Bolingbroke.

It is probable that from their first acceptance of office they intended to put an end to the war, but they could not well publicly declare this intention; and whilst they were still feeling their way, an event occurred which promised to provide them with an excellent excuse. The Emperor Joseph died; and his brother, the Archduke Charles, after due formality of an election and a delay of nearly six months, succeeded him as Emperor; so that it now became

Archduke Charles becomes Emperor.

doubtful whether it would be in accordance with the views of the allies to continue a war which had been begun nominally in order to give him the crown of Spain. But such a feeling was gradual, not immediate. In order to secure the election at Frankfort from any fear of a French invasion, Eugene received orders from Vienna to withdraw with all his troops from the army under Marlborough in Flanders. Villars, the French marshal, had fortified his position with great care, and boasted that Marlborough could not pass into France. He called his lines the *Non plus ultra*. Marlborough, however, although the allied forces were weakened by Eugene's withdrawal, entered the *Non plus ultra* with ease. He then laid siege to Bouchain, and captured it; but these were the only military achievements of the allies during the year 1711. Coming events were already casting their shadows before.

Marlborough's last campaign.

The ministers planned an expedition against Quebec, and entrusted the command of it to Colonel Hill, the brother of Mrs. Masham, the queen's favourite. It was thought that if this expedition was successful, it would act as a counterpoise to the great achievements of Marlborough. But the fleet of transports was badly provided with supplies, and had great difficulties in procuring pilots skilled in the navigation of the dangerous seas at the mouth of the St. Lawrence. Unfortunately it met with a violent storm, and several of the ships were wrecked. The result was that the expedition returned to England a failure.

Expedition against Quebec.

Meanwhile negotiations had been secretly opened with France, as the ministers had determined on peace—in concert with the allies, if the allies preferred; if not, without them—and upon terms as favourable for themselves as possible; but the consideration of terms was not to be allowed to stand in the way of peace. One obstacle it was necessary to remove. The great general who had won four great battles for the cause, who had never besieged a town without taking it, who had been the heart and spirit of the alliance, must be sacrificed. To break the blow, the queen did him the honour of writing a letter with her own hand, dismissing him from all his employments. The reason alleged was that an accusation had been made against him, that he had taken perquisites from a Jew, who had contracted to supply the army with bread, and that during the ten years this allowance amounted to the sum of 63,000*l*. There was also a charge that Marlborough had deducted 2½ per cent. from the pay which England gave to foreign troops, and that this amounted, in the ten years, to no less than 177,000*l*. His letter of reply was very dignified. He made answer, first, that the payments were quite according to precedent, and, secondly, that he had taken the money, not for his private use, but to obtain secret intelligence about the enemy. There can be no doubt that this defence is perfectly satisfactory, but his opponents were bent on his disgrace.

margin: Disgrace of Marlborough.

Prince Eugene hastened to England to endeavour to prevent its falling away from the alliance. He was received with all civility and even cordiality, but no representations that he could make could have any effect in reinstating his old companion in arms. Within a year of Marlborough's disgrace, his old friend and colleague, Godolphin, died at his house. Partly from sorrow, partly because of the unpopularity into which he had now fallen, Marlborough went abroad.

margin: Death of Godolphin.

The ministers, being determined to have a majority in both Houses of Parliament, strained the royal prerogative, and induced the queen to make twelve peers. Some were eldest sons of peers, who would have become peers in the course of nature; two were prominent lawyers; one of them was Mr. Masham. All of course were Tories. When they appeared in the House, an opponent, alluding to their number, asked sarcastically whether they voted separately or by their foreman.

Twelve peers.

Meanwhile the Duke of Ormond was appointed to an unpleasant post. It was difficult enough to succeed Marlborough as commander-in-chief, but it must have been absolutely humiliating for him to hold that office, and yet to receive secret orders, tying his hands and bidding him do nothing. "A general of straw," he was called. As no one likes to be a dummy, the duke must have felt it a positive relief when an armistice between the English and the French was declared. He received orders to separate the troops in the pay of England from the army of the allies. But many of these troops, acting under orders from their own Governments, refused to obey, and he withdrew with the native English soldiers. Eye-witnesses have described the indignation with which the English soldiers and officers received the orders, and the shame with which they parted from their former comrades in so many fields. Ormond was followed by only 12,000 soldiers. The smallness of this number points to the fact that England had been fighting in this war with money rather than with men. The number of native British soldiers was very small compared with the number of foreign mercenaries that England paid—Hessians, Pala-

Ormond Commander-in-Chief.

Separat on of English troops.

tines, and Germans of other small States, especially in the Rhine valley, where a century of wars, beginning with the terrible Thirty Years' War, had ruined their homes, and implanted in their breasts the love of a military life.

Notwithstanding the departure of the English troops, Eugene was still at the head of an army of 100,000 men in an excellent position. His lines were called the "road to Paris," because it seemed that when once he had taken Landrécies, a town which he was besieging, nothing could stop him from entering France. General alarm was felt in that country, and the king wrote to Marshal Villars that he trusted all to him, but that if defeat should await him, he himself would mass all his troops, and at their head perish or save the State.

<small>Eugene.</small>

It is curious that King Lewis should have thought such extreme language necessary, when the alliance was breaking up, and deliverance was so near. Eugene's lines were so widely extended, that if one part were attacked it could not quickly receive succour from another. Villars made a feigned attack on Eugene's camp before Landrécies, and then, hurling all his strength upon Denain, there won a brilliant victory. It is said that Eugene himself came up in time to witness, but not to stop, the defeat. There can be no doubt that this battle had a great influence in determining the Dutch to make peace. They saw that, with the English troops, victory had departed. Eugene was compelled to raise the siege of Landrécies, and Villars retook three towns from the allies, one of them being Bouchain, the sole conquest of the previous year.

<small>Victory of French at Denain, July 24, A.D. 1712.</small>

CHAPTER XV.

PEACE OF UTRECHT.

IN January 1711 a messenger arrived from London at Paris, who, calling upon Torcy, the Minister for Foreign Affairs, began his conversation with these words: "Do you wish for peace, sir? If so, I bring you the means of procuring it." "It was," says Torcy in his memoirs, "like asking a dying man whether he would wish to be cured."

Peace at hand.

It is not necessary to describe in detail all the negotiations which had preceded and which followed this. After Ramillies and the year of victory, terms had been indirectly offered by the French, including the surrender of Spain to the archduke, on condition that Philip had Naples, Sicily, and Milan as a separate kingdom. Marlborough thought that the offer of France was insufficient, and would not allow it even to be made the basis of a conference.

Negotiations:
(a) After Ramillies.

In 1709, after the defeat at Oudenarde and the capture of Lille, the bad harvest, and the terrible frost, the position of Lewis was so much worse that he was prepared to surrender even the condition of a monarchy for Philip. He was ready to accept all the terms of the allies laid down at the Conference of the Hague, except the article in which they insisted that, if his grandson did not resign the Spanish Crown, he should himself compel him by force of arms.

(b) The Hague.

Next year, after Malplaquet, the French king made another effort. A conference was held at Gertruydenburg, a small town near the mouth of the Waal, which place the Dutch rulers selected lest at any more important town the envoys might incline the natives towards peace. But the allies insisted on the same hard condition, and this conference was as abortive as that of the Hague.

(c) Gertruydenburg.

But, in January 1711, for the first time, the proposals were made from the side of the allies, and not from that of France; and as Lewis was always well informed about the state of English parties, he began the new negotiations with quite a different hope. Terms which he would gladly have accepted in the previous year he would not hear of now. The English ministry, thinking the allies intractable, were now negotiating without them, and had signed the preliminaries even before Marlborough's disgrace and Ormond's appointment. A congress was held at Utrecht, to which the allies at last consented to send representatives. Diplomacy was very long-winded, but after many months the Peace of Utrecht was signed in March 1713.

(d) Utrecht.

Peace of Utrecht signed.

There were several treaties made between the different belligerents, which, together, form what we call the Peace of Utrecht. Charles VI., the new Emperor, held out obstinately. He did not wish for peace, and was very angry with the allies, especially with the English, that they were not willing to continue fighting his battles. But what could he do, single-handed? He held out for nearly one year longer, but Villars vigorously turned his forces against him, and seized a town or two. Then, in the following spring,

Emperor holds out.

Peace of Rastadt, 1714.

the Emperor accepted the peace, which he could have enjoyed earlier. The peace between France and the Emperor personally was called after the town Rastadt, that between the French and the Empire after that of Baden.

The Spanish monarchy—the main point in dispute—together with the vast American possessions, was left in the hands of Philip V. If the allies had been fighting to take it from him, they had missed their object. Solemn renunciation was, however, made by the King of Spain of all his claim to the French Crown, at least as long as he retained the Spanish Crown. Both Lewis and Philip swore that the Crowns of France and of Spain should never be united. Lewis swore, "on the faith, word, and honour of a king," that he would acknowledge Queen Anne and the Protestant succession, and that he would give no further assistance to the Pretender, but induce him to leave France. He agreed also to demolish the fortifications and to fill up the harbour of Dunkirk.

The Spanish monarchy.

Though the English seem to have regarded Dunkirk as a standing menace to their commerce, and to have eagerly desired this article, it was never carried out. England was to keep Gibraltar and Minorca, but she promised that they should not be a place of refuge either for Moor or Jew. England also gained from France certain ice-bound territories in North America, which France did not value - the Hudson's Bay Territory, Newfoundland, and Nova Scotia. They were valuable as fishing grounds, and also for the fur-hunters; but the French reserved in the treaty the right to fish. There had been, indeed, as many English as French settlements in these places, and perhaps more English settlers. The possession of the first

England's gain.

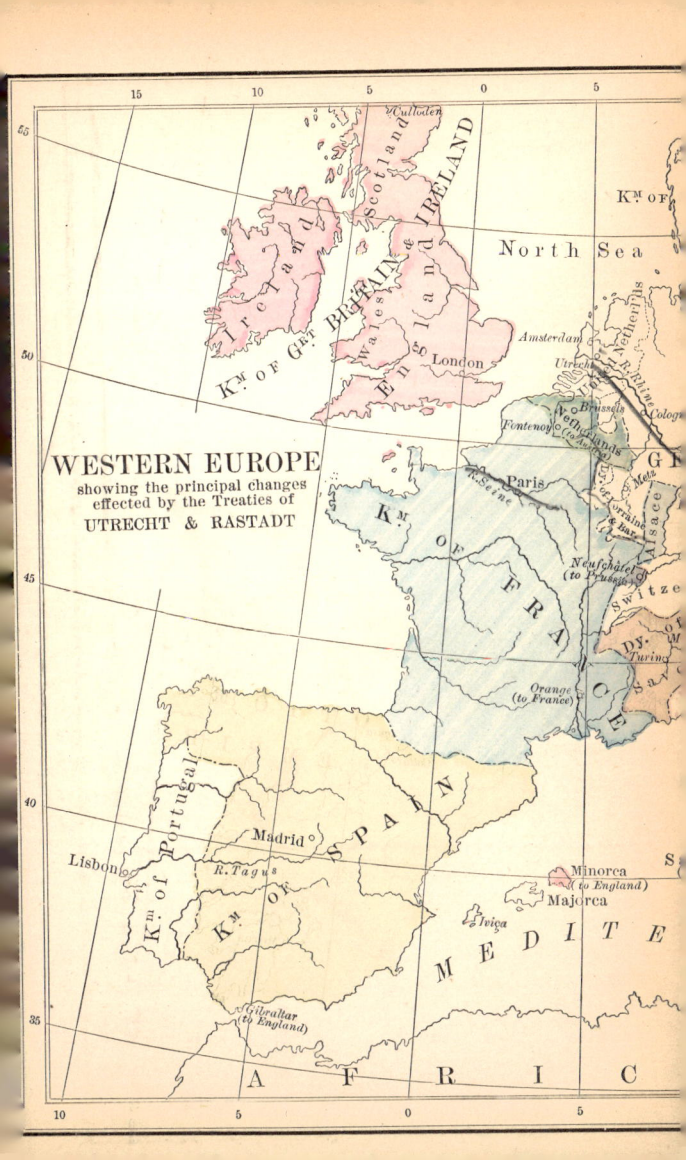

WESTERN EUROPE
showing the principal changes effected by the Treaties of UTRECHT & RASTADT

two had been long in dispute; but Nova Scotia—called by the French Acadia—had been formally ceded to the French in the reign of Charles II. It is important to notice that, in this article, England was commencing a policy of colonial aggrandisement which brought later wars on her. England further obtained from Spain the *Assiento* contract, which France had before enjoyed, viz. the privilege of importing 4,800 negro slaves into America within thirty years.

In addition to these treaties there was further proposed a treaty of commerce between England and France, but the House of Commons threw it out. It shows how enlightened a statesman Bolingbroke could prove himself, for it would have established free trade between England and France. Neither of the nations were to tax each other's manufactures, and each was to grant to the other whatever privileges it conferred on the most favoured nation.

France, it may be seen, suffered little by the treaty, for she lost no territory, and was left with the same boundaries that she had reached in the year of the English Revolution. Spain lost her possessions in Italy and in the Netherlands, of which Milan, the Kingdom of Naples, and the Netherlands fell to Austria, while Sicily, which was afterwards exchanged for Sardinia, fell to the Duke of Savoy, who was further, indulged with the title of King. The Elector of Bavaria, France's luckless ally, was reinstated in his dominions and at the same time the Elector of Hanover was fully and finally recognised.

Spain's loss.

Prussia, which a month before the treaty of Utrecht passed under the rule of its second king, famous in history as the eccentric father of Frederick the Great, secured its own recognition as a king-

Prussia.

dom by the King of France. Moreover, its territory of Orange was exchanged for land that lay more convenient in Guelderland. On the death of our William III. without children, his claim to Orange had passed to his sister, who married the first King of Prussia. The little principality of Orange was surrounded entirely by France, into which it was manifestly more convenient that it should now be swallowed up. Whether it belonged to a king of England or a king of Prussia, the French could at once overrun it with troops in case of war.

Lastly, the Dutch obtained certain towns, and had the satisfaction of seeing the Netherlands in the hands of Austria, a barrier between them and France.

Dutch.

It was not a very substantial result of all their efforts, but, if the English would not go on fighting, it was not in the power of the Dutch to obtain better terms. Holland, however, learnt the futility of engaging in wars like this, and henceforth pursued a policy of non-interference, and her influence declined in Europe.

The Peace of Utrecht has been often criticised, and generally in a sense hostile to its promoters—the English ministry. It may be as well to express shortly the arguments on both sides.

Those who supported it said that the war was becoming a great burden upon England; that her national debt was growing to such an enormous size that posterity would not be able to pay it; that in consequence of the peculiar spirit of the Castilians, Spain could never be conquered nor taken from Philip except at a terrible cost, and that Englishmen who did not want the Pretender had no right to force a king upon reluctant Spain; that the terms of the treaty secured Europe from the danger of a union of the Crowns of France and Spain, indeed, that a similar

Arguments for Peace of Utrecht.

danger was more to be feared on the other side, for the Grand Alliance was intended to prevent the union of the Spanish Crown with that of any other first-rate power, and that the Austrian claimant was now Emperor. France, therefore, being humbled and threatening no danger to Europe, if England continued to fight, she would be fighting the battles of her allies, not her own.

To these arguments answer was made: Debt or no debt, commerce flourishes. France, which has been for half a century a source of danger, is now at our mercy. Her fortresses are broken down, and Marlborough has cleared his road to Paris. Let us bind her now, so that she never can be dangerous again. It will never be safe to have France and Spain under kindred kings. The Bourbons are all of a piece, and this Philip may yet succeed his grandfather. In such case renunciations are valueless; we know that France always regards them as invalid. After all Marlborough's victories, the allies are wrong not to secure results more substantial. *Arguments against it.*

As the Peace of Utrecht ends the war, this is the right place to ask the question—was this a just and necessary war? And the answer must be that it was. We must place ourselves in the position of the statesmen who knew Lewis and his ambition, or of the people who had suffered and seen others suffer from his encroachments. Even after the Peace of Ryswick, there can be no doubt that he was dangerous to the liberties of Europe. But as decidedly the war should have been ended earlier. Peace ought to have been made after the battle of Ramillies. The war would then have lasted four years instead of eleven, and much would have been saved. It was the heartfelt mistrust of Lewis that made Marlborough, Eugene, and *General consideration on the war.*

Heinsius, the Whig ministers in England, and the Dutch statesmen, refuse to treat. But they could then have obtained the same terms that they secured afterwards, or better. From that time forward the allies were in the wrong, and at each negotiation, at the Hague and at Gertruydenburg, they plunged more deeply into it. After the disaster at Villa Viciosa, all claim on Spain should have been surrendered. The allies asked too much, and they were forced to take too little. For, that Bolingbroke and Oxford granted terms too easily, and mismanaged the negotiations, there is no manner of doubt.

When peace was proclaimed in London there was a grand Te Deum in St. Paul's Cathedral, Handel's music probably being played. But the Te Deum raised by Lewis and his courtiers should have been louder, for in the Peace of Utrecht Lewis gained the most.

Te Deum.

CHAPTER XVI.

THE UNION WITH SCOTLAND.

Section I.—*The Union itself.*

ONE of the most important works of Queen Anne's reign was the Union with Scotland. Until that was carried out, Great Britain was divided into two unequal kingdoms, with the same sovereign, but in every other respect distinct. There was no real security that even the union under the same sovereign would be permanent, and that under different sovereigns the old hostility, perhaps even war, would not arise. Statesmen had therefore long wished that

Earlier attempts at union.

the two kingdoms should be fused into one. Oliver Cromwell, who may be said to have anticipated the principle of Parliamentary Reform, also anticipated the Union, and summoned representatives from Scotland to one assembly with those of England. But the Restoration overthrew his arrangement, and perhaps the memory of Cromwell's change caused in the times that followed a prejudice against any imitation of his policy. William III. had been strongly in favour of the change, but other matters had occupied his time and attention. In his last message to Parliament he had recommended the project of Union to the members. In the first year of the reign of Queen Anne commissioners were appointed and met. But they were not in earnest about their work. It was often difficult even to procure the attendance of a quorum of the English commissioners, and so the matter dropped.

A step of the Scottish Parliament, the passing of the Act of Security, made the absolute necessity of the Union evident not only to statesmen but to all thinking men in England. As Queen Anne was childless, steps had been taken *The Act of Security.* even in her predecessor's reign to settle the devolution of the English crown. In the last year of William's life the Act of Settlement was passed, by which it was decided that the sovereign of England must be a Protestant, and that in the case of the death of Anne without heirs, the crown should devolve upon the Electress Sophia, grand-daughter of James I., and upon her heirs who were Protestant. This measure excited no enthusiasm, and yet all parties in England seemed to acquiesce in it. In the Scotch Parliament no such bill was passed, but two years later the Act of Security was carried, the effect of which was quite opposite. It declared that, on the death of the queen without issue, the Estates (that is, the Scotch Parliament) should name a successor from the Protestant descendants of the House of Stuart, but not the same as should succeed to the crown of England, unless certain securities were given for the religion, freedom, and trade of Scotland. The Government, however, instructed the queen's commissioner not to touch the Act with the sceptre. It did not therefore become law; but the irritation in the Scotch Parliament was so strong because of this refusal that the commissioner prorogued it without obtaining any subsidy. Next year (1704) the Act was passed again by the Parliament. Godolphin yielded to their persistency, and the measure became law. The effect, however, not on his mind only, but on that of almost all Englishmen, was that it was no longer safe to postpone the Union.

In the summer of 1706 commissioners met in London, thirty-one from each kingdom. Lord Somers presided over their meetings: to his bland temper and moderating wisdom much of the success of their treating was due. Once or twice the queen attended at the deliberations to encourage the commissioners by her presence; and it was evident that they were animated by a different spirit from that of the first year of her reign.

Commission appointed.

It is a law of physics that a larger body attracts a smaller. As England was three times as large, four times as populous, and probably forty times as rich as Scotland, it was evident that the latter kingdom would have to adopt the constitution of the former. But the English commissioners were prepared to treat the Scotch in a liberal spirit. The doctrine that the minority must yield to the majority required that the English weights and measures and the

Arrangements proposed.

English coinage should be the standard for the United Kingdom. As, however, the Scotch might lose by these and similar changes, it was proposed that a sum of money should be paid by the English Parliament, to which the name of the Equivalent was given. Elaborate calculations were set on foot to fix its amount, which was ultimately settled at 400,000*l.* It was to be thus employed. All the debts of the kingdom of Scotland were to be paid off, and for this it was estimated that 160,000*l.*, or about a year's revenue of that kingdom, would be required. The shares of the Darien Company were to be bought up with a second portion, and the company then dissolved. A third portion was to recoup the losses caused by the change in the coinage. But when the gold arrived in Edinburgh, there was a riot, and the waggons that brought it were near being plundered. The people regarded it as a bribe.

In England there was hardly any real opposition to the Union, but in Scotland there was a great deal. This may have been partly due to the anger of shopkeepers and citizens of Edinburgh, indignant that their beautiful city should cease to be a capital; partly to that of members of Parliament, who would lose their importance when the capital went south. There was also a general feeling, strongest amongst the uneducated, but not confined to them, that Scotland was going to be placed in subjection to England. The ancient glory of their kingdom was departing. But the strongest feeling was aroused on the question of their religion: there was a general fear lest by union with England, which had an Episcopal Church, the Presbyterian constitution of the Scotch Church should be in danger. And to this feeling a sort of echo was heard in England when the High Churchman seemed to regard

Opposition in Scotland.

it as unworthy to ally themselves with a Presbyterian body. It was determined that no change should be made in either Church; and Acts of Parliament were passed, both by the Scotch and by the English Parliaments, to secure that each Church should preserve its constitution and its independence. There was to be one State, but two Churches.

The Scotch share of the land tax was fixed at one-fortieth. If taxation had been taken as the basis of representation, the Scotch would not have been allowed more than thirteen representatives in the House of Commons. But it was felt that this number was insufficient, considering the population and the ancient reputation of the northern kingdom. After some negotiation the number was fixed at forty-five. Of these thirty were assigned to shires, fifteen to towns. Edinburgh had a member to itself. Sixty-six other boroughs formed fourteen groups. No shire had more than one member, nor has this system been altered by later reforms. The total number of forty-five has been increased to sixty, eight having been added by the great Reform Bill in 1832, and seven more by the Reform Bill of 1867. This number of sixty is now divided thus—shires, 32 (two or three shires being divided, but still having only one member for each division); towns, 26 (Glasgow having three members, Edinburgh and Dundee two each); and two being assigned to the Universities in two groups of two each. The Scotch peers and representatives sat in one house. Henceforward they would follow the practice of England, and sit in two. The number forty-five formed one-twelfth of the enlarged House of Commons of the United Kingdom. This proportion was therefore adopted for the Upper House also. Sixteen peers were to be elected as representatives for each Parliament. It was

Representation.

decided that no more peers of Scotland should be made. The peers who were not representatives were not allowed to sit in the Lower House either for English or Scotch constituencies, and an old Scotch restriction that the eldest sons of Scotch peers could not be elected was retained. This latter, however, was repealed in 1832.

The Scotch law and administration of justice was to remain unchanged. In many important points, notably in the law of marriage, there is still a wide difference between the Scotch and English law, the former following the old Roman law. *Law.*

Other matters caused less difficulty. It was easily settled that the national flag should be formed by a junction of the crosses of St. George and St. Andrew. This was a flag which James I. *Union Jack.* had tried to introduce upon succeeding to the English throne, but without success. Henceforward it became the flag of which both nations are proud, under the name of the Union Jack. At the Union with Ireland this flag underwent a further change, the red cross of St. Patrick being laid upon the white cross of St. Andrew. The arms of the two countries, the three lions of England and the lion rampant of Scotland were to be quartered according to the laws of heraldry. A new seal was to be made. This United Kingdom was to receive the name of Great Britain.

This scheme, which was drawn out by the commissioners in 1706, met with much opposition in the Scotch Parliament. But it was firmly maintained and eventually carried in 1707. It is said that bribery was extensively used, as was certainly the case at the Union with Ireland nearly a century later, but this charge has been investigated and disproved. If there was any bribery, it was on a very small scale.

In spite of the opposition then made to the Union, an opposition which died away only gradually in the minds of Scotchmen, there has not for generations been even a semblance of a wish for a repeal of the Union. This cannot be said for the Union with Ireland; and if the proof of the goodness of political work is the way that it stands the test of time, no work of the kind was ever so effectively accomplished. No act of the Government of Queen Anne so much deserves the honour and respect of succeeding generations, whether English or Scotch. England was strengthened by having a warm ally instead of a lukewarm neighbour, who might prove a dangerous foe. Scotland shared in the prosperity which she had often envied, acquired a large share of commerce, and yet did not lose the separate features of the Scottish character or in any way smother the individual glory of her historic memories.

Results.

It may be well to add a note on the difference between the Union with Ireland and that with Scotland with respect to the peerage. No more Scotch peers were to be created, and no Scotch peer is permitted to sit in the House of Commons. In the Irish peerage, one new peer may be created for every three peerages that become extinct, and an Irish peer may sit in the House of Commons, but not as representative of an Irish constituency. Ireland has now 105 members in the House of Commons, and 28 representative peers. The total number of Scotch peers is now 82, of Irish, 185; but of these so many are also peers of the United Kingdom, that only 26 Scotch and 80 Irish noblemen are without seats in the House of Lords. In the Union with Scotland, moreover, the two national Churches were kept distinct, whilst in that with Ireland they were united. But in the latter case the

Compared with Union with Ireland.

Churches were alike Protestant and Episcopalian. The injustice rather consisted in the fact that the dominant Church in Ireland was not the Church of the people, a very large majority of whom were Roman Catholics. It is certainly a fact that requires notice, that whilst the Scotch do not desire a repeal, the Irish as a nation do.

Section II.—Attempt for the Pretender.

The immediate unpopularity of the Union in Scotland suggested to the minds of the Jacobites that an attempt might be made in that country in favour of the Pretender. An avowed Jacobite, Colonel Hooke, moved about the country sounding other Jacobites, and returned to Versailles when he had obtained promises that a force of 30,000 men should rise in Scotland, if only Lewis would send a French army to form a nucleus. Lewis, not unmindful of the ancient friendship between Scotland and France, assented. He may have known that in the present state of Scotch feeling there was a good chance of success, or that at any rate a diversion would be created in the war, and that possibly Marlborough, certainly some of Marlborough's army, would be recalled from the Netherlands. The Jacobite cause had always more supporters in Scotland, especially in the Highlands, than in England. The feeling of loyalty was encouraged by the clan system: the Stuarts were a Scotch family. *(Jacobite rising.)*

James Francis Edward, son of James II. and Mary of Modena, was born in 1688, the year of the Glorious Revolution. Indeed his birth may be counted one of the immediate causes of that Revolution, for as long as James his father had no son, the English people felt that, however tyrannous his reign might be, upon his death the tyranny *(The Old Pretender.)*

would be overpast; for his daughters, Mary and Anne, following the religion of their mother, were Protestants and members of the Church of England. When this prince was born, all was changed. He would be brought up, men said, in the religion of both his parents: a long line of Roman Catholic sovereigns stretched itself before the eyes of their excited imaginations. King James, moreover, had unwisely not taken the usual steps on the birth of an heir to the throne. The high officials of State and Church, whose duty it is to be present, were not invited. A story, therefore, for which there is no evidence except this omission, and which has long been abandoned even by the strongest opponents of the House of Stuart, gained credence, that this prince was no prince at all, but that he had been brought into the royal bedchamber in a warming-pan. In honour of this belief it is recorded that on his birthday in each year, whilst Jacobites wore white roses in their button-holes, staunch Whigs wore little farthing warming-pans.

This young prince it was whom Lewis XIV. had promised the exiled James upon his death-bed that he would recognise as King of England: which promise had drawn this long war upon his head. At St. Germain's, the place which Lewis had granted to James and to his family, he had been brought up as a Catholic prince, and amidst the despotic ideas of the Court of Lewis. He was not trained to acquiescence in the exile of his house. All around him called him King of England; and he certainly made it the object of his life to become king in reality. In English history, to distinguish him from his son, he is known as the Old Pretender. But a title which friend or foe alike might give him, and which was therefore used in negotiations with the French Court, was the Chevalier de St. George. That he was not deficient in personal bravery he had no opportunity in this attempt to show; but he showed it afterwards when fighting (one might think somewhat unwisely), against his countrymen at the battles of Oudenarde and Malplaquet. He was now nearly twenty.

The French force that King Lewis was going to send to aid him consisted of five men-of-war with transports, conveying about 4,000 soldiers. Just as it was about to sail from Dunkirk, when secrecy and speed were all-important to such an expedition, the young prince fell ill of the measles. The ships could not start without him. During the delay the English Government received information, and sent Admiral Sir George Byng with a fleet of fifteen ships which blockaded Dunkirk. The army in Scotland was small, but large forces were collected at York. Byng's fleet was driven from its moorings by high winds, and the French ships escaped. When they appeared off the coast of Scotland, signals were made according to agreement, but the Jacobites on shore made no answer to the signals. The French admiral thereupon insisted upon returning. He had received positive orders not to risk a landing unless there was a rising of the Jacobites to co-operate with the French troops. The Chevalier and many of those with him wished very much to land to try the effect of their presence, confident that his friends would rise then if not before. The French admiral returned, however, to France as quickly as possible, for Byng's ships had followed, and were close behind him. They caught the rearmost of his vessels, but the others escaped. As the result of this attempted rebellion, to be followed after seven, and again after thirty seven years, by others, which were more successful for a time, and finally more disastrous, two bills were passed through

Failure of attempt.

Parliament, one a temporary suspension of the Habeas Corpus Act, so that the Government might be enabled to arrest people upon suspicion; the other, a law that a Justice of the Peace might make anyone appear before him and take an oath abjuring the Pretender.

It is as well to notice that though this attempt was a miserable failure, its chance of success was probably better than either in the Fifteen or in the Forty-five Rebellion. The attack of measles and the unpreparedness of the Jacobites on shore were fortunate for the United Kingdom. At that time, it must be remembered, the feeling of irritation against the Union was exceedingly strong in Scotland, and England was engaged in a great Continental war which taxed her strength. Time was the healer of the first wound. Against this we must set the reflections that in the rebellion against George I, the house was new to the throne, and that even by the reign of his son it had done nothing to gain the affections of the people. After the accession of George III., "born and bred a Briton," not "an Englishman," there is no more suspicion of disloyalty in Scotland.

Its chance of success.

CHAPTER XVII.

PETER THE GREAT AND CHARLES XII.

Section I.—*The North Eastern State-System.*

IN the north-east of Europe there was a group of countries which, though not without influence upon the history of the rest of Europe, for nations cannot live separate lives without intercourse with their neighbours, may yet be regarded as forming a separate State System. This

North-Eastern State System.

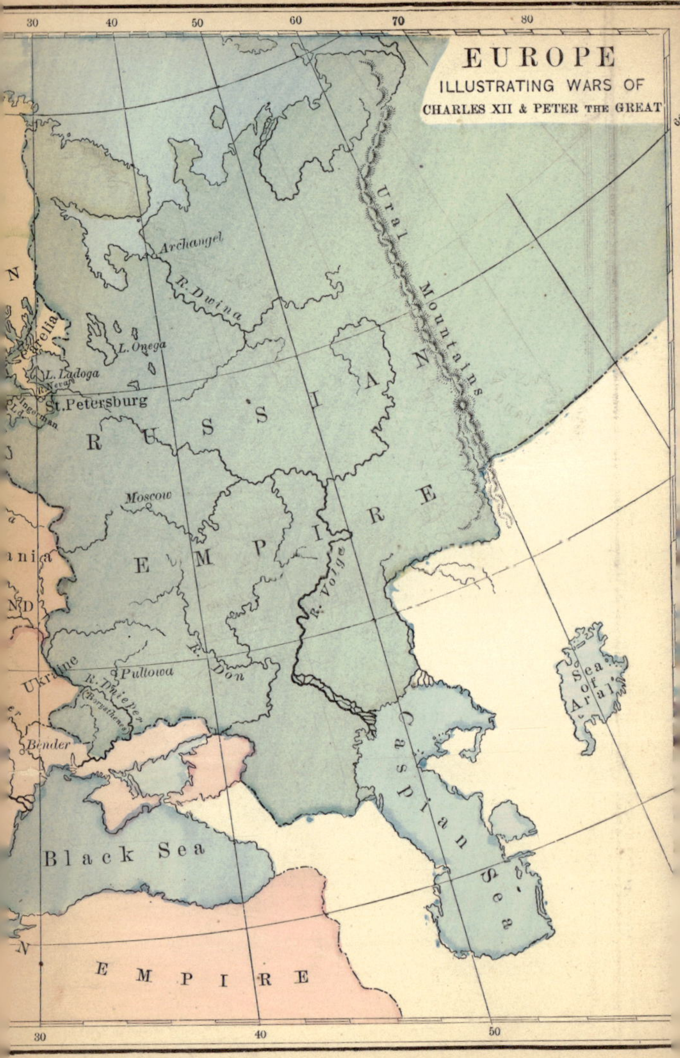
EUROPE
ILLUSTRATING WARS OF
CHARLES XII & PETER THE GREAT
30
40
50
60
70
80
Archangel
R. Dwina
Ural Mountains
Carelia
L. Onega
L. Ladoga
R. Neva
St. Petersburg
Ingerman Ld.
RUSSIAN EMPIRE
Moscow
R. Volga
R. Don
Pultowa
Ukraine
R. Dnieper
(Borysthenes)
Bender
Black Sea
Caspian Sea
Sea of Aral
EMPIRE
30
40
50

group must not, however, be left undescribed, partly on account of this connexion, but more especially on account of the remarkable character of two monarchs, one of whom influenced the future of his own country, and, through it, of Europe, to an extent which has been granted to few in the whole course of history.

This State System consists of Denmark, Poland, Sweden, and Russia. Just as the nations that occupy the stage of what we call ancient history are grouped around the Mediterranean Sea, so are these nations gathered round the Baltic.

Round the Baltic.

Of the four, Russia had as yet no territory on the shores of the Baltic, but she had already turned her eyes in that direction, seeing the advantage which a footing on the coast would give. Her rulers had already shaped their policy; her opponents, notably the famous Gustavus Adolphus, had planned resistance to it. Poland had two provinces, West Prussia and Livonia, on the coast of the Baltic. She had also a feudal suzerainty over two others.

Russia.

The three countries, Denmark, Poland, Sweden, had for about two centuries preserved a balance of power in the Baltic basin. At one time one of them would be stronger, then another. Of the three, Denmark was now the least important. Nearly two centuries had elapsed since it had been at the height of its power, but its territory was still much larger than that which it has to-day. The kingdom of Norway was under its crown, and the duchies of Schleswig and Holstein had the King of Denmark for their duke, an arrangement which remained in force until the Danish war of 1864. Yet, although separately Denmark was not to be feared by its neighbours, it might become important at any time as a factor in a combination.

Denmark.

Sweden, also, had passed the epoch of her greatest
power, but very substantial results remained
behind. Not only did she hold all the country which is now Sweden, but also the province of Finland, on the east of the Gulf of Bothnia, which had long been hers, but which now belongs to Russia; and in Germany, upon the other side, to the south of the Baltic, she still held part of Pomerania. The period of Sweden's greatest power was during the two years when her king, Gustavus Adolphus, placed himself at the head of the Protestants of Germany, and turned back the tide of defeat from the Protestant cause. Whatever may have been his motives, and those who have studied his history most are agreed to place them very high, the aggrandisement of his country was certainly the result of his campaign. During the remainder of the century Sweden was looked upon as the chief Protestant power in Europe. England, indeed, alone of other States, was capable of disputing the position. Under Cromwell, England was the chief Protestant State, and Cromwell valued the alliance of Sweden. In the reign of Charles II., when the counsels of Sir William Temple prevailed over baser counsels for a short year, and England determined again to assume that position, it was Sweden that with Holland joined England in the Triple Alliance, the mere formation of which was sufficient to bring France to terms. Sweden, however, did not join the Grand Alliance, probably because she felt that she had work to do nearer home; by that time, moreover, her influence in Europe was beginning to wane.

Sweden.

The kingdom of Poland had large territory, and yet did not exercise much influence on the politics of Europe. The reason for this is to be sought in the nature of its government. Poland was an

Poland.

Elective Monarchy. During the fifteenth and sixteenth centuries the monarchy had been nominally elective but really hereditary. But on the extinction of the house of Jagellon, which during that time had been on the throne, the nominal character of the monarchy became real. At each vacancy of the throne there had been the form of an election by the Diet, but after 1572 this form became a reality. The evils to which an elective monarchy is liable showed themselves in Poland. All the nobles had a right to elect, and all the sons of nobles were nobles themselves. A hundred thousand armed men appeared on horseback at the elections. The candidates, before election, pledged themselves to increase the privileges of their electors, until all the kingly power was given away, and Poland became what has been well termed a democracy of nobles. Foreign powers also interfered and used every means in their power by bribery, corruption, intimidation, to influence the elections. Defeated candidates raised up factions: and ultimate dismemberment of Poland, after two centuries of this experience, however unjustifiable on the part of those engaged in it, was the natural fruit of the form of its government, and of the conduct of its own nobility.

Of the four nations forming the north-eastern group, Russia, though on the eve of a forward start which would in an incredibly short space of time make it a first-rate power in Europe, was the least known. It was usually called Muscovy, from the name of its capital city. It possessed very little of European civilisation. The often quoted phrase of Napoleon—"If you scrape a Russian, you will find a Tartar," which means that under a superficial European polish the Russian is still at heart an Asiatic, would, before the accession of Peter the Great, have required the modification of omitting the first clause. The superficial polish was not there. Few in the West of Europe knew anything about Russia. It was not an element in the calculations of statesmen. The Russians in return knew nothing about Europe. They were a nation of uncivilised barbarians closely connected with Asia, slightly connected with Europe. The Russian empire had spread only in the direction of the north and east. At the accession of Peter it had none of the coast line either on the Baltic or the Black Sea. Yet Peter's predecessors had already begun to covet it. There is extant a letter by Gustavus Adolphus, in which he showed that Russia would become formidable, a dangerous neighbour to Sweden, if it held certain places which he regarded as the keys of the Baltic. He thought he had taken measures sufficient to secure these from falling into the hands of the Russians. It certainly is a tribute to his foresight that those very places stand about St. Petersburg.

The rise of Russia to a prominent place amongst European kingdoms, however the way may have been prepared for it, was due to one man, Peter the Great, whose character and work we proceed to describe.

Section II.—Peter the Great.

PETER'S father was married twice. He had two sons by the first marriage—Feodor, a delicate invalid, and Ivan, who was half an idiot, besides several daughters, of whom the most remarkable was the Princess Sophia, an ambitious and talented woman; by the second marriage, he had only Peter and one daughter. When Feodor succeeded his father, Sophia obtained all the real power in the State, and when he died, after a short reign, she managed still to preserve power as regent and guardian of her two brothers. Lest Peter should

Early life.

wrest it from her, she did her best to stunt his education; she dismissed the tutor in whom his father had placed confidence, and surrounded him with worthless companions. But it was all in vain. When he was nearly seventeen, the party in the State who were opposed to his sister encouraged him to throw off her tyrannous regency. He sent her into a convent, and her advisers into exile. This was in 1689, the year after the English Revolution.

Real accession to power.

Peter owed nothing to education. But by the mere force of genius, on taking up the reins of power, he immediately saw the state of his country, and made up his mind to reform it. He recognised that Russia was backward as compared with European nations; and his policy, conceived at the first and resolutely followed, may be summed up in the one phrase that he wished to make Russia European. With this object he sent many of his subjects abroad, to study how Russia could learn improvements from the other nations of Europe, and after a time he determined to travel himself.

His policy.

We know his appearance almost as well as if he lived in our own days, so often has it been described. He was very tall and had the figure of a powerful, strong man. His features were strongly marked, a fine, massive forehead over which great clusters of jet-black hair would hang, massive brows, from under which his black eyes flashed, now fierce, now piercing, as if he would read the very secrets of the heart. His mouth gave tokens of power. His smile was very gracious, but his frown terrible to behold. When at rest there was majesty about his face; but at times a troubled, nervous look would come over it, then would follow a wild twitch of face and of hands, then a convul-

His appearance.

sion during which he was ungovernable. This seems to have been hereditary; he tried to conquer it, but never could.

His visit to England was well remembered. In his travels, the countries that he most wished to see were England and Holland, for he desired to make Russia a maritime power, and he thought that from these two countries he could learn useful lessons. There was something very far-sighted in this desire, for in the whole of his dominions there was only one port, Archangel, and that was in a sea which was inaccessible for half the year. The Russian navy had to be created from the very beginning, for there was not, as yet, a single ship. Moreover, owing to an accident which he had suffered when a child, he had a great distaste, almost amounting to a nervous horror, of water. But he conquered this so completely that, in a storm, he once was able by his calmness to quiet the terrified seamen. "Fear not! Who ever heard of a Czar being lost at sea?"

His travels.

Desire for a navy.

He visited Holland first, and there, in the dockyards of Zaandam, he worked with his own hands as a ship's carpenter. He lived as the other workmen, and worked very hard. Thus he learnt the arts of shipbuilding and navigation. After nine months in Holland he passed on to London. At first he lived in a house in Norfolk Street which overlooked the Thames. He was anxious to see everything in England, but he did not wish to be seen himself. At the theatre he witnessed the play from the very back of his box, screened from public gaze by his attendants. He looked down upon a sitting of the House of Lords through a small window, where the king and the lords saw him and burst out laughing. When he

Holland.

England.

went to the king's palace, he was admitted at a back door. He "went privately to Oxford, but, being soon discovered, he immediately came back to London without viewing those curiosities he intended." He moved from London to Deptford, where he occupied the house of John Evelyn, an English gentleman of letters, who has left a diary that gives considerable insight into the social life of his day. He says that the Czar and his people were "right nasty" in their habits. At Deptford Peter spent his time as at Zaandam. But neither in England nor in Holland did he confine himself to the work of a ship's carpenter. He was making inquiries about State matters, about laws and law courts, about religious matters. He was inducing Englishmen, Scotchmen, Dutchmen, to settle in Russia, and take their skill with them. He visited Sweden and Brandenburg, and returned to his dominions after an absence of about a year and a half.

The most significant of all Peter's reforms was the removal of the capital. The traveller from Moscow to the shores of the Baltic sets his face westward. Peter was looking to the west for his model, and wished Russia to be European and no longer Asiatic. The old associations of Moscow drove him from it: the connexion with Europe enticed him to the Baltic. But it well illustrates the power of Peter over his subjects that he could make them quit their old capital. For the Russians loved Moscow with peculiar love. They call it still "the City of God," they reverence it as their "Holy Mother." At the first sight of its towers and pinnacles the Russian pilgrim falls upon his knees in awe. Yet, notwithstanding this affection and the consequent opposition of nobles, citizens, and priests, Peter carried out his plan. Nor was he even deterred by the physical difficulty of his task. The ground on which Petersburg is built was a marshy swamp. The city had to be built on piles, like a Dutch city. Thousands, it is said, lost their lives during the building, but Peter did not hesitate, and Petersburg, called after his own name, stands as a monument of his firmness.

Change in calendar.

The alteration of the calendar also was another of Peter's reforms. The Russians hitherto had dated from the creation, but he adopted the system in use in the rest of Europe. It is to be noted that the Russians still reckon by the old style.

Peter the Great was a reformer in ecclesiastical as well as in political matters. He abolished the Patri-

Abolishes Patriarchate.

archate, thus making the union of Church and State complete. Hitherto the Patriarch had power over the Church as despotic as that of the Czar over the State. Henceforth there was to be but one head. On the death of the last Patriarch he kept the see unfilled; and when the priests, disconsolate at seeing the vacant chair, asked him to appoint another, he said "I will be your Patriarch."

Even the fashions of Europe were to be imitated by his subjects. The habit of shaving the beard, the

Fashions.

smoking of tobacco, the very shape of dresses, the bringing the women out of seclusion, all of these he forced upon his reluctant people. There was so much resistance to the fashion of shaving that at length a tax was imposed upon those who wished to retain their beards, and a medal, bearing a head ornamented with beard and whiskers, was given as a token that the tax had been paid. Tobacco-smoking was not unknown in Russia before, having been introduced by English merchants at Archangel. The chief opposition to it was raised by the priests, on the ground that "not that which goeth into a man but that which cometh out of a man defileth him." Patterns of dresses were hung up at the entrance to a town, and the inhabitants were to be punished if their clothes were not cut in accordance with the Government pattern. But the social change which did most mischief was his determination that the women were to be drawn from their Oriental seclusion, a change for which they were wholly unprepared, and which, coming suddenly, could only do them harm.

The most important of his domestic reforms was the institution of the *Tchin*. From early times there has been a powerful hereditary nobility in Russia. A custom had almost grown into a law that no man whose ancestor had held a higher place than the ancestor of another man could serve under him without a stain upon his honour. The inconvenience of such a custom is manifest. Peter's predecessor had caused all the nobles to bring the records of their genealogies as if to compare them, and had then publicly burnt them. This was a severe blow to the principle of hereditary nobility; but Peter substituted for it an official nobility, called the Tchin, publishing a table of fourteen degrees, civil and military, by which all questions of rank were to be decided, the lower grades being duly subordinate to the higher. Thus he substituted what is called a Bureaucracy for an Aristocracy. *The Tchin, a bureaucracy.*

On his return from his first journey Peter found a formidable conspiracy against his authority. He put it down with great severity, actually assisting with his own hands at the execution of the conspirators. A corps of troops called the Strelitzes, holding a position of great importance in the *The Strelitzes.*

State somewhat analogous to that of the Prætorians at Rome, formed the centre of this conspiracy. Peter abolished the corps.

With the help of artisans from Holland and England he created a navy. When a child he delighted in a little boat which he saw upon the river that flows through Moscow. He made that little boat the germ of the Russian navy. He christened it "the Little Grandsire," and had it removed to Petersburg.

Section III.—Charles XII.

OF the States which formed the North-Eastern State System, there is no doubt that at the end of the seventeenth century Sweden was the most powerful. Its very power, and the fact that the power was of recent growth, excited the animosity of its neighbours; and when, in 1697, Charles XII. succeeded his father, at the early age of fifteen, they thought that they saw their opportunity. Each one of the neighbours wanted some part of the Swedish dominions. The Czar Peter wanted the Baltic Provinces, without which it would be impossible for him to keep up intercourse with Western Europe. Frederick Augustus the Strong, Elector of Saxony and King of Poland, wanted to rescue the Provinces of Livonia and West Prussia, which had formerly belonged to Poland, but had been wrested from her by the Swedes. Frederick, King of Denmark, wanted Holstein. The Duke of Holstein was brother-in-law of Charles of Sweden, as well as his boon companion; in spirit similar to Charles, he had been his associate in every mad exploit. Holstein, as was natural, stood under the protection of Sweden, although not part of the dominions of Charles. These three neighbours formed a league; from different quarters they were to make a simultaneous attack on Sweden.

According to his father's will, Charles was to remain for some time under a regency. But the States met and declared him no longer a minor, although he was only fifteen. Until the arrival of the news of the triple league which had been formed against him, he was contented to allow the Council of Regency to govern for him. He sat at the council table—some say "on it"—but appeared to take no interest in the the business transacted. But when the news was brought that the league had been made against him, he suddenly said:—"I am resolved never to begin an unjust war, nor to finish a just one except by the destruction of my enemies. My resolution is fixed. I will attack the first who declares against me, and, having conquered him, I shall be able to strike terror into the others."

<small>Beginning of his reign.</small>

The inert beginning of his reign was, indeed, no clue to the extraordinary character of this young prince. He was very self-willed, and had apparently set his aims clearly before him quite early in life. When he was a boy, Q. Curtius was his favourite author, Alexander the Great his favourite hero. To play the part of Alexander, in the altered circumstances of the world, was his ambition. It has been well said he was not Alexander, but he should have been Alexander's first soldier. Among his predecessors, Gustavus Adolphus was the one whose career he wished to imitate, especially in the two glorious years when he was victorious arbiter of the fortunes of Germany. But he differed from Gustavus, in that he made military glory the end rather than the means of his ambition. Napoleon the Great denied the right of Charles even to the title of a

<small>His character.</small>

great general. He was certainly a born soldier. He loved fighting. He loved danger. He said the noise of musket balls was the sweetest of music to him. He could endure all hardships, hunger, cold, fatigue. The pleasures and the splendour of a court had no attraction for him. He was simple, almost mean, in his attire, Spartan in his way of life. But he was self-willed and headstrong, and would not take advice. It is said that at his coronation he snatched the crown from the hands of the Archbishop, and placed it himself upon his head.

It had been agreed that the attack of his three opponents should be simultaneous, but either their arrangements were imperfect, or the quickness of Charles defeated them. He kept his word and attacked the first who invaded his territory. He began with Denmark, whose king was invading Holstein. Charles himself attacked Copenhagen, and in six weeks the King of Denmark was at his feet, promising to leave Holstein unmolested, and to quit the alliance.

He fights Denmark.

Frederick Augustus the Strong was the second. He could not persuade the Polish nobility to bear any part in the invasion, and was therefore obliged to fall back upon his hereditary dominions, his subjects in which were not so independent. The unfortunate Saxons had no interest in the war, but they were obliged to submit. The inhabitants of the provinces which he wished to recover were not pleased to see his army, and kept quickening his footsteps. He had just commenced besieging Riga, when he found that the victorious Charles was coming against him, and he hastily retreated.

The King of Poland.

He then turned towards the Czar Peter, who was laying siege to the town of Narva. His army was intrenched and defended with 140 pieces of cannon. Charles's army amounted only to 8,000 men, whereas that of Peter consisted according to some accounts of ten times the number, according to his own account, of about 45,000. But the Swedes had still the admirable discipline of Gustavus Adolphus, whilst very few of the Russians had any discipline at all; they were raw recruits, serfs, fresh from the woods, who had never smelt powder. On the day before the attack of the Swedes, Peter left the camp to hasten the arrival of some reinforcements. The Russian officers were angry that he left a foreigner in command; there was a spirit of mutiny among the Russian troops, and the whole army, in spite of its intrenchments, fell an easy prey to Charles. The battle was fought during a snow-storm, and there seems to have been a good deal of confusion in the Russian ranks.

Russians at Narva, 1700.

But the ease with which he won the battle of Narva was the cause of Charles' ruin. Thinking that he could at any time finish the struggle with Peter, for whom he entertained a profound contempt, he turned aside to follow and to dethrone the King of Poland. The Czar could have desired nothing better. This breathing time enabled him to recruit and drill his army: from their enemies, the Swedes, Peter was learning how to beat them. Charles, meanwhile, followed Augustus the Strong into Poland, and then into his hereditary kingdom of Saxony. Five years Charles wasted in needless campaigns, but at length he compelled Augustus formally to renounce the crown of Poland. His ministers wished him to take the crown of Poland himself, but in that unquiet monarchy he preferred the part of king-maker, and he forced the Diet of Nobles to elect, as king, a young Polish nobleman, named Stanislaus Leczinski.

Objection being taken to the candidate's age, Charles silenced it by saying, "He is as old as I am."

Charles kept his camp at Alt Ranstadt, near Leipzig. He was now at the summit of his career, and his position was very proud. The destinies of Europe may be said to have been in his hand. On the one side he was tempted to imitate his ancestor, Gustavus Adolphus, and, declaring himself the "protector of the Evangelical religion," to form a great Protestant confederation, which would be the Grand Alliance with the Austrian element omitted. On the other hand, Lewis XIV., who was with difficulty resisting the combination against him, had sent ambassadors to implore his aid. Had Charles turned his steps westward, it is not easy to predict what would have resulted from his interference. The Grand Allies knew the danger, and Marlborough himself paid a visit to the Swedish conqueror, with more than his usual honey of flattery on his lips. Conqueror of Blenheim and of Ramillies, he told Charles that he would gladly take lessons from him in the art of war. But Marlborough soon understood that Charles would not interfere, and that all his preparations were designed against Russia. Amongst the lessons in war which Charles could teach, we may wonder whether it was one to allow a defeated enemy time to gather up his strength again?

Charles arbiter of Europe.

Section IV.—*Pultowa.*

WHILST Charles XII. was campaigning, king making, sitting as arbiter of Europe in his camp at Alt Ranstadt, Peter was steadily preparing to fight him again. His soldiers were overcoming their fear of the Swedes, for, in the absence of their king, Peter had beaten them once, had captured Narva itself, and had conquered the province of Ingria. He took a Swedish town, and, whilst he strengthened its fortifications, he renamed it Schlusselburg or Key-town, because he said that it was the key to Sweden.

When Charles at length determined to carry on the war with Russia, it is probable, if he had known his own mind clearly and carried out his plan, that he must have prevailed. Napoleon criticised this campaign very unfavourably. There is no doubt that Charles should have marched straight upon Moscow, for, when once he had reached the Russian frontier, a fortnight's hard marching would have brought him under its walls. On account of his delay the Russians were enabled to lay waste the country. With a strange fatality Charles turned southwards, having been tempted by the promise of a remarkable, though not a trustworthy, ally.

Charles's campaign against Russia.

Mazeppa was by birth a Pole. Having been found guilty of misconduct, he had been tied naked on a wild horse, which carried him amongst the Cossacks of the wild barren country called the Ukraine. The Cossacks received him kindly. He enjoyed their warlike, roving mode of life, and rose amongst them till he became their hetman, or chief. He had been a great favourite of Peter, but he wanted to become an independent sovereign. On this account, and because of an insult which he suffered at the hands of the Czar, he intrigued with Charles, and promised that he would join him in the Ukraine, at the head of 30,000 Cossacks. But the Cossacks, when they discovered his intention, refused to desert the Czar, or to follow Mazeppa; and when, after weary marching, Charles reached the trysting place, Mazeppa could only bring to him a mere handful of men.

Mazeppa.

The Swedish army was by this time suffering terribly from the want of supplies, and from the frequent attacks of the Russian mounted skirmishers. Throughout the severe cold of the Russian winter Charles would not let his army rest in winter quarters. He was very ignorant of the country, and wasted his strength in fruitless marches and countermarches. His only hope now lay in the reinforcements and supplies which he hoped that one of his generals was bringing to him; for he had made a strategical mistake in coming so far from his base of operations without a proper line of communication. The reinforcing army was beaten by the Russians; its remnant suffered terribly as it struggled on, and at length joined the main body, few in numbers, without supplies, and, in many cases, even without shoes.

Reinforcements for Swedes defeated.

The town of Pultowa is situated upon a branch of the Dnieper, called the Vorskla. It was a magazine of stores. For this reason Charles thought it his best chance to attack it, and Peter was equally determined on its defence. Peter had much the larger army, and his soldiers were better equipped and well entrenched. Peter contrived that Charles's army should fight with their backs turned towards the angle made by the Vorskla falling into the Dnieper. Charles had been wounded in the heel in a skirmish a few days before the battle. He was obliged to be carried about during the battle in a litter. It gives some idea of the fury with which the battle raged, when we hear that it only lasted a few hours, and that, out of twenty-four bearers of this litter, twenty-one were killed. Both of the kings fought bravely, for they knew that the future of their countries depended on the issue of the fighting. The battle began very early in the

Battle of Pultowa. July 8, A.D. 1709.

morning, and the Swedes charged with such impetuosity that they broke the Russian lines. But by some mistake the Swedish cavalry was not ready to follow up this advantage. The Russians had time to rally. Peter brought up a great force of cannon, and, at the same time, sent a general to attack the Swedish reserve. A final charge of the Russians followed, and the Swedes were completely overcome. Mazeppa himself went up to Charles, and, knowing that persuasion was vain, made a sign to his attendants to place him on a horse; then, holding the bridle, he made their horses swim the river. They fled to Turkey. Four days later the whole Swedish army surrendered. There was no alternative for the proud troops that had always been conquerors. Peter expressed great admiration of them, but sent them into Siberia.

The results of the battle of Pultowa are very important. On the very day of the battle Peter wrote, "Thank God, the foundations of Petersburg at length stand firm." The province of Livonia and part of Finland fell at once into his hands. Demark laid claim to Scania, Prussia to Pomerania. The Swedish monarchy was reduced to its original limits, from which the genius of one man had raised it, and to which the folly of another had now brought it back again. Sweden's financial difficulties made her regret that she had attempted work that was too much for her. But the country in which most joy was expressed was Poland, where Charles's nominee was at once driven off the throne, and Augustus the Strong resumed his place.

Results of battle.

But before Peter could consolidate his conquests, he had one more serious crisis through which to pass, and one which almost overwhelmed him. Partly because Charles had taken refuge in Turkey, and partly because Turkey was jealous

War between Russia and Turkey.

of the growing power of Russia, a war sprang between those two powers. It was by no means the last of such wars, and some people think that it is the traditional policy of Russian statesmen never to cease struggling for the possession of Constantinople. On this occasion Peter imitated his late antagonist's rashness and contempt for his enemy. Promises had been made by traitorous subjects of the sultan; he believed them as Charles had believed Mazeppa. He crossed the Pruth with his army, but found himself hemmed in by a much larger number of the enemy. The Russian army was rescued by the Czarina Catherine, a Livonian woman of humble birth, who had been taken prisoner by the Russians on the very day of her marriage to a Swedish sergeant who was killed at the same time. After various vicissitudes of fortune she had attracted the notice of the Czar by her beauty and her wit: and he had publicly announced his marriage to her when setting out from Moscow on his expedition against Turkey. She was a woman of very sweet temper, and had remarkable influence over her husband, being the only person who could control him during his fits. He had not wished her to accompany the army; but she had begged hard, and to the great delight of the soldiers she was allowed to go with them. In the great strait of the Russian army it was Catherine who proposed that a very rich present should be sent to the Grand Vizier, giving her own jewels for the purpose and encouraging others to give. Negotiations followed.

The affair of the Pruth.

Treaty. The Czar surrendered all claim to Azov and to the Black Sea; and he further engaged not to interfere in the affairs of Poland.

Section V.—End of Charles XII. and of Peter.

Since Pultowa Charles had been at Bender, a town not far from the frontier of Turkey. When he reproached the Grand Vizier with letting Peter the Great escape, he received in reply the taunt: "It is not good that all kings should be away from their peoples." The Turks had made their illustrious guest an allowance, but this was now stopped. A little later he received a direct order to depart, and when that failed he was actually besieged in his own house at Bender by the Turkish troops. He fought them from room to room. When he was at length overpowered, he was carried to a place where he feigned illness for some months. After this madness, having received pressing letters from Sweden, and hearing of her reverses, he suddenly determined to go home. He travelled through Germany on horseback, in disguise, with only two companions. In sixteen days he arrived before Stralsund, and it is said that he had ridden so fast that his boots had to be cut off from his legs. Stralsund was the last town that the Swedes had been able to retain on the south of the Baltic, and very soon a force was besieging it, composed of Danes, Saxons, Prussians, and Russians. He was obliged to escape secretly from the town, and immediately after his departure it surrendered.

Charles XII. at Bender.

Not even his terrible experiences were sufficient to teach the fiery Swede. He had learnt nothing, he had forgotten nothing. With enemies enough around him, and with his country exhausted, he proposed to invade England and restore the Pretender. He actually did invade Norway, and met his death at the siege of Fredericshall.

Death, December 11, A.D. 1718.

> His fall was destined to a barren strand,
> A petty fortress, and a dubious hand;
> He left the name, at which the world grew pale,
> To point a moral or adorn a tale.
>   Johnson, "Vanity of Human Wishes."

The later history of Peter the Great need not detain us long. He made another journey through the different countries of Europe, in which he visited Holland again, and Prussia, and spent six months in France, where he romped with the young king, and stood in admiration before Richelieu's picture. "Great man," he said, "I would gladly give thee half my dominions if thou wouldst teach me to rule the other half." While he was visiting the mint in France, a medal dropped at his feet: picking it up he found on it his own likeness, with the motto, *Vires acquirit eundo*.

Peter the Great. Second journey.

One dark cloud hangs over this part of Peter's life. He had a son by his first wife, a boy of strange temper, who, sympathising with the party of rebellious priests, had always opposed his father. On Peter's return his son ran away, first to Vienna and then to Naples. He was brought back by promises that he should not be punished, but on his return he was condemned as guilty of conspiracy. It was given out in a proclamation that Alexis had died in a convulsive fit, but there were many who thought that the father himself had put him to death.

Death of his son.

Not long after, to his great grief, he lost his other son, Peter, the son of Catherine, and in February 1725, he died himself. He died in the faith of a Christian. "Lord, I believe, help thou mine unbelief," and then, "hereafter." These were his last words. What he meant by them no one

Death of Peter the Great.

can say, but they certainly may be taken as a motto of his work. It was for posterity, not for himself: therein lies his true claim to the name of Great. The later history of Russia is his best monument.

Yet the civilisation which he gave to Russia was superficial, and there is a world of meaning in the phrase of the witty Frenchman, who said, "The Russians were rotten before they were ripe."

CHAPTER XVIII.

THE PROTESTANT SUCCESSION.

AFTER the great war England was exhausted and glad of rest. From the Peace of Utrecht to the end of Queen Anne's reign it may be said that there is no incident of historical importance, except the events connected with the question of the succession to the throne, and of this the interest culminates towards the end.

End of reign.

Bearing in mind what the Revolution of 1688 wrought for England, and what it prevented, it was felt to be important that its work should not be undone. During William's life the cause of the Revolution, or, to put it in other words, of constitutional government, had been quite safe. As long, also, as Anne should live, there was no danger; but the friends of the cause felt that there was a risk with respect to her successor. Immediately after the Revolution the Bill of Rights, the first statute of William and Mary, had decided that the crown should pass first to the heirs of Mary, then to Princess Anne and to her

Measures to secure Protestant succession.

JAMES I.=Anne of Denmark.
b. 1566, succ. 1603, d. 1625.

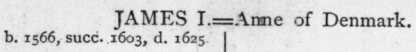

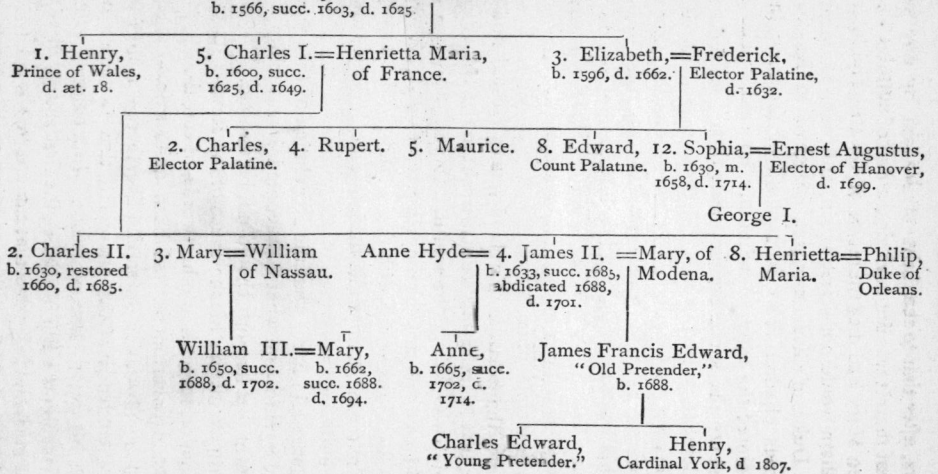

1. Henry, Prince of Wales, d. aet. 18.
5. Charles I.=Henrietta Maria, b. 1600, succ. 1625, d. 1649. of France.
3. Elizabeth,=Frederick, b. 1596, d. 1662. Elector Palatine, d. 1632.

2. Charles, Elector Palatine. 4. Rupert. 5. Maurice. 8. Edward, Count Palatine. 12. Sophia,=Ernest Augustus, b. 1630, m. Elector of Hanover, 1658, d. 1714. d. 1699.

George I.

1. Charles II. b. 1630, restored 1660, d. 1685.
3. Mary=William of Nassau.
Anne Hyde=4. James II.,=Mary, of b. 1633, succ. 1685, Modena. abdicated 1688, d. 1701.
8. Henrietta=Philip, Maria. Duke of Orleans.

William III., b. 1650, succ. 1688, d. 1702.
Mary, b. 1662, succ. 1688. d. 1694.
Anne, b. 1665, succ. 1702, d. 1714.
James Francis Edward, "Old Pretender," b. 1688.

Charles Edward, "Young Pretender."
Henry, Cardinal York, d. 1807.

heirs, after that to the heirs of William by any subsequent marriage. But towards the end of William's reign, when Mary had died childless, when it was evident that William would not marry again, and when the death of the Duke of Gloucester, the only one of Anne's numerous children who reached even boyhood, had disappointed the hopes of the nation, new steps were taken to secure the succession in safe hands. By the Act of Settlement, passed in 1701, the provisions of the Bill of Rights were strengthened by the declaration that upon failure of heirs to Anne and William, the Electress Sophia was to succeed, and that her claim should pass to her heirs. As her grandson was a grown man, it seemed as if heirs in this line would not be likely to fail. The principle upon which the Parliament, both in the Bill of Rights and in the Act of Settlement, proceeded was that of selecting the nearest heir to the English throne who was a Protestant. It was stipulated as a further security that the sovereign must be in communion with the Church of England.

There was no descendant of King Charles I. who satisfied these conditions. If there had been, the English people, with their affectionate memory of him, would have very much preferred such an one. But besides the family of James II., Henrietta Maria, alone of the children of Charles I., had left issue; but, as she married the Roman Catholic Duke of Orleans, their children were excluded from the English crown. In order, therefore, to find a satisfactory successor for the throne it was necessary to turn to the descendants of Elizabeth, sister of Charles I. Her name takes us back some distance in English and in Continental history. When her father, King James I., ascended the English throne,

Who was the Electress Sophia?

Her mother, Elizabeth.

uniting the crown of England and Scotland, she was a little girl not quite seven years of age. She grew up a very beautiful princess, whose praises poets sang, and wearing whose colours, soldiers of fortune were ever ready to fight. Her hand was sought for a dauphin of France, but without success. She was not seventeen when, in February 1613, she married Frederick, the Elector Palatine of the Rhine, whose capital was Heidelberg. From that time forward her life was stormy and full of trouble, intimately mixed up with the early part of the disastrous Thirty Years' War, then with the difficulties of her brother Charles and his house. But living through these she survived the Restoration, and came with her nephew to England, dying two years after it in London.

Elizabeth's husband, Frederick, the Elector Palatine, was elected King of Bohemia by the Protestant party in that country. But the house of Austria had regarded the process of election as a mere form, and claimed that the succession to the crown of Bohemia was theirs. A war was the result. Germany at that time being in a state of disunion and hostility between the two great religious parties, the war became a religious war, and continued to spread until the dispute about the succession in Bohemia had set the whole of Europe in a flame. But the first portion of the Thirty Years' War was entirely a triumph for the house of Austria and the Roman Catholics. Not only was Bohemia in a few months wrested from the hands of Frederick, called in derision the Winter King, but he was driven forth an outcast from his own hereditary dominions, and his electorate was given to the Duke of Bavaria. At the peace of Westphalia, in 1648, part of these dominions was restored to Frederick's family, and an eighth electorate established to avoid disputes.

Her father, Frederick.

Frederick and Elizabeth had a large family, the Electress Sophia, who inherited her mother's claim to the English crown, coming twelfth out of thirteen. Amongst her elder brothers and sisters, two have names famous in English history, Prince Rupert and Prince Maurice. Prince Rupert, who commanded the right wing of the royalist army at the Battle of Edgehill in 1642, and whose impetuous charge carried that wing triumphantly forward, regardless of the rest of the battle, was brother to the Electress Sophia, who, if Queen Anne had died in the spring of 1714 instead of in the summer, would have been Queen of England. His impetuosity led to the defeats of Marston Moor and Naseby, and to the surrender of Bristol. The license in plundering which he allowed his soldiers was a reminiscence of his early experience in the German wars. After the conclusion of the Civil War Prince Rupert had distinguished himself, first as a naval commander, and later in the domain of science.

Her brother, Prince Rupert.

The Electress Sophia was born at the Hague in 1630, some three months after Gustavus Adolphus landed in Germany. She married Ernest Augustus, titular bishop of Osnaburg, Duke of Brunswick-Luneburg, who in 1692 was raised by the Emperor, in return for services rendered, to the dignity of Elector of Hanover. Sophia had her mother's beauty, and was remarkable for the evenness of her temper and for her acquirements. When English ambassadors came to her they found that she spoke English as fluently as themselves. But she was equally well versed in other languages—in French and Italian as well as in Dutch and German, about which there might be a dispute which should be called her native tongue. At first she was not particularly eager to accept the succession to

Life of the Electress Sophia.

the English crown. When the Act of Settlement was passed, in which she was named as successor, she did not think it likely that she would survive Anne, and she doubted whether her son George was not of too despotic a nature loyally to recognise the limitations of sovereignty in England. Her opinion was that it would be better for the Prince of Wales, as she called him, that is the Old Pretender, to change his religion and accept parliamentary government. When, however, the Act of Settlement was formally presented to her she accepted the position, and expressed a hope that her descendants "would never give the English people cause to be weary of them." All who stood nearer in point of blood to the English throne were excluded as Roman Catholics, but Sophia cannot be regarded as a very strong upholder of the Protestant faith if the story be true that, when a French agent asked what religion her daughter professed, she answered, "She is of no religion as yet." She was waiting to see what would be the creed of her future husband. Later, when the aged Electress still lived, and it became doubtful whether she might not survive Anne, it is said that she used to declare that she would die happy if she could have "Queen of England" written on her coffin. But it was fortunate for England that her wish was not gratified, and that the two deaths, which followed each other within less than eight weeks in the summer of 1714, fell as they did. The Electress was in her eighty-fourth year, and, as there was some danger that the change of dynasty might lead to a rebellion, it is evident that two successions coming close together would be still more dangerous.

It is somewhat difficult to estimate the real strength of the Jacobite party. Exaggerated on the one side by the zeal of friends and accredited

The Jacobites.

agents, who wished to show that the party was strong enough to be up and doing, it was exaggerated also on the other side by the real or feigned alarms of enemies, who wished violent measures to be adopted against it. Certainly many who had been loyal subjects of William and of Anne were prepared passively to accept the Old Pretender upon his sister's death; many even might have taken active measures to secure his succession. Probably if the young man would have consented to change his religion, a large majority of the English people would have argued that the Stuarts had learnt lessons enough to make them refrain from any further attack on constitutional government. Yet the atmosphere of the despotic court in which the prince had been trained was not calculated to make him a good constitutional king. "The uses of adversity" are sweet only if we accept its lessons, and those cannot be taught who are determined not to learn. At any rate it must be said in James's honour that he never for an instant entertained the proposal to renounce his religion. The Jacobites may be regarded as an extreme wing of the Tory party. Their opponents used unfairly to say that all Tories were Jacobites, and indeed an air of suspicion that they were in favour of the exiled family hung over all the more prominent and staunch members of the Tory party. The country gentry were mostly Jacobites, and it was asserted that at their gatherings they drank the health of "The king across the water."

Their connection with the Tories.

During the last years of the queen's reign a Tory ministry was in power, and its opponents confidently asserted that the object of the ministers was to restore the Pretender. When with the new reign these opponents came into power

The Tory ministers.

the Tory ministers were impeached; but though the facts elicited by the Committee of the House of Commons are quite clear as to the misconduct of the ministry with respect to the Peace of Utrecht, and prove that they had sullied the honour of England, there is no real evidence of a formed design to restore the Pretender. The evidence against the ministers Bolingbroke and Oxford falls under two heads—their own letters and the statements of Whig historians. The latter, if unsupported, may be dismissed as of no value; and with respect to the former it must be remembered that these ministers, like many other prominent men of the day, were anxious to stand well with both sides, and therefore to the Stuarts exaggerated or invented their services in the Jacobite cause. Of the two Oxford is generally acquitted of overt treason; but as Bolingbroke afterwards entered the service of the Pretender, and became his Secretary of State, this is generally taken as a proof that his treason began at an earlier date. It is, however, only a presumption and not a conclusive proof. It may be true, according to the usual story, that Bolingbroke was scheming to restore the Pretender; that, finding Oxford would not go the whole length with him, he determined to oust him from the ministry, and that it was only the sudden death of the queen and the promptitude of the leading Whigs which prevented the scheme from being carried into effect. But if Bolingbroke's heart had been in such scheming, it is difficult to believe that he could not have done more. The following feeling also actuated him: If he was not in favour of the Pretender, he certainly wished to secure the continuance of his party in power; but he knew that the Elector George was likely to call the Whigs to office, and he had been constantly impressing upon Oxford that gradually every

A.D. 1714. *The Protestant Succession.* 183

position in the State, whatever its seeming importance, should be given to a Tory, so that when the new king came he might find the Tories too powerful and united to remove. As Oxford was half-hearted in this scheme, his rival at length resolved to drive him from the ministry.

The last week of Queen Anne's life was an exciting time. In the early part of it there was a quarrel in the ministry, which led to the ejection of Oxford. Oxford had nominally higher power than Bolingbroke. Holding the office of Lord High Treasurer, he was what we should now call Prime Minister, and Bolingbroke seems almost from the first to have been jealous of him upon this ground; and this jealousy was increased by the contempt which he did not care to conceal for Oxford's understanding. Moreover, Oxford, whose strength lay in Court interest, had the misfortune to offend one who had been his chief ally, Lady Masham. Herewith he fell also under the queen's displeasure. It is said that an open quarrel between Oxford and his rival took place in the presence of the queen and Lady Masham, and that Anne dismissed Oxford with contumely, taking from him the white staff, the badge of office, and afterwards telling the council her reasons—that he was unpunctual; that she could seldom understand him, and when she could, that no dependence was to be placed on what he said; that he was often tipsy; and that his conduct to her was improper.

The last week. Quarrels in the ministry.

The question now arose, who was to succeed Oxford as Lord High Treasurer? and after long deliberations it was decided to put the office into commission. But before anything could be settled the queen was taken ill, from which illness she never recovered. She had long suffered from a complication of diseases, gout and erysipelas; now apoplexy followed.

We must now give an account of a man in whom at this time the queen was much inclined to trust. Charles Talbot, Earl of Shrewsbury, was born in the year of the Restoration.

Shrewsbury. His previous career.

He was a man of such winning manners that King William gave him the pleasant name of "King of Hearts." He was not, however, made of the stern stuff that public life requires, and though he was a good deal mixed up with affairs of State, he was never happy in them. His timidity of character not only caused him to shrink from office, but made his conduct as a statesman uncertain. He early became a Protestant, though his family was Catholic, and this conversion brought the ill-will of King James upon him. He was one of the seven who signed the declaration inviting William of Orange to come over to England. As a friend to the Revolution he became Secretary of State with the title of Duke of Shrewsbury under William III., and though he more than once expressed a wish to be released from office, the king would not consent to it. Shrewsbury was accused of treasonable correspondence with the Stuarts, and though there was reason to believe that the accusation was not wholly unjust, William, with great magnanimity, would pay no attention to it. Shrewsbury's conscience, however, would not let him rest, and he not only retired from office, but, leaving England, went to live at Rome. After five years' absence he returned in Anne's reign, bringing with him an Italian wife. At first he acted with Marlborough and the Whigs; but the great Whig ladies treating his wife with disdain, he was estranged, and Harley seized the opportunity to win him to the other side. He voted with the Tories on the

Sacheverell trial. The queen liking him personally appointed him Lord Chamberlain. Later he was also made Lord Lieutenant of Ireland.

In the crisis at the end of the reign he assumed a very prominent position. Almost the last words that Queen Anne uttered were in giving to Shrewsbury the staff of Lord High Treasurer: "Use it for the good of my people." Who it was in the Council that proposed Shrewsbury's name for recommendation to the queen is a point in dispute. Some say that it was Bolingbroke himself, seeing that his own policy had become impossible; others that it was the work of two Whig lords, who, without summons but with the connivance of Shrewsbury himself, had entered and taken their seats at the Council. *He is appointed Treasurer.*

Whatever may have been the veerings in Shrewsbury's career, to one point he was staunch at the end as at the beginning of it—his loyalty to the Protestant succession. If he had been guilty of treasonable correspondence with the exiled family, he had quite made up his mind now. With Shrewsbury, one of the original inviters of King William, at the head of affairs, it was felt at once that the Jacobites had no chance. They themselves seem to have been thoroughly taken aback. Every preparation was made to secure the Hanoverian succession, and when the queen died, August 21, 1714, George Lewis, Elector of Hanover, was quietly proclaimed King of Great Britain and Ireland. It was said that a Jacobite bishop offered himself in lawn sleeves to proclaim King James III. at Charing Cross, but his friends induced him to abstain from so mad a project. *The Protestant succession safe at last.*

George I., the new King of England, was born in the year of the Restoration. He was therefore fifty-four years old when he began his reign. He had been trained as a soldier, and had served in campaigns against the Turks, and in the late war had commanded in one campaign the army upon the Rhine. He was one of the allies, though it usually required English money to set the Hanoverian, as well as other German troops, in motion. His son, afterwards George II., fought bravely at Oudenarde, as he did later at Dettingen. Even their enemies never accused either George of want of courage.

George I.

Very brave.

He succeeded his father as Elector of Hanover in the last year of the seventeenth century, and was very much beloved in his own hereditary dominions. These he was very slow to leave when he heard that the English crown had fallen to him; and when he did arrive in England he was never popular with the English people. They looked upon him as a necessity, and perhaps were even thankful to him for saving them from the Pretender and French influence in England, but how could they love a king who could not speak a word of their language! Sir Robert Walpole, who was Prime-Minister during the greater part of his reign, could not speak German, so that the conversations between the sovereign and his minister were carried on in bad Latin. George I., like William III., was never happy in England, and always rejoiced when he could return to Herrenhausen, as his palace near Hanover was called. His manners in public were cold and phlegmatic, but it is said that in private he could be very sociable. Over his private life there hung a great cloud. When only just of age he had married Sophia Dorothea daughter of the Duke of Zell; but, finding her guilty of unfaithfulness, he

Good Elector.

Unpopular; could not speak English.

Phlegmatic.

caused her to be shut up in a castle in the midst of a desolate heath, from the name of which she was called the "Princess of Ahlden." For twenty-eight years she was shut up in this dreary place, surrounded by soldiers with drawn swords whenever she went forth. She died shortly before the king, whom she is said to have summoned to meet her at God's throne.

His wife.

George I. was not liked in England, and his private life was not fair to behold, but he did not prove a bad king for the country. His mother's doubt about him was unfounded; so far from desiring to be despotic, he left the English people alone to govern themselves. His reign was a time of peace, a peace policy being emphatically that which the king, as well as Walpole and his supporters, wished to pursue. The material prosperity of the country went forward with great strides during the thirty years which followed the accession of the House of Hanover. "Happy," says the proverb, "is the nation that has no history." This interval seems barren in our annals, but on that very account it was doubtless a better time for people to live in. In all other reigns, from William III. to Victoria, the National Debt has increased—it was the glory of George I.'s reign that in it alone the debt was diminished.

Good king for England.

CHAPTER XIX.

END OF LEWIS XIV.

Lewis XIV. died September 1, 1715, just thirteen months after the death of Queen Anne. He was seventy-seven years of age, and had reigned for the enormous number of seventy-two years. His reign began in May 1643.

It was just one month before John Hampden fell mortally wounded in the skirmish in Chalgrove Field. Lewis was nominally reigning over France soon after the Great Rebellion began in England. He lived to see its principles triumph in the Commonwealth, and fall at the Restoration, to see them reasserted in a more moderate and therefore more durable form in the Glorious Revolution. Of these principles he had been the determined enemy, as he had been constant to the cause of the Stuarts. But this enmity and this support had cost him dear, and in his old age Lewis acknowledged the principles of constitutional government as finally triumphant by the recognition of Queen Anne which he made in the treaty of Utrecht, and in the peaceful recognition which he so soon afterwards accorded to the House of Hanover.

Lewis XIV. Events in England parallel with his life.

The last years of Lewis were clouded and overcast. Beyond the precincts of the Court were disaster and defeat, which during the whole war of the succession had been his portion, an empty treasury and an exhausted country. Famine had done its work, driving men into the army from sheer impossibility of obtaining food. In his family relations the king had grievous trouble, blow coming after blow upon his unfortunate head. In 1711 sickness raged through Europe. The same epidemic of small-pox which served to bring the war to an end, by the death of the Emperor Joseph at Vienna, proved also fatal in Paris to Lewis the Dauphin a man of fifty. He had not indeed played a very important part in the Court, but he was heir to the throne. His eldest son, the Duke of Burgundy, the elder brother of the King of

Troubles at the end.

Death of Dauphin.

Duke of Burgundy.

Spain, was a prince of whom high hopes were entertained. Great care had been taken with his education, and that of his brothers, the superintendence of which had been entrusted to Fénelon, afterwards Archbishop of Cambray, a man famous alike for learning and for the gentleness of his character. The Duke of Burgundy was Fénelon's favourite pupil, and the one whose character he had been able to mould most nearly after the pattern of his own. Fénelon's famous romance, the "Adventures of Telemachus," was written to serve as a model for this young prince. Its author did not wish to publish the book, but a servant stole a copy from which it was printed. Passages in it, finding fault by implication with matters in France, were too outspoken for the Court of Lewis, and the work was for a time suppressed. But Fénelon hoped that the princely virtues which he had inculcated would not so readily pass from the mind of his pupil. Three years before his father's death the Duke of Burgundy was in the field, the nominal commander of the French troops before Oudenarde. Want of harmony between him and Marshal Vendôme may be considered as one of the chief reasons of the loss of the battle there fought. He married the daughter of Victor Amadeus, of Savoy, his brother the king of Spain marrying her sister. The Duchess of Burgundy was a graceful, winning princess, the life of the whole Court and the especial darling of the old king. But in less than a year after the death of the Dauphin, the Duchess of Burgundy was carried off by malignant fever; and within a week her husband fell a victim to the same disease. Then their eldest son died; and their second son, Lewis, Duke of Anjou, was now heir to the throne.

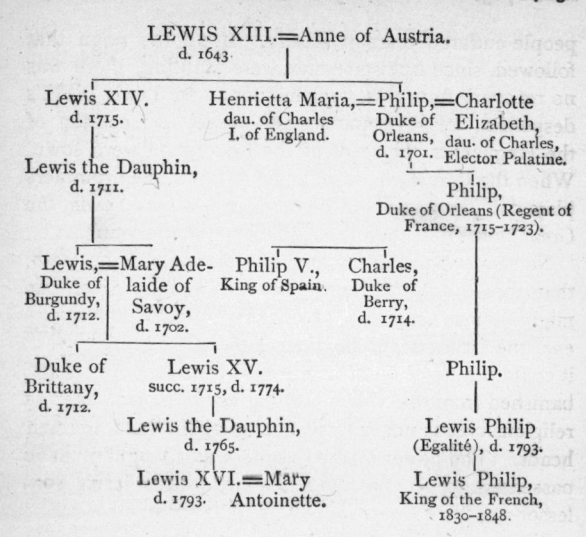

```
                LEWIS XIII.=Anne of Austria.
                   d. 1643.

Lewis XIV.     Henrietta Maria,=Philip,=Charlotte
d. 1715.       dau. of Charles   Duke of  Elizabeth,
               I. of England.    Orleans, dau. of Charles,
                                 d. 1701. Elector Palatine.
Lewis the Dauphin,
d. 1711.
                                      Philip,
                                 Duke of Orleans (Regent of
                                   France, 1715-1723).

Lewis,=Mary Ade-  Philip V.,    Charles,
Duke of | laide of  King of Spain.  Duke of
Burgundy,| Savoy,               Berry,
d. 1712. | d. 1702.             d. 1714.

Duke of      Lewis XV.                   Philip.
Brittany,   succ. 1715, d. 1774.
d. 1712.
             Lewis the Dauphin,
             d. 1765.                 Lewis Philip
                                      (Egalité), d. 1793.
             Lewis XVI.=Mary
             d. 1793.  Antoinette.    Lewis Philip,
                                      King of the French,
                                        1830-1848.
```

On these losses in the royal family of France followed the Peace of Utrecht, which Lewis survived a little more than two years. His great-grandson suc‑

Lewis XV. Contrast.

ceeded him. Born in 1710, he was now five years old. Lewis XIV. also had been five when he succeeded to the throne: but what a contrast the beginning and close of that long reign presents, and what a lesson does the contrast read upon the hollowness which its so-called magnificence hid! Lewis had succeeded to a throne with power consolidated by wise government. He had squandered its resources in the attempt to extend that power and to prop up falling causes. He possessed all the externals of a king, but he was lacking in the true virtues of a ruler. His condemnation is that he left France exhausted, and that under him her people endured years of misery. In all the reign that followed, since true statesmen were wanting, there was no recovery from this wretchedness. In Lewis XIV.'s despotism, misgovernment, and cruel persecution of the Huguenots, the seeds of the Revolution were sown. When the Camisards were being tortured, the drummers played. Drums were beaten also when Lewis the Great's own descendant perished by the guillotine.

No sooner had the old king closed his eyes in death, than there passed through France a sigh of relief, one might almost say a cry of delight. Whatever the future might be, men thought that it could not be as bitter as the past. Nobles banished from the Court were glad to return; men of religious creeds not tolerated in it again held up their heads. The power of the Jesuits was thought to have passed away; so that even the late king's Jesuit confessor was hardly safe from the popular fury. *Joy at death of Lewis XIV.*

The new king was five years old. Who then was to govern the country during his infancy? Of the princes of the blood royal, the nearest akin to him, except the King of Spain, was Philip, Duke of Orleans, a man of considerable ability, but unscrupulous, an avowed infidel, and of dissolute life. *Who shall be regent?* The last years of Lewis XIV. had been embittered with the thought that this man, his nephew, was the rightful regent to his grandson. He had therefore made a will, by which a Council of Regency was appointed, with the Duke of Orleans as president, for in France at least the hereditary principle must not be entirely set aside; Lewis however, even when drawing his will up, did not deceive himself as to its value. "As soon as I am dead," said he, "they will put it aside. I know too well what was done with my own father's will."

His prophecy came true. The Duke of Orleans became regent without any council to limit his power. His policy also was in many respects a reversal of that of the old king. He formed a close alliance with England, under George I. and his Whig ministers, and a little later with Holland against Spain, whose king disputed his title to the regency. The duke caused strict investigation to be made into the finances, and often by harsh and unjustifiable measures materially reduced the burden on the country. But the reign of Lewis XV. had received from its predecessor too vast a heritage of disorder, and before its distant close it was marked by terrible and costly wars, and by misgovernment greater than the nation could endure.

<small>Duke of Orleans. His policy.</small>

CHAPTER XX.

THE FRAGMENTS THAT REMAIN.

THERE are several who have played parts more or less important in this history, and whose later careers we must follow to an end before parting with them.

The great Duke of Marlborough had lived in dignified retirement on the Continent during all the latter part of the queen's reign. Hearing that the queen was not likely to live, he made preparations to return to England. Having been for some time detained by contrary winds at Ostend, on landing at Dover he received the news of the queen's death and of the quiet accession of the new sovereign. When George I. reinstated the Whigs in office, Marlborough was made captain-general or commander-in-

<small>Duke of Marlborough.</small>

chief of the army. In that capacity he superintended the military arrangements that suppressed the rising of 1715. A little later he suffered from a severe attack of paralysis, but not such as to hinder his attendance in the House of Lords and the performance of official duties. In 1722 he died, and was honoured with a splendid funeral in Westminster Abbey. The Duchess of Marlborough survived her husband many years, and died at the advanced age of eighty-four. She occupied herself in drawing up a vindication of the duke's conduct and her own, which offers valuable material to the historian.

In the treaty of Utrecht, the interests of one people had been shamefully neglected by the allies. The people of Catalonia had taken up arms at the instigation of the English, especially of Lord Peterborough. They had fought valiantly for the cause of the Austrian claimant. But in the negotiations the allies deserted them. When the English made peace they withdrew the remnant of their troops from Barcelona. When the emperor continued the war by himself, in order to concentrate his forces he was obliged to withdraw his soldiers also. The King of Spain was about to treat them as subdued rebels. But the inhabitants determined to resist to the uttermost. They fought valiantly, and gallantly defended Barcelona; but the Spanish king was able to procure French soldiers, and the services of Marshal Berwick; and thus the heroic resistance was in vain. In the September after the death of Queen Anne, Barcelona was stormed and taken. *[margin: The Catalonians.]*

By the treaty of Utrecht, Victor Amadeus, Duke of Savoy, was made King of Sicily. Five years later, Sicily was exchanged for Sardinia. His descend-

Victor Amadeus, Duke of Savoy and King of Sicily, then of Sardinia.

ants remained kings of Sardinia, until in our own time the title was merged in the greater title of King of Italy. During this period of peace he displayed as great talents for administration of his kingdom as he had previously shown for war.

In 1730 he determined to abdicate in favour of Charles Emanuel, his only surviving son. By no means an able man, Charles had hitherto been kept at a distance by his father, who frequently avowed his dislike of him.

His abdication.

A little more than a year after his father's abdication, the new king of Sardinia held a meeting of his council, at which it was decided that the old king should be placed under arrest. He was very harshly treated, soldiers being sent in the night-time, who tore him from his wife and hurried him away to prison. In a little more than a year again, he died in confinement. It was said that he had shown a desire to regain the crown which he had surrendered, but he had no force at his disposal, and there is no evidence that the charge was true. He really fell a victim to the ambition of a minister who wished to establish a greater influence over the young king.

In Spain a singular act of abdication took place. Philip, who remained king as the result of the War of Succession, abdicated in 1724 in favour of his son, and retired to a monastery, but upon his son's death in the next year resumed power, though professing that it was against his will.

Philip V. in Spain. His abdication

It remains to give an account of the other and unsuccessful claimant of the Spanish crown, whom we have known as Archduke Charles, and after the death of his brother, Emperor. He never could be induced quite to give up his claim on Spain, and the result was that he was never on good terms with that country. But his latter history is chiefly famous on account of the war that ensued upon his death. He had no son that lived beyond infancy, but he had a daughter, the beautiful and famous Maria Theresa. On this account he prepared a document called the Pragmatic Sanction (a name given to certain very important State documents), by which he decreed that, failing male issue, his daughter was to succeed to his hereditary dominions. To securing promises of adhesion to this Pragmatic Sanction, Charles seems to have devoted all the energies of the last fifteen years of his life. His diplomacy seemed successful; but when he died in 1740, the promises were not kept, and a tedious war arose, England taking the part of Maria Theresa, France and Prussia supporting the Duke of Bavaria against her.

The Emperor Charles.

CHAPTER XXI.

ECONOMIC AND SOCIAL.

Section I.—Population. Towns. Architecture.

BEFORE we consider the social and economic condition of the people of England in the reign of Queen Anne, it would be advisable to discover how many people there were. Unfortunately there is no census to guide us, as it was not until the beginning of this century that statesmen had the wisdom to require an accurate calculation on which taxation could be based. The elements for an estimate are twofold. First, we

Population.

know the number of houses that paid the hearth tax, which might have been called a house tax, for it was a certain sum from every house; and we can multiply that by what is known to be the average number of inmates of a house, viz. five. Secondly, there was a register of deaths, and a calculation can be based upon the average rate of mortality. This information is not as precise as a census, and the calculations make the population of England and Wales vary between five and seven millions. It is now about twenty-four millions. He was a wise man who wrote—

> It is not growing like a tree
> In bulk, doth make man better be;

and a country is not to be considered as necessarily in a better condition because its population has increased; on the contrary its condition is worse, unless the growth has been proportionate in other respects.

Of the whole population of England and Wales one-tenth was at that time included within London, but with

Country rather than town.

that exception the country had a very much larger share than the towns. Bristol, the next town in population, was only one-seventeenth of London, and many towns which were considered of importance had populations which would now be thought very small. During the period from Queen Anne's time to our own the growth of manufactures has been continually drawing the people from the country into towns. If a line be drawn from the mouth of the Severn to the junction of Ouse and Trent, where the river Humber commences, one might say that, roughly speaking, it would now divide the manufacturing from the agricultural parts of the country, that with the exception of London the great towns lie to the north and west of the line, and that the preponderance of political power rests with them. With equal confidence one might assert that in Queen Anne's time this line separated the important from the unimportant parts of England, all that lay to the north and west being comparatively unimportant.

The facilities of locomotion which have helped the growth of manufacture, brought about, first, by the improvement in roads, then in coaches and waggons, lastly in railways, have also conspired to send the country people into the towns, have emptied the small into the larger towns, have in favour of London destroyed the social prestige of country capitals, and of towns which were social centres of large districts. The following may be regarded as a list of the chief English towns, after London, in the order of their importance, during Queen Anne's reign :—Bristol, the chief sea-port; Norwich, the largest manufacturing city; York, the capital of the northern counties; Exeter, the capital of the western district; Shrewsbury, of the counties along the Welsh border, and well situated for intercourse with Wales; Worcester, in which the porcelain manufacture was beginning to rise. To these would have to be added Derby, Nottingham, Canterbury. {Important towns.}

The population of London was then about 700,000, that is, one-tenth of that of England and Wales. Modern London, with all its suburbs, in the widest circuit that is called London, that is to say, the postal districts, covers a much larger area, and contains about 4,000,000 inhabitants. This makes it considerably more than one-tenth of the United Kingdom, and one-sixth of England and Wales, so that if the growth has been remarkable elsewhere, it has been portentous in London. The earlier growth had been {London.}

noticed, and had caused concern to the Government. In the reign of Elizabeth, and under the Stuart kings, building had been prohibited. But it was found impossible to stop the growth of London; it would have been as practicable to stop a tree from putting out its branches and its leaves. A great calamity befell London in the reign of Charles II. It was burnt down; but far from checking the growth, this only made room for a fresh start. Here was an opportunity to build the city anew on a systematic plan, and the Government of the day commissioned the greatest living architect, Sir Christopher Wren, to draw up such a plan for the city. This can still be seen, with his own Cathedral of St. Paul's standing in a free space in the centre, broad wide streets leading from it, spacious squares at due intervals, wide and convenient quays along the banks of the Thames; but, building in accordance with the plans not being strictly enforced, the opportunity was lost.

London was built hastily after the fire, and many conveniences which are now thought necessary, and which might have been supplied had a little more time been taken, were neglected. Not only were the streets narrow and irregular, but there was no arrangement for sewers, and there were no gutters to the streets. The police service also was very bad; "the watch" was wholly insufficient in numbers, and was composed chiefly of old men. The streets were badly lighted of a night, and it was quite easy for anyone bent on mischief to overpower the watch. Of course thieves and robbers availed themselves of the power; but others also, who should have known better, took occasion not to rob but to riot. Young men of birth and fashion used to form themselves into clubs, banded together for the sole purpose of creating disturbances. The most fashionable of these, the Mohawks, were a terror to all peace-loving citizens, their name being taken from the wild tribe of North American Indians. An ancient writer mentions it as a sign of progress in civilisation when men cease to wear swords. This stage had not been reached in Queen Anne's reign, when the young bucks and dandies of society were always ready to draw their rapiers, and the honest citizens had to arm themselves with bludgeons.

The London of Queen Anne's day consisted of two parts, then more distinct than now, the City and Westminster. The space between them was not built over. But London proper, what is strictly called the City, was no longer sufficient to contain all the inhabitants, and fashionable life had already begun that movement to the West which is so remarkable a feature in the history of London. The fashionable quarters then were the neighbourhood of Great Ormond Street and Queen's Square. To the West lay Kensington, a separate village where was King William's Palace. Both London and Westminster may be said each to have had two centres, one secular and the other ecclesiastical: London, the Exchange and St. Paul's; Westminster, the Parliament Houses and the Abbey, or Minster, whence the place had its name.

The City and Westminster.

The Exchange was the commercial centre, and indeed may be said at this time to have become the centre of the commerce of the world. In the Middle Ages Venice was the centre of the world's trade. The invention of the compass took away this supremacy from Venice, as mariners were no longer confined to coasting voyages. The extreme commercial activity of the Netherlands next made Bruges and Antwerp the centre, and they retained

The Exchange and London's commerce.

this supremacy during the Reformation period. The persecution of the Protestants by the Spanish Government, and the fierce fighting which followed the Revolt of the Netherlands, destroyed this. Commerce was driven from Antwerp through the long siege by the Duke of Parma, which ended in the year that followed Elizabeth's death. During the next century, the seventeenth, the supremacy of trade lay between Amsterdam and London, the former having the best of it until the English Civil War was over; but in the latter half of the century London was beginning to prevail. The commercial rivalry between the English and the Dutch was very keen, and their commerce was nearly equal; but the plan was slowly though surely passing to England. Tyre in Fénelon's "Télémaque," is supposed to be Amsterdam; but if he had written a quarter of a century later he would probably have described London. The following passage from the "Spectator" gives Addison's picture of the Exchange, which, it must be remembered, is neither the Exchange that now is, nor that originally built by Sir Thomas Gresham, but the second, namely, that which was built after the Great Fire, and which was itself destroyed by fire in 1838:—

"There is no place in the Town which I so much love to frequent as the Royal Exchange. It gives me a secret Satisfaction, and in some measure gratifies my Vanity, as I am an Englishman, to see so rich an Assembly of Countrymen and Foreigners consulting together upon the private Business of Mankind, and making this Metropolis a kind of Emporium for the whole Earth. I must confess I look upon High Change to be a great Council, in which all considerable Nations have their Representatives. . . . I have often been pleased to hear Disputes adjusted between an Inhabitant of Japan and an Alderman of London, or to see a Subject of the Great Mogul entering into a League with one of the Czar of Muscovy."

The only art that really flourished in Queen Anne's time was Architecture, and that because England happened to possess an architect of consummate genius. Sir Christopher Wren was a man of great attainments, being especially learned in astronomy and in mechanics, and one of the first members of the Royal Society founded in the reign of Charles II. He was as modest as he was learned, and perhaps would have been treated with more respect in that age if he had more firmly asserted his own rights. He was not especially educated for the profession of an architect, but when he was appointed king's surveyor he at once showed himself a master of the art. With all the architects of his day, he evidently preferred the classical style. Before the Fire, he was asked to restore old St. Paul's, which was in the Gothic style, and he did add some towers to Westminster Abbey, which are amongst his least successful productions. But whilst the question of the restoration of St. Paul's was being debated, and the battle of the styles being fought, the Great Fire put an end to the controversy. St. Paul's is Wren's greatest work, though some say that the church of St. Stephen's, Walbrook, is a more perfect specimen of his art. It was a dean of St. Paul's that wrote of the Cathedral: "What eye, trained to all that is perfect in architecture, does not recognise the inimitable beauty of its lines, the majestic yet airy swelling of its dome, its rich, harmonious ornamentation?"

As the subscriptions for the rebuilding of St. Paul's did not come in fast enough, Parliament voted that a

Cost. portion of the duty on coals should be applied to the purpose. The total cost of the cathedral was 747,661*l.* 10*s.* 5*d.* The first stone was laid in Wren's presence, June 21, 1675, the nine years since the fire having been spent in making designs, and the highest stone of the lantern in the cupola was also set by his son in his presence in 1710. It is rare in the history of great buildings, especially of cathedrals, that they should be finished in the lifetime of the original architect. Indeed, it was a marvel both on account of its cheapness, and because of the short time in which it was built. After the completion of the cathedral, it was voted by the Parliament in 1711 that fifty new churches should be built, and that the portion of the coal duty which had been expended on St. Paul's should be applied to that purpose. It is not known how many of these churches were actually built. Yet we may say that most of the London churches, built since the Fire, are of Wren's designing. Fault is found with him because his churches are not Gothic, an objection which seems to imply that there is only one order of ecclesiastical architecture, and surely narrows the art; and also because he mixed the styles in putting steeples, which are a feature of Gothic architecture, over buildings, and especially over porticoes, in the Greek style. The defence is this, that architecture having had its full development, and absolutely new invention being impossible, the originality of a modern architect consists in skilful composition and harmonious proportions. If the combination does not offend the eye, it is pedantry to object that it runs counter to the traditions of the art.

Wren's style.

By way of contrast with Sir C. Wren, it may be well to mention another architect of the day. Sir John

Vanbrugh had distinguished himself as a writer of very coarse comic dramas. As men used to change from soldier to sailor, so Sir J. Vanbrugh became an architect. He built his own house out of the ruins of Whitehall. A brother architect compared it to "a flat Dutch oven," and Swift has a funny little poem about the house, describing everyone as hunting for it up and down the river banks and unable to find it, until at length they did—

> In the rubbish spy
> A thing resembling a goose-pie.

This was the architect who was chosen to build for a grateful nation, at an expense of half a million pounds, Blenheim Palace, near Woodstock, to be presented to the victorious Duke of Marlborough. It is imposing chiefly on account of its size, but the style is very heavy, and justifies the epigram written on the architect:

> Lie heavy on him, earth, for he
> Laid many a heavy load on thee.

The immense improvement in one city should be mentioned, because it began within this period. Bath was known as a watering-place as long ago as the Roman occupation of Britain. It seems always to have preserved its reputation, but it was so uncomfortable that no one cared to stay there, unless for the purposes of health. In the first year of Queen Anne's reign a man of fashion—one Richard Nash, nicknamed Beau Nash—paid it a visit, as some say, in order to replenish a purse emptied by gambling, as well as to mend health broken by dissipation. He at once set to work to increase the cheerfulness of the place, and to provide amusement for those who resorted to it. His genius for organization was quickly recognised, and he was appointed Master of the Ceremonies in 1704. From that time, for a period of nearly fifty years, he may be described as king of Bath, whilst squares and terraces, pump-rooms and public buildings, rose almost like magic; till under his auspices Bath became the well-ordered city that it now is, deserving, with its magnificent situation, the title of the queen of watering-places.

Section II.—The Poor Statistics.

It seems advisable to collect under one head some scattered information on the history of the English poor.

History of the poor. Serf.

Under the feudal system the poor man was a serf. The difference between a slave and a serf is that the former is a personal chattel and might be sold, the latter could not be sold away from the estate, but had no personal liberty. He was not able to move from the place where he was born, and he was obliged to serve one particular lord. In A.D 1346 came the pestilence known as the Black Death, which cut off half the labouring population of England, and by a

Black Death.

well-known economic law raised the position of those that were left, because as there were fewer labourers their services were more in demand. The result was that Parliament passed the Statute of Labourers to compel the labourer to work for certain wages. That the position of the labourers was improved is shown by the fact that their class, under Walter the tiler and others, raised an insurrection at the opening of the next reign, a thing which their grandsires would never have dreamt of doing.

The next great event in the history of the poor was

the suppression of the monasteries. There can be no doubt that the monasteries supplied bed and board to those who asked, thus conferring a great blessing on those who could not, and an equally great bane on the idle who would not, work. The suppression of these religious houses in the reign of Henry VIII. had the effect of letting a flood of poor loose upon society; and its necessary results may be seen in two Acts of Parliament—the first Poor Law and the first Statute of Vagrants.

Suppression of monasteries.

The statue against vagrants in Henry VIII.'s reign enacted that the "sturdy and valiant" beggar, the man who can work and will not, was to be whipped at the cart's tail; the statute of Elizabeth enacted that he was to be whipped and branded in the ear, that whoever liked might put a collar on him and make him a servant; the statue of Charles II., that he should be transported to the English plantations beyond the seas. In Queen Anne's reign a statute was passed that beggars should be put into the army, and as soldiers were well paid, they should certainly have felt that this was kind treatment.

Statute of Vagrants.

The Poor Law of Henry VIII. was modified in the reign of Elizabeth, but the statute then passed lasted until the great Reform Bill. Churchwardens and overseers were to "provide work, build poor-houses, and apprentice paupers."

Poor Law.

It is generally allowed that what the poor can fairly claim is relief for the sick and the infirm, who cannot work, and work for those who are able-bodied, but who are absolutely unable to find it. It is with the latter in view that what used to be called the poor-house is now called the work-house. The work-house should not be made too comfortable, because men should be taught that they ought to support themselves, and not be supported by others. In Queen Anne's reign there were 1,330,000 paupers, or nearly one in five of the whole population. Men often complain, now-a-days, of the burden of pauperism; but the proportion of paupers has very much diminished. In the year 1873 there were, in round numbers, 890,000. It is thought that this number is too large, and with discreet measures can, and will be reduced. Yet, this is only one in twenty-seven of the population. Side by side with this calculation one must, however, place the cost. The paupers of Queen Anne's reign cost 900,000*l.* in the year, or about 14*s.* apiece, whilst the poor rate in 1873 amounted to 13,000,000*l.*, or 14*l.* apiece. Now, the decrease in the value of money since that time is not nearly in the ratio of one to twenty. This shows, therefore, that the pauper is more expensively housed and cared for in the present day, and probably, also, that he is a more permanent charge; for the pauper of Queen Anne's day can only have been at times "upon the parish," as the 14*s.* would not suffice to keep him more than a third of the year. As some must have been permanently upon the parish, others, who were but a temporary charge must be included in the calculation.

Pauperism in Queen Anne's reign.

There is no doubt that the value of money has considerably decreased since the reign of Anne, but it is not easy to find the exact figure by which our money should be multiplied. It is said that the price of a sheep was 7*s.*, and of an ox 2*l.* This would make meat rather less than a penny a pound. The same observer says that 2*l.* 5*s.* would keep a labouring man in food for a year. But prices varied from year to year much more than they vary now, because the country was much more depend-dent on its own harvest than it is now. In the present day so much corn is imported, that the deficiency of an English harvest can be made up, without a great or sudden change in general prices. The fluctuations in the price of wheat were remarkable: at 56s. 6d. a quarter in 1699, it went down to 25s. 6d. after the abundant harvest of 1702. There was a deficient harvest next year, and prices doubled. In 1706 again we are told that the kingdom was blessed with plenty, and the people cheerfully contributed to the expenses of the war. But the winter of 1708 in England, as in France, was terribly severe; it was noticed that the wheat was all destroyed on the north-east side of the furrows, a fact which points to the prevalence of cutting north-east winds. Wages averaged about 10d. a day. The pay of a soldier was 8d., whereas the French soldier only had 3d. A private in the present day receives 1s. 2d., besides barrack-room, pension, and facilities for buying food cheaper. The labourer probably had better wages, but he had no facilities for saving beyond an old stocking. There were no investments open to him, and no savings bank.

England and Wales may be said roughly to consist of thirty-seven million acres; and a glance at the following table will show how these acres were and are distributed:— *The land.*

	Then.	Now.
Arable	9	14½
Meadow (including park)	12	12
Woods	6	2
Unfit for cultivation	10	8½

The staple produce of England was corn. The popula-

tion being so much smaller, and, at the same time, a
larger part of it being employed in agriculture, the country was easily able to supply her own needs of wheat.

Corn.

The second produce was wool. England had long been a wool-growing country; her meadows were famous for the breed of sheep; her chancellor sat upon the woolsack. But it had been the custom to send all the wool over to the Continent to be manufactured. Many English statesmen had regretted this, but the wool still went over. Then came small beginnings of the cloth manufacture in England. Edward III. had imported families of cloth-workers from the Netherlands; and it is said that, in his reign, the name "worsted" was given to the yarn made from spun wool, after a small town of that name in Norfolk. In order to foster the manufacture in England, various statutes were made to encourage the natives to exclude the foreign cloth: in 1696 the latter was absolutely prohibited, and in the reign of Charles II. it had been decreed that everyone was to be buried in woollen cloth. In old church registers one may find the entry, "buried in wool." Further, Irish wool was prohibited, and not only Irish wool but Irish linen. Of course Englishmen could not complain when the same protective policy was repeated in another country, and British as well as Irish woollen goods absolutely prohibited in France. Of the English manufacture Leeds was already the centre, but it was a town of very different size from the Leeds of to-day. Its population is now thirty-seven times as large. But in our days the woollen manufacture is only the third of English manufactures—that of cotton being about two and a half times as large, and iron standing second.

Wool.

Cotton was then beginning to raise its head, and the policy that had always discouraged all rivals to English wool was repeated. A statute was passed in 1700 (the year in which Charles II. of Spain died), prohibiting the importation of cotton goods, such as Indian muslins and chintzes. The competition, however, most to be feared was not the manufactured goods, but the fibre imported from America to be made in England into goods; and that business must have assumed some dimensions when, in 1701, cotton goods worth 23,000*l.* were exported. The amount is now three and a half times as many millions as thousands then.

<small>Cotton.</small>

Other manufactures were still very young. The coal fields were not largely worked, as coal was only required for domestic purposes. That from Newcastle-upon-Tyne was considered the best. Sheffield, famous for its "whittles" even in Chaucer's time, kept up its reputation for cutlery, though the manufacture was on a small scale. The French refugees who settled in England, and who vexed the Tories because their Protestantism was not that of the English Church, introduced several valuable branches of manufacture; silk weaving was the chief, but to these also must be added, glass, paper, and hats. All the gold and silver came into Europe from America, through Spain, entering by Cadiz, "the golden gate of the Indies."

<small>Manufactures.</small>

There can be no doubt, as regards the standard of comfort, that the English people were far beyond other European nations. Ambassadors wrote to express astonishment that the food was so good, that the consumption of beer, spirits, and foreign wine was so large, and that articles of luxury imported from distant lands were in such general use. An

<small>Standard of comfort.</small>

English writer of the time estimates, indeed, that only half the labouring class ate animal food more than twice a week, but in proportion to wages meat was much cheaper then than it is now. The consumption of beer seems enormous. It was calculated that in the year after the Revolution a quart a day was brewed for every man, woman, and child in England; whereas the same calculation makes the amount in the present day sixty quarts per annum, or just one-sixth. It would not be a fair conclusion that the English are now a more sober people because less beer is drunk, for a great deal that was brewed was very small beer. The majority of the English people have three meals a day—breakfast, dinner, and tea, and it is only at one of these that the larger portion ever touch beer. The choice then lay between wine or spirits, cider, beer, milk, or water. It is to two

Tea.

beverages that have since passed into common use, tea and coffee, that the diminution in the amount of beer is due. Tea, or as it was then always pronounced, *tay*,

(And gentle Anna, whom three realms obey,
Does sometimes counsel take and sometimes tea.—POPE.)

was first brought into England by the Dutch nearly a century earlier, but during the whole seventeenth century it was regarded as a rare luxury. Mr. Pepys drank his first cup of tea on September 25, 1661, describing it as—" A China drink, of which I had never drunk before." In the reign of Charles II. the East India Company presented the king with two pounds of tea. But during the latter years of the century and through the reign of Queen Anne its use as a beverage was rapidly spreading. We have an estimate of the consumption just after the accession of George II. It amounted in the year to 700,000 lbs., and the price, depending on the quality, varied between thirteen shillings and twenty shillings a pound. The amount imported into England in 1872 was 185,000,000 lbs.

Coffee was making its way at the same time. Coffee was imported from the Levant, which it easily reached from Arabia, its home. It was first brought into England by a Cretan gentleman, who made it his common beverage at Balliol College, Oxford, in the year when the Long Parliament first met. Coffee became a social power earlier than tea. The Greek servant of an English Turkey merchant from Smyrna is said to have started the first coffee-house in London in the time of the Commonwealth. About the end of the seventeenth century, coffee-houses were very common, and important as a means of social and political intercourse amongst men. They filled the place that is now filled by the London clubs. Some were chiefly political places of resort for only one party; others, especially the famous Wills', in Covent Garden, were literary. Those who wished to see, to hear, or perhaps to bow to a prominent literary man, such as Dryden or Addison, would find him at the coffee-house. These houses had great influence in the formation of opinions. Men now-a-days often take their opinion from their club or their newspaper; then they took it from the coffee-house.

Coffee.

On the general question of the far-brought supply of luxuries one may, with advantage, read the following passages from the paper in the "Spectator" which begins with the glories of the Exchange:—

Luxuries.

"Almost every Degree produces something peculiar

to it. The Food often grows in one Country, and the Sauce in another. The Fruits of Portugal are corrected by the Products of Barbadoes, the Infusion of a China Plant sweetened with the Pith of an Indian Cane. The Philippick Islands give a Flavour to our European Bowls. The single Dress of a Woman of Quality is often the Product of a hundred Climates. The Muff and the Fan come together from the different Ends of the Earth. The Scarf is sent from the Torrid Zone and the Tippet from beneath the Pole. The Brocade Petticoat rises out of the Mines of Peru, and the Diamond Necklace out of the Bowels of Indostan.

"Our Ships are laden with the Harvest of every Climate: our Tables are stored with Spices and Oils and Wines: our Rooms are filled with Pyramids of China, and adorned with the Workmanship of Japan: our Morning's Draught comes to us from the remotest Corners of the Earth: we repair our Bodies by the Drugs of America, and repose ourselves under Indian Canopies. My Friend Sir Andrew calls the Vineyards of France our Gardens: the Spice Islands our Hot-beds: the Persians our Silk-weavers, and the Chinese our Potters."

England and Wales consumed eleven million pounds of tobacco, and sent on no less than seventeen millions to the Continent, all of which came from the English plantation in Virginia.

One other point should be especially noticed—the change in the taste for wine which was brought about during this reign. Since the days of the Black Prince, and earlier, there had been a large English trade with Bordeaux. The favourite wines in England were the French, which passed then, as often now, under the general name of claret. In the year before the English Revolution, the amount of French wine imported was three and a half times as much as that from Spain and Portugal together. The Methuen Treaty with Portugal, however, decided that the tax upon Portuguese wines admitted into England should always be one-third less than that on French, for which privilege Portugal was to import no woollen goods but English. The old Tories, and especially those in Oxford Common Rooms, were very strong in favour of their Burgundy, and would gladly have seen the Methuen Treaty cancelled: but the result of that treaty was a change in the public taste; and for more than a century port reigned supreme, until that in its turn became a sort of emblem of Toryism. One evil followed. The port was much stronger than the claret, but men drank the same quantity with very bad results: a great deal of the hard drinking which distinguished the eighteenth century can fairly be traced to the Methuen Treaty.

Port ousts claret.

> Firm and erect the Caledonian stood;
> Sweet was his mutton and his claret good.
> "Thou shalt drink port," the English statesman cried;
> He drank the poison, and his spirit died.

Section III.— National Debt.

The account of this time would not be complete without some statement of the debt of the country. It was not indeed in this reign that the practice of making posterity pay began, but in this reign the practice was vigorously carried on.

The principle of a National Debt is just the same as that of a debt incurred by a private individual. If some-

General principle of a debt.

thing has to be done, the advantage of which is not confined to one year, there is no reason that a man should pay for it out of income. It is quite fair to make posterity pay in part for advantages which posterity will enjoy: and circumstances may arise which justify placing part of the burden of a war on the future. Strictly, however, such a war should be defensive, for in self-defence the nation is defending posterity's freedom as well as its own; but, with respect to other quarrels, posterity may be expected to have its own. There was a small national debt in England before the Revolution, Charles II. having taken the money of the goldsmiths and having told them that he would pay interest, though he would not repay the principal. The payment of interest was so neglected by the Treasury, that the owners of the money had well-nigh given up hope, when the Revolution took place. The debt was then acknowledged, and became the nucleus of the Funds. Whatever blessings the Glorious Revolution conferred upon England, it is to the Revolution that we owe the National Debt. The system of funding was brought from Holland, and the policy of interference in Continental wars was commenced by the Revolution. This is not the place to consider how far England was bound in honour to enter upon those wars, or whether the "balance of power" was a delusion. It is in Queen Anne's reign that we first hear of stocks going up or down, forming what has been described as a national pulse, so that the skilful man may be able to tell whether the state of the nation is healthy. The creation of the public funds has undoubtedly helped in the formation of a moneyed class in opposition to the landed interests.

But unfortunately when once the rulers had learnt

how easy it was to raise a loan, and throw the payment on the future, the necessity for care was removed. They were spending another generation's money, not their own. The following table will show with what fatal readiness the lesson was learnt. The figures represent millions of pounds :— {Later history of the Debt.}

Loans, or posterity's share.

William's War, ending with Peace of Ryswick	13½
The Spanish Succession War	38
The wars in George II.'s reign, and including the whole of the Seven Years' War	86
War of American Independence	121
Great French or Napoleonic War	600

In the earlier wars the taxation was nearly equal to the loans. But in the worst and most unnecessary, the American, the taxation did not amount to one-third of the debt incurred. The example has been followed also by other nations, and the debts of the world now amount to no less than 4,000,000,000*l.*

The change of public sentiment on the subject of the debt is shown by the fact that Swift thought the amount so great that he was in favour of repudiation. The Whigs always made out that such a policy would have been pursued if the Pretender had been restored. Addison, with his usual felicity, describes a dream which fell upon him after a visit to the bank. It is a vision of Public Credit, a beautiful virgin, whose touch could turn what she pleased to gold. Magna Charta, the Acts of Uniformity, Toleration, and Settlement are on the walls. She is easily affected by news, wastes quickly away, and recovers with equal quickness. Then, in a dance, entered hideous phantoms, two by two, at sight of which the lady fainted. {Repudiation.}

They were Tyranny and Anarchy, Bigotry and Atheism, the Genius of a commonwealth, with a young man about twenty-two years of age. He had a sword in his right hand, which in the dance he often brandished at the Act of Settlement. A citizen whispered that he saw a sponge in his left hand. This was the Pretender, and the sponge was to wipe out the national debt. The scene vanished, and a second dance entered of amiable phantoms, Liberty and Monarchy, Moderation and Religion, a third person (whom Addison had then never seen, the Elector of Hanover), with the Genius of Great Britain. Whereupon Public Credit revived, and there were pyramids of guineas.

Statesmen of the present day see the need of making a provision for repayment, though, as money continually decreases in value, the burden continually becomes of less weight in proportion. When the French war ended the amount was 840 and it is now 780 millions.

"Woe to England," has been the warning of thinkers, "when the coal fields are exhausted and the national debt remains unpaid!"

Section IV.—*Strength of parties. The Clergy.*

As it was in the reign of Anne that parties began to assume the shape which they have kept almost to our own times, it seems advisable to consider the classes of society from which the two parties respectively drew their strength. One must premise that the great bulk of the English people belongs to no party, but, being as it were between the two, sways from one to the other, according as their sense of justice or the prejudices of passion may incline them. When the Long Parliament met, the bulk of the people were opposed to the Court. Twenty years later at the

Parties. The bulk of no party.

Restoration they were as certainly for the Stuarts, and as surely at the Revolution against them. We may note also the sudden change in the queen's reign, when the same mob that had cheered Marlborough shouted for Dr. Sacheverell. The same reflection helps to explain sudden changes of our own as well as of other days.

The strength of the Tories lay in the country rather than in the towns, in the small boroughs rather than in the large towns, in the agricultural rather than in the moneyed interest. The tenant farmers were mostly Tories. Almost all the clergy, and especially the country clergy, were to be found in the Tory ranks. As an extreme wing of the Tory clergy must be ranked the non-jurors, those who resigned place rather than take the oath of allegiance to William and Mary, a sect numerically unimportant, but comprising several men who were distinguished for learning and for piety.

Tories.

The Whigs were strong in the large towns, London being especially staunch to them. The merchants and bankers, as well as most of the small freeholders in the country, were Whigs. A good many of the lords and of the bishops belonged to that party; but this was because the former had been created, and the latter appointed, by King William. To these must be added the whole body of the Dissenters, who were estimated to amount to 4 per cent. of the population.

Whigs.

As the Universities were the recruiting ground of the clergy, we should expect that the Tory party would be strong in them. It was, however, much stronger at Oxford than at Cambridge. Shortly after the accession of George I., at the time of the rising for the old Pretender, it was found necessary to send soldiers down to

Oxford to keep order. At the same time the king happened to be sending a present of books to the sister University.

An Oxford epigram was written—

> The king observing, with judicious eyes,
> The state of both his universities,
> To Oxford sent a troop of horse; and why?
> That learned body wanted loyalty;
> To Cambridge books he sent, as well discerning
> How much that loyal body wanted learning.

A Cambridge man replied—

> The king to Oxford sent a troop of horse,
> For Tories own no argument but force;
> With equal skill to Cambridge books he sent,
> For Whigs admit no force but argument.

There was a great difference between the clergy of the towns and of the country; the London clergy, especially, were often men of mark. But the great majority of the clergy were both in learning and in social position far below the standard of the present day. It was estimated that not one benefice in forty was worth 100*l.* a year, so that the "passing rich on 40*l.* a year," of Goldsmith's poem would not then have excited the smile that it now does; and as the Church of England wisely allows its clergy to marry, there was very general misery and distress amongst their families. Bishop Burnet claims the credit of having suggested a method of improving their position, first to William and then to Anne The humane heart of Anne at once approved the suggestion, and Parliament was found quite willing to sanction the plan. In the times before the Reformation it had been the practice to give to the Pope first-fruits and tithes, that is, the whole of

The clergy.
Queen Anne's Bounty.

the first year's revenue, and a tithe of all later years. When Henry VIII. pillaged the Church this revenue was seized by the Crown, and Burnet's suggestion was to apply this fund to the improvement of the livings of the poorer clergy. It is still called Queen Anne's Bounty.

CHAPTER XXII.

LITERATURE.

Section I.—*French Literature.*

THE age of Lewis XIV. is often called the Augustan Age of French Literature. That name compares it with the time when under the rule and patronage of Augustus, Roman literature reached its most polished if not its most original epoch, and when the masterpieces of most of the great Latin authors were written. The period is often made to include works which really belonged to earlier times. Nor did the system of State patronage begin with Lewis. Some of his predecessors had encouraged literature. To one of them, Cardinal Richelieu, France owes the establishment of the Academy, which, itself to a great extent the creature of patronage, was intended in a sense to be the vehicle of the king's patronage to others. Pensions were freely bestowed on authors, and literature was intended to become a branch of the civil service. The Academy was to draw up a code of laws for the literary, by producing treatises on rhetoric and poetics, and to compile a dictionary of the French language, which, in the seventeenth century, was assuming its present shape. Patronage certainly cannot create

Augustan Age of French Literature.

Patronage.

genius any more than rules can make a poet. It is within its power to promote culture; but it will be found that its tendency is to dwarf genius. Despotism cannot give genius, but it can stifle it; for really great men will not long endure to live in the atmosphere of a despotic court, and to shape their voices only to speech that is agreeable there. They may for a time be content to dedicate their works to a king who is their paymaster, and to let their dedications be fulsome. Racine died in disgrace because he spoke out about the miserable condition of the French peasantry, and Boileau left the Court saying, "What should I do there? I know not how to flatter."

It is impossible to separate from the system of patronage the most marked characteristic of the era, that everything must be done according to rule.

All according to rule.

If patronage stifled genius on one side, rules stifled it on the other. The drama was hidebound by the doctrine of the three unities—of time, of place, and of action, fetters to which Shakespeare had never subjected his genius. It was an age in which poetry was reduced to an art, that is, a body of rules which can be taught. Boileau, in imitation of Horace, wrote the "Art of Poetry." Pope, in turn, in the so-called Augustan Age in England, copied Boileau as well as Horace in the "Essay on Criticism."

An instructive lesson with respect to the age of Lewis XIV., is to be learnt in the fact that its great authors and artists fell within the first half of it. The year 1688, which witnessed the English Revolution, divides the real reign of Lewis XIV., that is, the time during which he himself governed, into two equal halves. It has been noticed that almost all the great ornaments of the time died be-

Greatness in first half of reign.

fore this year. It would seem to follow that the effects of patronage are only spasmodic and not permanent. The literary greatness of the reign was over at the same time as its military successes; and with the beginning of the new century, and in the general misery of the Spanish Succession War, the character of the literature changed. A new epoch had begun whose tone breathed rebellion against the previous spirit.

It is, however, necessary to sketch in outline the prominent features of the literature of the whole reign, in order to understand both its results, and the rebellion against its influence.

First, the reign was very strong in the drama, having, besides minor authors, three illustrious dramatists, Molière, Corneille, and Racine, of whom the first wrote comedies, the other two chiefly tragedies. At first *Molière* seems only to have had in view the amusement of an audience; but he soon learnt that the poet should also teach. Whilst standing well with the Court he attacked, in an exquisitely ludicrous style, the follies and foibles of the day; at one time the pedantic affectation of the learned women, at another the cumbrous and antiquated jargon of the doctors, then the pious hypocrite, the citizen who imitated the nobility, or the frivolous noble. *Corneille* has the title of Father of French Tragedy. He is distinguished for simplicity. He paints the conflict between private and public passions, the conflict between love and honour, or religion or duty. He drew both the subjects of his plays and his method of treatment from Spain; whilst *Racine* who succeeded him drew his inspiration rather from ancient Greece. In his hands French tragedy was framed upon Greek models, and almost all his subjects are taken either from classical or from sacred antiquity. "Andromaque" was his first and "Athalie" his last play. His plays are remarkable for grace of expression, rhythm and correctness. He always conforms to the three unities, that there shall be no impossibilities on the stage, no asking the audience to pass over time or space.

The age of Lewis XIV. is, secondly, famous for the development of French prose, and therein especially for the composition of letters and of memoirs. The letters of *Madame de Sevigné* and the memoirs of the *Duc de Saint Simon*, chief chamberlain at the King's Court, may be selected as representatives. The former are witty, tender, and always in good taste. The latter, which belong, perhaps, rather to a later age, are full of the gossip of this and the succeeding reign, every species of anecdote, everything small and great being recorded by a vivacious eye-witness.

French prose.

It was to be expected that theology would flourish; but it was for the most part a courtly theology, and inspired by the Jesuits. The eloquence of the pulpit became very famous. *Bossuet*, Bishop of Meaux, was the chief of the preachers, and his excellence lay especially in funeral orations. Bossuet may be said to have applied to religion the teaching which Lewis inculcated in politics. With him all opposition was wrong, whether it took the form of Protestantism and absolute revolt from the Church, or the minor form of holding different views within her pale. Such a revolt was shown in *Pascal*, who, after displaying a precocious and extraordinary genius for mathematics, at an early age turned his attention to theology, and just before Lewis took up the reins of government, published his "Provincial Letters," a book which attacked the teaching and views of the Jesuits.

Theology. Bossuet.

Pascal.

Pascal belonged to a sect called the Jansenists, because its members held certain views first promulgated by a Bishop Jansenius on the subject of predestination. There was a fierce controversy between them and the Jesuits. But the latter having the ear of the Papal Court were enabled to procure from the Pope a Bull against their opponents. It was called from its first word, the Bull *Unigenitus*, dated September 1713, in which the Jansenists were condemned, and the king insisted on the acceptance of the Bull throughout France.

One of the leading theologians was *Fénelon*, Archbishop of Cambray. On account of the saintliness of his character he had been appointed tutor to the young Duke of Burgundy. "Télémaque" is a book which he wrote for the use of his pupil, and, under veil of describing antiquity, it contains a strong condemnation of the Government, as well as a sort of programme for reform, which his pupil would probably have carried out if he had reached the throne.

Fénelon.

As a result of the age of Lewis XIV. the French language acquired a great ascendency in Europe. It became the language of diplomacy and of polite society. Its influence upon English literature is well worth notice. Pope, the leading poet of the time, shows many traces of a study of French writers. Addison spent a long time in France, and one can see the same influence in his polished and easy style.

Influence of French on English literature.

After the peace of Utrecht, the current of influence seemed to pass the other way. Many Frenchmen visited England and conceived the greatest admiration for the spirit of English politics, English laws, and English society. It would be hardly too much to say that some of the

French literature afterwards inspired by England.

seeds of the French Revolution were sown in their minds and the admiration first acquired, of which they afterwards gave such practical expression, of the way in which the English treated their kings in general, and Charles I. in particular

When Lewis XIV. died, Voltaire was a young man just of age, and Jean Jacques Rousseau was in the nursery. Though the former never quite shook off his feeling of reverence for the king, one cannot help feeling that it was opposition to the spirit of the French Government and knowledge of its results that led both these thinkers and writers to fan the spirit of liberty. So that here, also, the Revolution was being prepared, though there were years and years of weary misgovernment before its outbreak.

Section II.—English Literature.

The reign of Queen Anne, likewise, is usually called the Augustan Age of English Literature. It was a time when England was as great in literature as in war. Writers of deeper tone and weightier calibre have lived at other times; but there is probably no period so short in which so many famous books have been given to the world, or in which forces have had their roots destined so powerfully to influence the future. There are many who regard the name as wholly inappropriate, for the Latin literature was fostered by the judicious patronage of Augustus. However great may be the affection of posterity for "good Queen Anne," it cannot be included amongst her virtues that she cared for or helped literature. But Augustus was assisted in the exercise of his patronage by the taste and discrimination of his great minister Mæcenas. Was there, then, a Mæcenas in Queen

Anne's reign? Was there any influential subject who made it his pride and his pleasure to help men of letters? The only subject who could be compared in extent of power to Mæcenas was Marlborough; and he did not care for poetry, and was nervously sensitive to the least attack on himself.

But if there was no one great patron standing out above the rest, alike prominent and anxious to make the assistance of literature his glory, it would yet be fair to say that the time of Queen Anne was, like the Augustan age, a time of patronage, a time, not of one, but of many patrons. *Patronage with many patrons.* There probably never was a time in which successful literature was so well rewarded: probably never a time in which the alliance was so close between politicians and literary men. Intimacy even must have been great when a poet like Prior, and a statesman like Bolingbroke, would write to and of each other as Matt and Harry.

Pope was the representative poet of the age, and he is proud to boast of his friendly intercourse with Bolingbroke (who supplied him with the subject-matter of one of his greatest poems), and of the assistance that Peterborough gave him in gardening— *Connection of literary men with statesmen.*

> There my retreat the best companions grace,
> Chiefs out of war, and statesmen out of place.
> There St. John mingles with my friendly bowl
> The feast of reason and the flow of soul;
>
> And he, whose lightning pierced the Iberian lines,
> Now forms my quincunx, and now ranks my vines,
> Or tames the genius of the stubborn plain,
> Almost as quickly as he conquered Spain.

No "statesman out of place" probably ever had nobler eulogy passed upon him than that with which Pope honoured Harley—

> A soul supreme in each hard instance tried,
> Above all pain, all passion, and all pride,
> The rage of power, the blast of public breath,
> The lust of lucre, and the dread of death.

Pope.

Alexander Pope was born in 1688, the year of the Revolution. His father was a London linen-draper, who, on retiring from business, went to live near Windsor. The boy was deformed, and almost a dwarf: throughout his life he suffered a great deal from disease. An undercurrent of unhappiness, caused by his bodily ailments, and a nervous irritability, which is not uncommon with very short men, can be traced through all his life. Unable to engage in the sports of boyhood, he showed poetical talents at a very early age:

> I lisped in numbers, for the numbers came.

So great was his reverence for Dryden, the poet of his boyhood, that, in the last year of the seventeenth century, when he was twelve years old, at his own express desire, he was taken up to London, to Wills' coffee-house, in order to see him. Dryden died in that very year. His mantle and a double portion of his spirit fell upon Pope.

The following are his most famous works, given in the order in which they were composed: "Essay on Criticism," "Rape of the Lock," "Messiah," Translation of Homer's Iliad and part of the Odyssey, "Dunciad," "Essay on Man," "Imitations of Horace," and "Epistles." Most of these were written after the reign of Anne, at the time of whose death he was engaged in translating the Iliad.

The "Essay on Criticism" may be said to be an imitation of the "Ars Poetica" of Horace, but there is this difference between the writers: Horace was an experienced and practised poet, Pope a young man of twenty-three. Though the former may claim the palm for originality in the treatment of such a subject, honour must also be given to the genius of the young man, which enabled him to utter thoughts worthy of the wisdom of age. *"Essay on Criticism."*

The "Rape of the Lock" is a playful poem, mock heroic. It has been called the true epic of the time. A young cavalier of the Court cut a lock of hair from off the head of a beautiful maid of honour. The place that the gods occupy in epic poems, Pope supplies in this airy pleasantry with sylphs and gnomes, and the whole subject is treated in so graceful a style that the poem may serve as a model for this species of composition. *"Rape of the Lock."*

On Pope's "Homer," his best-known but not his greatest work, his contemporary Bentley, the greatest classical critic of all time, has passed a criticism to which, even now, we can add nothing. "A very pretty poem, Mr. Pope, but please don't call it Homer." The sonorous dignity of the original and its natural freedom have vanished, and been replaced by the stiffness of an artificial style. But it is the work of a true poet, and, if it does not reproduce Homer, is yet well worth reading for its own sake. *"Homer."*

It is said that Lord Bolingbroke supplied Pope with the material out of which he composed the four epistles that form the "Essay on Man," a treatise on the relation of man to the universe, to himself, and to society, and on man's pursuit of happiness. The matter is, however, certainly the *"Essay on Man."*

least valuable portion of it; as to treatment it may be regarded as Pope's masterpiece. The merits of Pope's poetry shine forth in it; these merits not being originality or sympathy with nature, or insight into character, virtues which distinguish greater poets, but grace, smoothness, correctness, the perfection of taste. He pays infinite attention to the form of his verses, making the subject-matter a secondary consideration. His lines remind one of the exquisite chiselling of a master sculptor. In few English poets can we find such melody of rhythm. Dr. Johnson compares his prose to that of Dryden in language which may be applied also to their poems. "The style of Dryden is capricious and varied, that of Pope is cautious and uniform; Dryden is sometimes vehement and rapid, Pope is always smooth, uniform, and gentle. Dryden's page is a natural field, rising into inequalities, and diversified by the varied exuberance of abundant vegetation; Pope's is a velvet lawn, shaven by the scythe, and levelled by the roller."

Pope's style.

Pope's influence upon English poetry may be said to have lasted to the end of the century, and it cannot be regarded as beneficial. Poetry consists of two parts—the outward form and the inward meaning. Some writers have neglected one, some the other. The absence of heart and of nature in the poetry of the last century seems to be due to imitation of Pope. For his style is like Ulysses' bow, it requires a master's hand to make it really effective.

Pope's influence.

The real strength, however, of the age of Anne lay not in poetry, but in prose; and its prose, still more than its poetry, influenced the times that followed, and is making its influence still felt in our own day. There was a close alli-

Prose. Party politics.

ance between politics and literature, but politics took more than ever the form of party politics. A great development had taken place in parties, for not only was there the contest raging between Whigs and Tories, and side by side with it the sister contest between Low and High Church, but also there was a new aspect of the fight between the Ins and the Outs. Before the end of the reign it came to be understood that all the ministers should be of one party, whilst the other was in opposition. This gave a new—almost a pecuniary—interest to the contest.

If there was no Augustus and no Mæcenas, party spirit took their place. The elections to the House of Commons were all-important, and the question arose—How were they to be influenced? Now-a-days, elections still being of importance, more influence is due to the speeches of a few eminent men, delivered in Parliament or in public places, and to the articles in the newspapers, than to the views of candidates at each election. But at the outset of Queen Anne's reign there were hardly any newspapers and no reporters. Nay, more, there was a law against reporting, and valuable debates are in consequence wholly lost to history. Even to our own times the practice lasted that any member might exclude reporters by merely calling the Speaker's attention to their presence. Members of Parliament might be influenced by speeches; those outside could be reached only by pamphlets. Able pens were therefore in demand for pamphlet writing, and able men, whether they liked it or not, were compelled to declare for a party. It is quite true that the best literary men protested against this compulsion. Swift made it a point in his satire of the contest between the Big endians and Little-endians,

Patronage by parties.

Addison humorously tells of the boy who, asking his way, was abused by one as a Popish cur in asking for St. Ann's lane, and cuffed for irreverence when he asked for Ann's Lane. Pope protests vehemently that the matters are not worth the fighting for:

> "For forms of government let fools contest,
> Whate'er is best administered is best."

Pamphlets were not a new invention. Our great Milton during the middle stage of his life was a pamphleteer. But the profusion with which pamphlets were poured forth was new, and formed a marked characteristic of the time.

Pamphlets.

We are so much accustomed to our daily papers that we sometimes wonder how people used to get on without them. At Athens of old they supplied the want by conversation in the market-place. In Queen Anne's reign it was done partly by pamphlets, partly by clubs and coffee-houses, which were beginning to have considerable influence on political and social life.

The greatest pamphleteer, probably the greatest genius of his time, was Jonathan Swift. He was of English extraction, but born and educated in Dublin. At the age of twenty-one, in the year of the Revolution, he entered the service of Sir William Temple, a distant kinsman, apparently in the capacity of secretary. His position seems to have been unpleasant to him, for he left it, and took holy orders; but he returned to it again, and though not proud of the connexion, yet he edited Temple's works when his patron died. Temple had retired from political life, but was often consulted by William III., when the king wanted an opinion less interested than that of the partisans who surrounded him. King William taught Swift how to cut asparagus

Swift.

in the Dutch fashion, and offered him a cornetcy in a troop of horse. It is said also that his name was entered in William's note-book for preferment; but William died, and Swift's own conduct prevented preferment coming from the king's successor.

His first work was the "Tale of a Tub," a very ludicrous story of three brothers, Peter, Jack, and Martin, who represent respectively the Roman Catholic, the Calvinist, and the Lutheran religion. The story is told of their attempts to carry out their father's wishes in agreement, and of their quarrel at the Reformation. The whole tendency of the book was to cast ridicule upon religion.

"Tale of a Tub."

Failing in his efforts for promotion, Swift changed his party, and went over to the Tories, who received him with open arms; but the queen would not consent to the wish of her ministers to make him a bishop. Ultimately he was appointed Dean of St. Patrick's, Dublin.

He was naturally of a sour temper, and the continued disappointments of his life made him very bitter. He is a furious assailant, sparing no insult to gain his point. He seems to have had little heart. His humour is wonderful, such that no English writer has ever equalled it. Ireland alone could have produced it. One could desire no addition to it but a little kindliness.

His pamphlets are indispensable to the historian of the reign of Queen Anne. Their name is Legion. One of them probably had greater influence than any other pamphlet ever had. When the Whigs were turned out of office, the public opinion in England, especially in the City, was still strongly in favour of the prosecution of the war. The effect of the "Conduct of the Allies," showing that the

"Conduct of the Allies."

English people were paying the allies that they might be allowed to fight their battles for them, was magical in turning the tide of opinion. Stocks fell when the Whigs were turned out; stocks were unaffected by the cessation of arms which showed that negotiations were genuine.

In King George's reign Swift wrote "Drapier's Letters," against a new Government Coinage, and the result was that the coinage was withdrawn, whilst Swift became the darling of the Irish people.

"Drapier's Letters."

But of course Swift's really greatest work is "Gulliver's Travels," which may be described as a satire upon humanity, with contemporary allusions. In the voyage to Lilliput is represented the littleness of mankind, as seen by beings of a larger growth. In Brobdingnag the absurdities of men are shown, seen, as it were, through a magnifying glass. Then Gulliver travels to other lands, wherein learning and science are satirised, and at length Swift bursts forth into terrible descriptions of the Yahoos, which read like a savage attack on mankind.

"Gulliver's Travels."

Swift outlived his genius, and before his death sank into absolute idiocy. The story is told how towards the end of his life he took up one of his own books and said, "Good God, what a genius I had when I wrote that book!"

Swift's death.

So Swift expired, a driveller and a show.

The following epitaph in St. Patrick's Cathedral he composed for himself:—

> Hic jacet Jonathan Swift, S. T. P.
> ubi sæva indignatio cor ulterius lacerare nequit.
> Abi, viator, imitare, si poteris.

Swift was the great Tory pamphleteer, famous as the

author of "Gulliver." A writer on the Whig side was none other than the author of "Robinson Crusoe."

Daniel De Foe was born in 1661, the year after the Restoration. His real name was Foe, for though he had this strange fancy for prefixing *de* to his name, he was a true-born Englishman. His father was a London butcher, a Whig and a Dissenter, and he was himself engaged in business as a hosier; but his strong sympathy with that extreme section of the Whig party which the Dissenters formed soon drew him from commerce, in which he was unsuccessful, to literature. He had a very facile pen, and it often got him into trouble; but neither pillory nor imprisonment could restrain him from writing again. As a faithful and extreme Whig he had joined Monmouth, and taken refuge abroad after the defeat of Sedgemoor. He was a great friend of the Glorious Revolution, and during the reign of William was always ready to defend the king and his cause, even with respect to acts which were unpopular. His career as a pamphleteer may be said to have begun one year before the Revolution, and to have ended about a year after the end of Queen Anne's reign. The two most famous of his pamphlets are "The True-born Englishman," which appeared in the former, and "The Shortest Way with Dissenters," in the latter.

"The True born Englishman" is a poem in which De Foe defends King William. The verse is not melodious, and may be said in parts to descend to doggerel; but its sterling sense caused a very large sale. Considering the services that William and his Dutch soldiers had conferred upon England, even a true-born Englishman can forgive him for liking his old friends better than his new subjects. The former at any rate had been true to him.

> The foreigners have faithfully obeyed him,
> And none but Englishmen have e'er betrayed him.

The writer vigorously maintains the principles of the Revolution against the tyranny which James had wished to establish. The claims of kings should be broad-based upon their people's will.

> Titles are shadows, crowns are empty things,
> The good of subjects is the end of kings.

The "Shortest Way with Dissenters" was a pamphlet called forth by the Occasional Conformity Bill. The Church party, knowing that the queen was on their side, were anxious to persecute the Dissenters, until they were entirely rid of them. They wished legislation to run in the groove of Charles II.'s reign, not in that of William's. De Foe wrote under the disguise of a Churchman, and his shortest way was this: "If one severe law were made and punctually executed, that whoever was found at a conventicle should be banished the nation, and the preacher be hanged, we should soon see an end of the tale." The Churchmen were delighted, and De Foe had to publish an explanation of his sarcasm, at which they were proportionately enraged. The result was the pillory and imprisonment. The pamphlet is really an argument in favour of complete toleration, for he also attacks his own friends the Dissenters, because when they had the power they did not respect their opponents. Now, like the cock in the stable, they are quite willing to propose to the horses, "let us all keep our legs quiet."

De Foe's greatest work is, of course, "Robinson Crusoe." He was nearly sixty when he wrote it. It is founded upon the adventures of Alexander Selkirk, a seaman who had been marooned upon the island of Juan Fernandez, that is to say, put on shore by his captain and left there on pretence that he had committed some great crime. The adventures of Robinson Crusoe, his shipwreck, his life upon the island, his attempts to provide himself with the common necessaries of life, his meeting with Friday, the boat too big to launch, and ultimately the escape, have delighted many generations of readers, young as well as old. Written in an exceedingly simple style, it has all the air of a real narrative.

But the most famous Whig writer of the time, and one whose life is closely mixed up with its history, is Joseph Addison. He was educated at the Charterhouse, which was then, and indeed until late years, a London school, but has now been moved into the country. A modern novelist, himself educated at the same school, writes with great pride of Addison, as the head boy at the Charter-house. Addison distinguished himself at school, and went thence to Oxford, where he obtained a fellowship at Magdalen College. He had a great reputation for Latin scholarship and especially for Latin verses. He also tried English verses, and some of them arresting the attention of Lord Somers, that enlightened nobleman procured Addison a pension, wherewith he travelled over France and Italy. He stayed a long time in France, and the influence of a close acquaintance with French literature can be plainly traced in Addison's style. On King William's death the pension ceased, and he returned to England. He published an account of his travels, which was not successful, and for some years Addison lived in poor, but dignified and contented retirement in lodgings in the Haymarket, up two pairs of stairs. When the battle of Blenheim was fought, its glory was sung by many poetasters in miserable verses, which seemed to the ministers to mar it. Godolphin, the Prime-Minister, did not know to whom to turn. A Whig nobleman suggested an application to Addison, on condition that all due respect be shown in making it. The Chancellor of the Exchequer was sent as a deputation to Addison, who consented to write, and when the Chancellor came again the poem was completed as far as the following passage:—

> But O my Muse! what numbers wilt thou find
> To sing the furious troops in battle join'd?
> Methinks I hear the drum's tumultuous sound
> The victor's shouts and dying groans confound;
> The dreadful burst of cannon rend the skies,
> And all the thunder of the battle rise.
> 'Twas then great Marlborough's mighty soul was proved,
> That, in the shock of charging hosts unmoved,
> Amid confusion, horror, and despair,
> Examined all the dreadful scenes of war:
> In peaceful thought the field of death surveyed,
> To fainting squadrons sent the timely aid,
> Inspired repulsed battalions to engage,
> And taught the doubtful battle where to rage.
> So when an angel, by divine command,
> With rising tempests shakes a guilty land
> (Such as of late o'er pale Britannia passed),
> Calm and serene he drives the furious blast;
> And, pleased the Almighty's order to perform,
> Rides in the whirlwind and directs the storm.

This simile carried the minister away with enthusiasm, and the same feeling was quickly spread throughout the country when the whole poem called "The Campaign" was published. All the critics allow that the merit of the rest of the poem is by no means equal to that of this passage, and that its great praise is that it recognises the truth, that in a modern battle the general does not engage hand to hand with the enemy, and slay thousands with his own sword, but is the directing mind of the whole.

By this poem Addison's career was made. He was appointed in turn Commissioner of Appeals, Secretary to Legation at Hanover, Under-Secretary of State, Secretary for Ireland, and ultimately, three years after the accession of King George I., Secretary of State. He married the Countess of Warwick, to whose son he had formerly been tutor, and lived at Holland House, which has been for so many generations the haunt of a brilliant literary society.

The character of Addison has made him almost the model of a literary man. He had only one weakness, inability to resist the temptation of wine, and that was, perhaps, the fault of his age rather than of himself. He was humane, genial, modest, and, in the best sense of the word, religious. The wits of his day used to call him "a parson in a tye-wig"—the layman's wig—as we might say, "a clergyman in a black tie:" indeed, the benevolent morality of his writings and their earnest Christianity have probably had more effect for good than many sermons.

Character.

Pope quarrelled with Addison, and inserted in one of his poems the following magnificent declamation against him:—

> Peace to all such! but were there one whose fires
> True genius kindles, and fair fame inspires;
> Bless'd with each talent and each art to please,
> And born to write, converse, and live with ease;
> Should such a man, too fond to rule alone,
> Bear, like the Turk, no brother near the throne,
> View him with scornful, yet with jealous eyes,

> And hate for arts that caused himself to rise:
> Damn with faint praise, assent with civil leer,
> And, without sneering, teach the rest to sneer;
> Willing to wound, and yet afraid to strike,
> Just hint a fault, and hesitate dislike;
> Alike reserved to blame or to commend,
> A timorous foe, and a suspicious friend;
> Dreading e'en fools, by flatterers besieged,
> And so obliging that he ne'er obliged;
> Like Cato, give his little senate laws,
> And sit attentive to his his own applause;
> While wits and Templars every sentence raise,
> And wonder with a foolish face of praise—
> Who but must laugh, if such a man there be?
> Who would not weep, if Atticus were he?

It is said that in the first draft, Addison's name stood without even the veil of "Atticus." There can, however, be no doubt that this attack is very unfair, and proceeded from the spiteful venom of the poet. It is quite true that Addison had a band of faithful admirers, to one of whom we shall presently advert. But jealousy was not Addison's failing, though it was Pope's.

The allusion to Cato would show that the passage was intended for Addison, even if there were no direct evidence. Cato was the name of Addison's single tragedy. It was first acted in 1713, the month after the Peace of Utrecht was concluded. A great deal of it had been written much earlier, but the play was only recently finished. Pope, then friendly to Addison, wrote a prologue to it, and as Addison surrendered all the profit of the performance to the actors, they did their utmost to make it a success. It was a time when party feeling ran very high. The Whigs applauded every passage in praise of liberty, and the Tories, not to be outdone, applauded also. Marlborough's application to be made captain-general for life being still fresh in men's memories, Lord Bolingbroke made a capital hit by sending for the chief actor between the acts, and presenting him with a purse of 50*l.* "for defending the cause of liberty so well against a perpetual dictator." The saying went round the Tory benches that the Whigs meant to make as good a present, when they could accompany it with as good a speech. The play is constructed after French models, and is certainly neither admired nor read in the present day; it is too frigid. But a few lines from it still pass as the current coin of every-day quotation.

A fellow-worker on the same side, and intimately connected with Addison, was Mr. Richard Steele. They were educated at the same school, and were contemporaries and friends at Oxford. But *Steele.* whilst Addison was steady, and distinguished himself, Steele was idle. At length, no longer able to bear the restraints of Oxford life, he ran away and enlisted as a private in the Blues. Later, he obtained a cornetcy, and we find him afterwards a captain in the Fusiliers. Steele's name, like Swift's, was down in William's note-book for promotion; but William's death destroyed the value of the entry. It has been said of Steele that he spent his life in "sinning and repenting." Whilst notorious for his gaiety and the dissipation of his life, he astonished the town by bringing out a little book called the "Christian Hero," which breathes the very spirit of piety.

When his party was in power, places were found for him, and at length Sir Richard Steele was appointed editor of the "Gazette." It occurred to him, that the early information which he thus *"Tatler."* obtained might be made of use in a paper, and that the dulness of news might be relieved by an occasional essay on some subject not political. This idea took form in the "Tatler," which, when the Whigs lost office and Steele his place, was merged afterwards in the more famous "Spectator," in which Steele received great assistance from Addison. The share which Addison and Steele had in this constitutes their chief claims upon the notice of posterity. It was a small sheet, published three times a week, at the price of one penny, containing a short essay on two of the pages and news on the others.

"Spectator."

The subjects of the essays were infinitely varied: now a criticism on manners, now on the hoops worn by ladies, on their absurd practice of wearing patches on the face, or on cherry-coloured ribbons. These lighter subjects would be matched by reflections on Westminster Abbey, on the Exchange, on the Bank, or by criticisms of decided value on Milton's "Paradise Lost," and on the old ballad of "Chevy Chase." But a sort of thread of connexion was given to the papers by the character of the Spectator, a quiet observer of men and and manners, and by the account of the club, with its types of English society of the day, the first sketch of which is due to Steele. The character of Sir Roger de Coverley, its leading member, the representative of the English country gentleman, was adopted and improved by Addison, who wrote all the later papers about him, until Steele again tried his hand, placing the old knight in improper company; and to prevent such a liberty being taken again, Addison wrote a very touching account of his death.

The influence of the "Spectator" has been very remarkable. One may regard the modern newspapers and the modern magazine as its children. For newspapers combine criticism with news, magazines present essays without the news.

Influence on the future.

Surely the most significant feature of modern literature is to be found in the merit and profusion of its periodicals that are poured forth daily, weekly, monthly, from the press. Their transparent fault is that they are transitory; but the gain is, that knowledge which once remained upon the mountain-height, is now brought down to water the plain. Who shall measure their influence?

INDEX.

ANN

ACADEMY, French establishment of, 218
Addison, Joseph, his sketch of the Exchange, 200; his dream, 215; early life, 235; his character, 237
Adolphus, Gustavus, 156, 158
"Ahlden, Princess of, 187
Aix-la-Chapelle, peace of, 18
Albigenses, the, 50
Allies, the, campaigns in Germany and elsewhere, 44; defeat the French at Blenheim, 65; victory at Ramillies, 79; Madrid relinquished by, 88; the year of victory, 76-89; the year of disaster, 89-95; defeated at Almanza, 91; results of their defeat 93; fighting in the Low Countries 95-109; victory at Oudenarde, 98; overtures for peace by France, 102; terms insisted on by, 102; victory at Malplaquet, 108; later campaigns in Spain, 109-119; victory at Almenara and Saragossa, 113, 114; advance and enter Madrid, 114, 115; retreat to Toledo, 116; return to Catalonia, 116; English defeated at Birhuega, 117; battle of Villa Viciosa, 118; end of the war. 131; separation of English troops from, 136; defeated at Denain, 137.
Almanza, battle of, 91; the positions of the armies and total defeat of the allies, 92; results of defeat, 93; effects of, 109
Almenara, battle of, 113
Anderkirk taken, 79
Anne, daughter of James II., Queen of England, succeeds to the throne, 25; her character, 25; her children and husband, 26; development of

BEN

English parties in her reign, 120; her impartial views, 122; her first Tory ministry, 122; gradually alienated from the Duchess of Marlborough, 126; change of her ministry, 127; dispute as to her successor, 171; the last week of her reign, quarrels in the ministry, 183
Antwerp falls into the hands of Marlborough, 80
"Arbuthnot's History of John Bull," a political satire on the dishonour to Spain, 7
Architecture, flourishing condition of, 201
Assiento contract, the, 141
Ath, siege of, 81
Augsburg, league of, 24
Augustan age, of French literature, 218; of English literature, 223
Augustus, Ernest, Duke of Brunswick-Luneburg, 179
Austria, trouble in, 57

BADEN, peace of, 140
Barcelona taken, 73; besieged by the French, 85; stormed and taken, 193
Bath, Beau Nash's improvements in, 203
Bavaria, Elector of, his alliance with France, 40; at the battle of Ramillies, 77; reinstated, 141, 142
Bavarians, routed at Schellenberg, 60
Beachy Head, battle of, 24
Beau Nash, 203
Beer, enormous consumption of, 210
Benbow, Admiral, 46
Bentinck, Duke of Portland, 6

243

CAM

Berwick, Duke of, commands the French forces, 49; enters Madrid, 88; defeats the allies at Almanza, 92

Black Death, the, 204

Blenheim, battle of, preparations for battle, 62; description of the ground, 62; position of the armies, 63; the battle begins, 63; the result, 67

Blenheim Palace, near Woodstock, 203

Bohemia, Elector of, 34

Bolingbroke, Lord (*see* St. John, Henry)

Bonn taken, 44

Bossuet, Bishop of Meaux, 222

Bouchain taken, 134

Boufflers, Marshal, his defence of Lille, 99; capitulates, 101; serves under Villars in Flanders, 105; named to the command at Malplaquet, 108

Brabant, duchy of, claims to, 16; inclining to French, 96

Brandenburg, Elector of, 34

Brihuega, battle of, 117

Bristol, proportion of population to London, 196

Bruges taken, 81

Brussels falls into the hands of Marlborough, 80

Burgundy, Duke of, commands in Flanders, 97; defeated at Oudenarde, 99; his education, 189; his marriage, 189; his death, 189

Burgundy, Duchess of, her death, 189

Burnet, Bishop of Salisbury, 26; credited with the improvement of the position of the clergy, 218

Byng, Admiral Sir George, 153

CABINET government, 128, 129

Cadiz, English expedition against, 46

Calendar, change in Russian, 162

Camisards, the, rebellion of, 52; persecuted by Dragonades, 54; their retaliation, 55; severity used to put down the rebellion, 55; appeal to foreign governments, 55; end of the war, 56; their bravery, 57

Campaign of 1702, 42; of 1704, 58; of 1705, 68; of 1706, 76; of 1707, 89; of 1708, 96; of 1709, 104; of 1710, 133

"Campaign, the," 236-7

CON

Carleton, Captain, 73

Castilians the, 7, 115

Catalans, the, 73

Catalonia subdued, 74

Catalonians, the, 193

Catherine, Czarina, rescues the Russian army, 172; married to Peter the Great, 172

Cato, 238

Cavalier, Jean, his daring character, 52; his chivalry and uprightness, 54; his later life, 57

Cevennes, the, 22; rising in, 50 58

Charles II. of England, secret treaty with Louis XIV., 17; his opinion of Prince George of Denmark, 26

Charles II. of Spain. claimants to the throne on his death, 2; his will, 9

Charles V., Emperor, 1

Charles XII., King of Sweden, visited by Marlborough. 90; his enemies, 164; beginning of his reign, 165; his character, 165; subdues Denmark and Poland, 166; defeats the Russians at Narva, 166; arbiter of Europe, 168; his campaign against Russia, 169; defeated by Peter the Great at Pultowa, 170; overpowered at Bender, 173; his death, 173

Charles Emanuel, son of Victor Amadeus, 195

Charles the Archduke, claimant to the throne of Spain, 4; joins Lord Peterborough. 70; refuses to enter Madrid, 88; takes part in the campaign of 1710, 113; enters Madrid, 115; becomes Emperor, 133; holds out against the peace of Utrecht, 139; his later policy, 194; his death, 195

Church, High and Low, origin of, 121

Churches of England and Scotland, unaffected by the Union, 147

Churchill, Lord John (*see* Marlborough, Duke of)

Claret, a favourite wine in England at this time, 212

Clergy, the, their position, 218

Coal-fields, 209

Coffee, introduction of, into England, 211

Cologne, Archbishop of, 35; Elector of, 41

Commerce, increase in, 200

"Conduct of the Allies," 231

Continental war, the, 24

ENG

Corn, the staple produce of England, 208
Corneille, 220
Cotton, importation of, 209
Cremona, victory of Prince Eugene at, 45
"Criticism, Essay on," 227
Cromwell, Oliver, his anticipated union with Scotland, 145
Cutts, Lord, 64

DARIEN Company, the, 8; proposed dissolution of, 147.
Daun, Marshal, 83, 93
Defoe, Daniel, his character and books, 233
Denain, battle of, 137
Dendermonde, siege of, 81
Denmark, her territory on the shores of the Baltic, 155
Dover, treaty of, 18
Dragonades, 54
Drama, French, the, 221
"Drapier's Letters," 232
Drunkenness in the eighteenth century, 213
Dryden, compared with Pope, 228
Dutch, application of the word, 35; their anxiety for peace, 96; effect of the war on, 142

ECONOMIC condition of the people of England, 195
Election, general, of 1710, 131
Electors, the, how they ranged themselves, 34
Elizabeth, sister of Charles I., her descendants, 177
England, indignation against William III. in, 8; foreign policy in the seventeenth century, 17; formation of league with Holland and Sweden, 18; revolution of 1688, 23; declaration of war, 42; victory at Schellenberg, 60; victory over the French at Blenheim, 65; defeats the French at Ramillies, 80; troops separated from the allies, 136; her gains by the war of Spanish succession, 140; social and economic condition of the people at this time, 195-218; compared with other European nations, 209; union with Scotland (see Union with Scotland)
English Literature, 224-241

FRE

Equivalent, the, 47
Eugene of Savoy, Prince, his character and intimacy with Marlborough, 32; his victory at Cremona, 45; his meeting with Marlborough, 59; his position in the battle of Blenheim, 63, 64; his attack on Lutzingen, 66; marches to Turin, 82; his victory at Turin, 84; besieges Toulon, 94; joins Marlborough in the battle of Oudenarde, 97; besieges Lille, 99; wounded at Malplaquet, 108; his mission to England, 135; separated from Ormond, 136
Evelyn, John, 161
Exchange, the, 199, 200

FENELON, Archbishop of Cambray, 223; his "Adventures of Telemachus," 189
Feodor, 158
Finland, falls into the hands of Russia, 171
Flag, national, changes in, 149
France, her position at the commencement of the eighteenth century, 4; injuries caused to, by the revocation of the Edict of Nantes, 21; her chance against the league, 40; her object in making the campaign of 1704, 58; defeated at Blenheim, 65; defeated at Ramillies, 80; commences the siege of Turin, 82; demoralization of troops, 84; defeated at Turin, 84; defeats the allies at Almanza, 91; her endeavours to win Brabant back, 96; defeated by the allies at Oudenarde, 97; public misery in, 99; intolerable proposal by the allies and appeal to the people, 103; and the answer to it, 104; troops withdrawn from Spain, 112; victory at Denain, 137; effect of the war on, 141
Frederick Augustus, the Strong, of Poland, 164; defeated by Charles XII., 167
Frederick, Elector of Brandenburg, 35
Frederick, the Elector Palatine, 34; 178
Frederick, King of Denmark, 164; defeated by Charles XII., 166
Fredericshall, siege of, 173
French Literature, 218-224
French prose, development of, 222

HES

GALWAY, Earl of, in Portugal, 48; enters Madrid, 86; junction with Peterborough at Guadalaxara, 88; defeated at Almanza, 92; his letter to Marlborough regarding his defeat, 92; appointed to the command in Portugal, 110

George I., Elector of Hanover, proclaimed King of England, 185; his early life, 186; his bravery, 186; a good Elector, 186; unpopular: could not speak English, 186; phlegmatic, 186; his wife, 187; a good king for England, 187

George II., son of George I., 187

George, prince of Denmark, marries Anne, 26; appointed Lord High Admiral, 27; his sympathy with the Occasional Conformity Bill, 123

Germany, weakness of, 14; campaign in, 44-45

Gertruydenburg, conference at, 139

Ghent taken, 81

Gibraltar taken by the English, 49

Godolphin, appointed Lord High Treasurer, 31, 122; his character, 31; goes over to the Whig party, 123; loses favour with Anne, 128; dismissal from office, 131; his death, 135

Grand alliance of the Hague, the, 11, 24; its component parts, 31-41; progress of, 36

Guadalaxara, junction of Galway and Peterborough at, 88

Guiscard, Marquis of, assails Harley, 132

"Gulliver's Travels," 232

HAGUE, the, conference of, 102, 138

Hampden, John, 188

Hanover, Electoral Prince of, 98

Hanoverian succession secured, 185

Hapsburg, House of, 33

Harley, Robert his ministry, 127; as Secretary of State, 128; as chief of the Tory party, 132; attack on his life, 132; made Earl of Oxford, 133; dismissed from office, 183; lines from Pope on, 225

Heinsius, Anthony, Pensionary, a friend of Marlborough, 32

Henry of Navarre, 21

Hesse, Prince of, 70; his death, 72; his successor invests Mons, 107

High Church, origin of, 122

LAG

Hill, Abigail, in favour with Anne, 126; marries Mr. Masham, 127; (see Masham, Mrs.)

Hill, Colonel, commands an expedition against Quebec, 134

Hochstadt, battle of, 45

Holland, invasion of, 18; formation of league with Holland and Sweden, 18; cutting of the dykes, 19; application of the word, 36; decline of her influence in Europe, 142

Holstein, Duke of, 166

"Homer," 227

Hooke, Colonel, 151

Horace, compared with Pope, 227

Hudson's Bay Territory, acquired by England, 140

Huguenots, effect of the revocation of the Edict of Nantes, 21; persecution and emigration, 22; geography of their country, 50

Hungary, its condition during the war of the Spanish succession, 57-58; revolt in, 58

Huy, fortress of, taken, 44

INGOLSTADT fortress, 61

Innsbruck captured by the Bavarians, 45

Italy, North, war in, 45; campaign in, 77; the allied cause in, 82

Ivan, 158

JACOBITES, the, rising of, 151; their real strength, 180; their connection with the Tories, 180

James II., King of England, 10, 23

James Stuart, Francis Edward, surnamed the Pretender, his character 151, 152; Jacobite rising in favour of, 151; acknowledged as king by Lewis XIV., 152

Jennings, Sarah, wife of the Duke of Marlborough, 27

Joseph, Electoral Prince, claimant to the throne of Spain, 4; his death 6

Joseph, succeeds his father Leopold I. as emperor, 34; his death, 133

Junto, the, 125

KAISERSWERTH, siege of, 42

Kidd, Captain, 125

Kufstein, fortress of, captured by the Bavarians, 45

LABOURERS, statue of, 205

La Gudina, battle of, 112

LIT

Landau taken, 45; retaken, 45
Landrecies, siege of, 137
Law, Scotch, not changed by the Union act, 149
Leczinski, Stanislaus, elected King of Poland, 168
Leopold, emperor, 34
Lewis XIV., renounces his rights to the throne of Spain, 2; his power in Europe, 4; his quarrels with William of Orange, 5; his negotiations with William of Orange, 6; his mistaken policy, 9, 10; claims the Netherlands, 10; his reign, 13; his ambition, 14; his character, 15; lays claim to the duchy of Brabant, 16; secret treaty with Charles II., 18; at war with Holland, 19; the title of "Great" bestowed on him, 19; his three symptoms of madness, 20; seizure of Strassburg, and revocation of the Edict of Nantes, 21; ravaging of the Palatinate, 23; "Hereditary Foe of the Holy Empire," 34; opposes the Duke of Savoy, 38; campaign of 1704, 58; his overtures for peace, 102; his appeal to the people of France concerning the terms of the allies, 103; the answer to it, 104; withdraws his troops from Spain, 112; his offers to the allies, 138; his new proposals, 139; his death, 187; events in England parallel with his life, 188; troubles at the end of his reign, 188; joy at his death, 191; disputes regarding the regent on his death, 191
Lewis XV., succeeds to the throne of France, 190; commencement of reign contrasted with that of Lewis XIV., 190-191
Lewis, Prince of Baden, 36; takes Landau, 45; his disputes with Marlborough, 60
Lewis the Dauphin, his death, 188
Liege taken, 43
Lille, siege of 101; surrenders, 101
Literature, English, Augustan age of, 223; connexion of literary men with statesmen, 225; alliance with politics, 228, 229
Literature, French, Augustan age of, 218; greatness in first half of reign, 220; influence on English literature, 223; afterwards inspired by England, 223
"Little Grandsire," the, 164

MAR

Livonia falls into the hands of Russia, 171
Loire valley, the, 50
London, population of, 197; disturbed life in, 198; divided into the City and Westminster, 199; the Exchange and commerce, 199; architecture, 200
Louvain taken, 80
Low Church, origin of, 122
Lutzingen taken, 66
Luxuries, far-brought supply of, in the eighteenth century, 211

MACAULAY, extract from, 19
Madrid, relinquished by the allies, 88
Mahon, Port, taken, 111
Maintenon, Madame de, 22, 103
Majorca declares for allies, 94
Malplaquet, battle of, preparations, 104; description of ground, 108; the battle, 108; and result, 109
"Man, Essay on," 227
Manufactures, growth of, 196, 209
Margrave of Bayreuth, 94
Maria Theresa, wife of Lewis XIV., renounces right to the throne of Spain, 2
Maria Theresa, daughter of the Emperor Charles VI., 195
Marlborough, Earl of, afterwards Duke, (John Churchill) as Governor to the Duke of Gloucester, 26; early life, 27; dismissed from all his employments, 28; aids James, 28; restored to favour, 28; his character and virtues, 29; appointed Commander-in-Chief, 41; in Flanders, 41-44; his object and first campaign, 42; result of campaign, 43; in danger, 43; results of second campaign, 44; made Duke, 43; his plans and meeting with Prince Eugene, 59; his victory at Schellenberg, 60; preparations for the battle of Blenheim, 61; report of his victory at Blenheim, 66; his designs upon Italy, 77; his campaign of 1706, 77; narrow escape of being taken prisoner, 79; his plans, 79; his victory at Ramillies, 80; takes Brussels and Antwerp, 80; proposed as Governor of Netherlands, 82; his campaign of 1707, 89; visits the King of Sweden, 90; in

NET

Flanders, 91; his campaign of 1708, 95; defeats the French at Oudenarde, 97; preparations for the campaign of 1710, 104; defeats the French at Malplaquet, 108; ascendency of, 112; change in his political views, 123; loses favour with Anne, 128; request to be made Commander-in-Chief for life refused, 129; his last campaign, 134; disgrace of, 135; libels against him, 135; returns to England and is again appointed Commander-in-Chief of the army, 192; his death, 193

Marlborough, Lady, the favourite of Anne, 27; her influence over Anne, 27; allied to the Junto, 126; dismissed from Court, 131; her death, 193

Marsin, Marshal, in Bavaria, 59; routed at Blenheim, 64; commands at siege of Turin, 83; defeated at Turin, 84

Masham, Mrs. (Abigail Hill), her influence over Anne, 127

Maurice, Prince, 179

Maximilian, Elector of Bavaria, at the battle of Blenheim, 63

Mayence, Archbishop of, 34

Mazarin, on Lewis XIV., 14

Mazeppa, 169

Menin, siege of, 81

Methuen Treaty, the, 40; hard drinking traced to it, 213

Milan, convention of, 85; ceded to Austria, 141

Minorca, taken by the English, 110

Mohawks, the, 199

Moliere, 224

Mona teries, suppression of, 205

Money, value of, in this reign, 206

Monjuich, capture of, 72

Mons, besieged, 107; taken, 109

Mordaunt, Charles, Earl of Peterborough (see Peterborough, Earl of,)

NANTES, Edict of, revoked, 21
Naples, makes peace apart from Spain, 85; secured by the Emperor, 93; ceded to Austria, 141

Narva, battle of, 167

Nash, Richard, 203

National Debt, the general principle of, 213; later history of, 214

Nebel, passage of the, 64

Netherlands, the war in, 77; ceded to Austria, 141

PET

Newfoundland, ceded to England, 141

Noguera river, 113

North-Eastern State System, comprising Denmark, Poland, Sweden and Russia, 154-158

Nova Scotia, ceded to England, 141

Nules taken, 75

Nymwegen, treaty of, 20

OBERGLAU, village of, 65
Occasional Conformity Bill, description of, 123; defeated in the House of Lords, 124; passed, 131

Orange, Prince of, takes part in the battle of Malplaquet, 108

Orleans, Duke of, commands at Turin, 83; succeeds to the command of the French forces, 111; becomes regent on the death of Lewis XIV., 191; his policy, 192

Ormond, Duke of, 46; appointed Commander-in-Chief, 136

Ostend, siege of, 81

Ottomond, tomb of, 79

Oudenarde, battle of, 96; battle begins, 97; sequel of battle, 99

Overkirk, Marshal, 98

Oxford, Earl of, impeached, 182

PALATINATE, ravaging of the, 23; Elector of, 34

Pamphlets, 230

Parties, strength of, 216; at the Universities, 217; patronage by, 229

Partition, first treaty of, 6; second treaty of, 6; results of these treaties in Spain, 7

Pascal, 222

Paterson, William, his expedition to Darien, 7, 8

Patriarchate abolished in Russia, 162

Patronage of French literature, 228; of English literature, 224; by parties, 229

Pauperism in Anne's reign, 206

Peace, negotiation for, 138

Peer ge, Irish and Scotch, 148

Pepys, Mr., his first cup of tea, 210

Peter the Great, his early life and real accession to power, 158; his policy, 159; his appearance, 159; his desire for a navy, 160; visits Holland and England, 160; changes the capital and calendar of Russia,

161; abolishes patriarchate, 162; adopts European fashions, 162; institutes the Tchin, 163; defeated by Charles XII. at Narva, 167; his victory over Charles XII. at Pultowa, 170; at war with Turkey, 171; his second journey to Europe, 174; death of his son, 174; his death, 174

Peterborough, Earl, of (Mordaunt), his early life, 67; sent to command in Spain, 68; his character, 68; progress of his expedition, 70; his proposals regarding Valencia, 70; before Barcelona, 71; takes Monjuich, 72; takes Barcelona, 73; subdues Catalonia and Valencia, 74; his energy, 71; his success at San Mateo, 74; his winter campaign, 75; relieves Barcelona, 75; raises the siege, 85, 86; junction with Galway at Guadalaxara, 88; quits the army, 88

Philip II. of Spain, 1

Philip, Duke of Anjou, Philip V. of Spain, claimant to the throne of Spain, 4; proclaimed King of Spain, 9; besieges Barcelona, 85; Spanish loyalty to, 84; heads the army at Villa Viciosa, 118; renounces claim to the French crown, 140; his abdication, 194

Piedmont, evacuated by the French, 85

Poland, her territories, 156

Police service, inefficiency of, in the eighteenth century, 198

Politics, alliance of, with literature, 228-229

Pomerania claimed by Prussia, 171

Poor law, the, 206

Pope, his life and most famous works, 225; compared with Horace, 227; his influence, 228; his style, 228; compared with Dryden, 228; his lines on Addison, 237

Population during this reign, 195

Port, a favourite drink in England, 213

Portoust's claret, 212

Portugal, joins the Grand Alliance, 39; subject to Spain, 39; accedes to the Grand Alliance, 46

Pragmatic Sanction, the, 195

Pretender, the (*see* James)

Prose, French development of, 222

Protestant Succession, measures to secure to it, 175; secured, 185

"Provincial Letters," the, 223

Prussia constituted a kingdom, 35; recognised by France, 141

Pruth, the affair of the, 172

Pultowa, battle of, 170; results, 171

QUEBEC, expedition against, 134
Queen Anne's Bounty, 218

RACINE, 22
Ramillies, battle of, the armies and ground, 77; the battle, 79; result, 80

"Rape of the Lock," the, 227

Rastadt, peace of, 139

Religious distinction between Whigs and Tories, 121

Representation of Scotland in parliament, 148

Repudiation, 215

Revolution of 1688, party views of the, 121

Rhone valley, the, 50

Rights, Bill of, 25

"Robinson Crusoe," 234

Rooke, Sir George, 47; captures Gibraltar, 49

Rousseau, Jean Jacques, 224

Rupert, Prince, 179

Russia, her territories, 155, 157; foundation of St. Petersburg, 161; patriarchate abolished, 162; European fashions adopted, 162; war with Turkey, 171

Ryswick, peace of, 5

SACHEVERELL, Dr. his sermon and parliamentary proceedings against him, 130

St. George, Chevalier, 99

St. John, Henry, as Secretary at War, 128; his character, 132; created Lord Bolingbroke, 133; his schemes, 183

St. Paul's, rebuilt by Sir C. Wren, 201; cost, 202

St. Petersburg, foundation of, 161

Saint Simon, Duc de, memoirs of, 222

St. Stephen's, Walbrook, 201

San Mateo, siege of, 74

Saragossa, battle of, 114

Sardinia taken, 110

Savoy, joins the Grand Alliance, 37; secured to the cause of the Grand Alliance, 85

STA

Savoy, Duke of, (*see* Victor Amadeus)
Saxony, Elector of, 34
Scania, claimed by Denmark, 171
Schellenberg, storming of, 60
Schlusselburg taken, 169
Scilly Isles, shipwreck ff, 95
Scotland, ill-will of, against William III., 8; union with England (*see* Union with Scotland)
Security, Act of, 145
Serf, a, 204
Settlement, Act of, 26, 145
Sevigne, Madame de, her letters, 222
"Shortest way with Dissenters,' 234
Shovel, Sir Cloudesley, is shipwrecked off the Scilly Isles, 95
Shrewsbury, Earl of (*see* Talbot)
Social condition of the people of England, 195
Somers, Lord, the leader and guide of the Whig party, 125; as president of the Council, 128
Sophia, princess, sister of Peter the Great, 158
Sophia, electress, her descendants, 177; her wife, 179; named successor to Anne, 180
Sophia Dorothea, of Zell, wife of George I., 186
Spain, monarchy of, 1; claimants to the throne on the death of Charles II., 2; anxieties regarding the crown, 4; and anger against William, 7; English expedition against, 46; invasion of, 49; Peterborough's campaign in, 70-76; later campaign in, 109; French troops withdrawn from, 112; defeated at the battle of Almenara, 113; defeated at Saragossa, 114; end of war, 119; her losses by the war, 141
Spanish galleons destroyed at Vigo, 48
Spanish monarchy in the hands of Philip V., 140
Spanish succession, the, 1-13; opening of the war, 41-56; the point of greatest success in the war, 86; general considerations on, 143
"Spectator," the, 240; its influence, 210
Stanhope, General, 88, 110; commands the British troops, 110; takes Minorca and Port Mahon, 111; advances and passes the river Noguera, 113; his victory at Almenara, 113; and Saragossa, 114; enters Madrid, 115; winters at Toledo, 116; defeated at Brihuega, 117

TOR

Staremberg, 110; colleague of Stanhope, 113; his victory a Saragossa, 114; gives battle at Villa Viciosa, 119
Steele, Richard, his character, 239, 240; his works, 239-240
Stradella, pass of, 83
Stralsund, siege of, 173
Strassburg, seizure of, 21
Strelitzes, the, 163
Sunderland, Earl of, as Secretary of State, 126
Sweden, formation of league with England and Holland, 18; her territory on the shores of the Baltic, 156; her power, 156; defeated at Pultowa, 170
Swift, Dean, on Lord Peterborough, 69; in favour of repudiation, 213; his life and works, 230-233; his death, 232

TACKERS, the, 124
Talbot, Charles, Earl of Shrewsbury, his previous career, 184; as Secretary of State, 184; retires from office, 184; appointed Lord High Treasurer, 185
"Tale of a Tub," 231
Tallard, General, 6; joins Marsin, 61; his position at the battle of Blenheim, 63; taken prisoner, 65
"Tatler," the, 239
Tavieres taken, 79
Tchin, the institution of, 163
Tea regarded as a luxury, 210
Te Deum in St. Paul's Cathedral, 144
Temple, Sir William, 17
Test act. the, 123
Theology, French, 222
Tobacco, great consumption of, 212
Toledo, winter quarters of the allies, 116
Toleration, Edict of, 50
Torcy, M. de, at the Hague, 102; anecdote of, 138
Tories their principles, 120; their views of the Revolution of 1688, 121; their religious views distinguished from the Whigs, 122; majority at general election of 1710, 131; election of twelve peers, 136; the Jacobites, connection with, 180; the ministry at the end of Anne's reign, 181; strength of, 216

VIC

Toulon besieged, 94
Toulouse, Count of, 85; besieges Barcelona, 85
Tournai taken, 106
Towns, important, 144
Townshend, Lord, 102
Treasure ships, destruction of, at Vigo, 47
Treves, Archbishop of, 34
Triple alliance, the, 17
"True-born Englishman, the, 233
Tu in, siege of, 82; state of the siege, 83; battle of, 84; result of the battle, 85
Turkey, war with Russia, 171

UNIGENITUS Bull, the, 222
Union Jack, the, 149
Union with Scotland, earlier attempts at union, 144; commissioners appointed, 146; arrangements proposed, 146; opposition in Scotland, 147; results, 150; compared with the union with Ireland, 150
Unterglau, 62
Utrecht, peace of, 138-144; congress at, 139; peace signed, 139; arguments for, 142; arguments against, 143

VAGRANTS, statute of, 205
Valencia, subdued, 74; recovered by the French, 92
Vaubrugh, Sir John, 203
Vendome, Duke of, 81; defeats the Imperialists at Calcinato, 82; commands in Flanders, 96; defeated at Oudenarde, 99; sent to command in Spain, 117; defeats the English at Brihuega, 117
Venloo, capitulation of, 42
Victor Amadeus II., Duke of Savoy, his character, 37; his part in the war before Ryswick, 37; in the Spanish succession, 38; his correspondence with Lewis XIV., 38; opposes him, 39; joins Prince Eugene, 84; made King of Sicily, 193; his abdication and death, 194

WYN

Vigo Bay, battle in, 48
Villadarias, Marquis of, 47; commander of Spanish army, 113
Villars, marshal, commands in the Cevennes, 56; defeats the allies on the Rhine, 94; commands in Flanders, 105; wounded at Malplaquet, 108; defeats Prince Eugene at Denain, 137
Villa Viciosa, battle of, 118
Villeroy, marshal, commands in Flanders, 77; defeated at Ramillies, 80
Voltaire, 224

WALPOLE, Sir Robert, as prime minister, 186
War of the Blouses, 52
Webb, General, his victory at Wynendale, 100
West Indies, war in, 46
Westphalia, peace of, 14
Wheat, fluctuations in the price of, 207
Whigs, their principles, 120; their views of the Revolution of 1688, 121; their religious views distinguished from the Tories, 121-122; strength of, 217
William III., prince of Orange, 36; his quarrels with Lewis XIV., 5; his negotiations with Lewis XIV., 6; opposition in England, Scotland to, 8; his death and character, 11; as a European statesman, 12; at war with Lewis XIV., 18; expedition against Cadiz, 46; his influence on foreign policy 121
William, Duke of Gloucester, 26
Wine, great change in the taste for, 212
Witt, De, massacred, 18
Wool, exportation of, 208
Wren, Sir Christopher, his plan for the city of London, 198; his character, 201; rebuilds St. Paul's, 201; his style of architecture, 202
Wynendale, skirmish at, 100